ANCIENT LAW

ITS CONNECTION WITH THE EARLY HISTORY OF
SOCIETY AND ITS RELATION TO MODERN IDEAS

BY

HENRY SUMNER MAINE

WITH INTRODUCTION AND NOTES BY

FREDERICK POLLOCK

Preface to the Beacon Paperback edition by
RAYMOND FIRTH

GLOUCESTER, MASS.

PETER SMITH

1970

First published in 1861
First published as a Beacon Paperback in 1963
Preface to the Beacon Paperback edition copyright © 1963 by
Beacon Press

Printed in the United States of America

Reprinted, 1970, by Permission of
Beacon Press

PREFACE

TO

THE TENTH EDITION.

THE theory of legal development propounded in this volume has been generally accepted; but it has been thought that, in his Fifth Chapter on " Primitive Society and Ancient Law," the Author has not done sufficient justice to investigations which appear to show the existence of states of society still more rudimentary than that vividly described in the Homeric lines quoted at page 110, and ordinarily known as the Patriarchal State. The Author at page 106 has mentioned " accounts by contemporary observers of civilisations less advanced than their own," as capable of affording peculiarly good evidence concerning the rudiments of society; and, in fact, since his work was first published, in 1861, the observation of savage or extremely barbarous races has brought to light forms of social organisation extremely unlike that to which he has referred the beginnings of law, and possibly in some cases of greater antiquity. The subject is, properly speaking, beyond the scope of the present work, but he has given his opinion upon the results of these more recent inquiries in a paper on " Theories of Primitive Society," published in a volume on " Early Law and Custom."

H. S. M.

LONDON : *November,* 1884.

PREFACE

TO

THE FIFTH EDITION.

WHILE further reflection and research have not led the Author of this work to alter his views on most of the matters of which it treats, he has convinced himself that the opinions expressed in the First Chapter on the difficult and still obscure subject of the origin of Customary Law require correction and modification. He has attempted to supply a part of the necessary corrections and modifications in a volume called "Village Communities in the East and West".

H. S. M

LONDON, *December*, 1873.

PREFACE

TO

THE THIRD EDITION.

———————

THE Second and Third Editions of this work have been substantially reprints of the First. Some few errors have, however, been corrected.

It is necessary to remind the reader that the First Edition was published in 1861. The course of events since that period in Russia and in Northern America has taken away much of its application to existing facts from the language employed by the writer on the subject of serfage in Russia, of the Russian village-communities, and of negro-slavery in the United States. It may perhaps be interesting to the reader to observe the bearing of the changes which have taken place on the argument of that part of the work.

H. S. M.

CALCUTTA, *November*, 1865.

PREFACE

TO

THE FIRST EDITION.

THE chief object of the following pages is to indi
cate some of the earliest ideas of mankind, as they
are reflected in Ancient Law, and to point out the
relation of those ideas to modern thought. Much
of the inquiry attempted could not have been prosecuted with the slightest hope of a useful result if
there had not existed a body of law, like that of
the Romans, bearing in its earliest portions the
traces of the most remote antiquity, and supplying
from its later rules the staple of the civil institutions by which modern society is even now con
trolled. The necessity of taking the Roman Law as
a typical system has compelled the Author to draw
from it what may appear a disproportionate number of his illustrations; but it has not been his
intention to write a treatise on Roman Jurispru
dence, and he has as much as possible avoided all

discussions which might give that appearance to his work. The space allotted in the Third and Fourth Chapters to certain philosophical theories of the Roman Jurisconsults has been appropriated to them for two reasons. In the first place, those theories appear to the Author to have had a much wider and more permanent influence on the thought and action of the world than is usually supposed. Secondly, they are believed to be the ultimate source of most of the views which have been prevalent, till quite recently, on the subjects treated of in this volume. It was impossible for the Author to proceed far with his undertaking, without stating his opinion on the origin, meaning, and value of those speculations.

H. S. M.

LONDON, *January* 1861.

CONTENTS

INTRODUCTION.

Sir Henry Maine's "Ancient Law" is now a classical text. The object of this edition is to reproduce it, accompanied by such help to right understanding and profitable use as a younger generation may reasonably require. More than forty years have passed since the book was first published in 1861. During those years, and to a great extent under the influence of Maine's own work, research into the early history of laws and institutions has been more active, systematic, and fruitful than it ever was before. Many new facts have been disclosed; our knowledge of others has been freed from error and misconception; as many, perhaps more, which were formerly accessible, but neglected as being insignificant or of merely local interest, have found their due place and importance in a wider field of knowledge. The materials thus acquired enable us to confirm and supplement Maine's work in many points. If they also show us that it calls for amendment in some places, no one who is at all acquainted with the progressive character of legal and historical learning will find in this any cause for disappointment. The wonder is not that Maine's results, after more than a generation, should stand in need of some correction, but that, in fact, they need so little as they do. Later speculation and research have, on the whole, confirmed Maine's leading ideas in the most striking manner, partly by actual verification of consequences indicated by him as probable, partly by new examples and applications in regions which he had not himself explored.

There is no better witness to the intrinsic weight of Maine's work than the nature of some criticism it has met with, from competent persons on the Continent rather than at home. So far as those learned persons complain of anything, they miss that symmetrical construction of a finished system to which their training has accustomed them. Now it is to be observed that no words of Maine's own ever gave his readers the promise of a systematic doctrine. Not one of his books professed on the face of it to account for the ultimate origin of human laws, or to settle the relations of jurisprudence to ethics, or to connect the science of law with any theory of politics or of social development. Yet it does not seem to have occurred to the critics in question to charge Maine with remissness in not having attempted these things. The disappointment expressed was that he did not fully accomplish them, or that, if he had a solution, he never sufficiently declared it. Regret that Maine's work was not more openly ambitious is legitimate, though I do not share it; expression of it might

have signified much or little. It might have been
thoroughly sincere, and due to imperfect understanding of the relations to time, circumstances,
and materials, which determined Maine's manner
of working, and, as I believe, determined it for the
best. It might also have been, in the critic's intention, the easy compliment of the professional and
disciplined scholar to a brilliant amateur. Very
different from this was the actual criticism. It assumed that the author had proved himself a master, and that, accordingly, the highest and most exacting standard was to be applied both to his
method and to his results. When we turn from
Dareste or Vanni to the original preface to " Ancient Law," we are astonished by the studiously
modest terms in which Maine defined his own undertaking: " The chief object of the following
pages is to indicate some of the earliest ideas of
mankind as they are reflected in ancient law, and to
point out the relation of those ideas to modern
thought." In like manner, on the first publication of the lectures on Village Communities, he
apologised for their fragmentary character, and in
the height of his mature fame he described " Early
Law and Custom " only as an endeavour " to connect a portion of existing institutions with a part
of the primitive or very ancient usages of mankind,
and of the ideas associated with those usages."
It is worth while to observe Maine's caution in dis-
claiming authority to lay down what ancient

usages, if any, are really primitive—a caution sometimes neglected by his followers, and often by the champions of other theories.

Maine's dignified and almost ironical reserve about his own work has certainly made it rather difficult for a student approaching it for the first time to form any general notion of what it has really done for legal and historical science. Although Maine himself was the last person of whom the answer to such a question could be expected, we who are in no way bound to reticence must say that he did nothing less than create the natural history of law. He showed, on the one hand, that legal ideas and institutions have a real course of development as much as the genera and species of living creatures, and in every stage of that development have their normal characters; on the other hand, he made it clear that these processes deserve and require distinct study, and cannot be treated as mere incidents in the general history of the societies where they occur. There have been complaints, often too well justified, of the historical ignorance prevailing among lawyers. " Woe unto you also, ye lawyers! " Freeman said—whether in print in those terms, I know not; but I have heard him say it—when he was grieved at the fictions about mediæval institutions that still passed current for history twenty-five or thirty years ago. But Maine has taught us that the way to impart a historical habit of mind to lawyers is

to show them that law has an important history of
its own, not at all confined to its political and constitutional aspects, and offers a vast field for the
regular application of historical and comparative
method. When once a lawyer has grasped this, he
is entitled to point out in turn that a historian who
is not content to be a mere chronicler can hardly
do without some understanding of legal ideas and
systems. And the importance of the legal element,
so far from diminishing as we retrace the growth
of our modern institutions into a semi-historic
past, rather increases. Others have shown this besides Maine, but none before him. It is easy to un-
derrate his originality now that his points have
been taken up by many teachers and become current in the schools. Any student who harbours
doubt as to the extent of Maine's contributions to
the historical philosophy of law may do well to ask
himself in what books, legal or historical, of earlier
date than " Ancient Law," he could have found
adequate perception, or any distinct perception, of
such matters as these: The sentiment of reverence
evoked by the mere existence of law in early communities; the essential formalism of archaic law;
the predominance of rules of procedure over rules
of substance in early legal systems; the fundamental difference between ancient and modern ideas
as to legal proof; the relatively modern character
of the individual citizen's disposing power, especially by will, and freedom of contract; and the still

more modern appearance of true criminal law. Nowadays it may be said that " all have got the seed," but this is no justification for forgetting who first cleared and sowed the ground. We may till fields that the master left untouched, and one man will bring a better ox to yoke to the plough, and another a worse; but it is the master's plough still.

It will now be proper to consider in a general way what resources were available for Maine's purposes when he wrote " Ancient Law," or rather when he prepared and delivered the lectures of which it was a revised publication ("Early Law and Custom," p. 194). We shall be pretty safe in taking legal and historical scholarship as they stood, for an English student who had not frequented Continental seats of learning, about the middle of the nineteenth century.

First, in Roman law Savigny, then still living, was the person of greatest authority; the historical school which he took a principal part in founding was dominant in Germany and beginning to prevail elsewhere. Savigny's work, as well as that of his contemporaries and immediate followers, dealt only with the Roman materials. Comparative investigation of archaic legal systems had scarcely been undertaken at all, certainly not on any considerable scale, and this may perhaps account for more than one conjecture of Savigny's which has not proved tenable. The work of Rudolf von Ihering, the character of whose genius, individual as it was, perhaps most nearly resembled Maine's in the same generation, was only beginning. His views on the evolution of modern from archaic law coincide remarkably with those of Maine in several points; for example, in the position that all jurisdiction, if we could trace it far back enough, would be found to be in its origin not compulsory, but voluntary. But there can be no question of borrowing either way. Maine had formed his own ideas before any part of Ihering's great work, " Der Geist des römischen Rechtes," was published; and Ihering was never in a position to make much use of Maine's work, even if he had the time; for, as I came to know from himself, he could not read English with any facility.

The literature of Roman law to be found in our own language was, with few exceptions, antiquated or contemptible, and such incidental references to Roman law as occurred in English text-books were almost always crude, often inappropriate or quite erroneous. Blackstone has some very bad mistakes in this kind. For many years after the publication of " Ancient Law " this state of things remained unamended. At the present time it is very different. In our own language Muirhead, Poste, Dr. Moyle, Dr. Roby, and Dr. Greenidge have made excellent provision of various kinds both for beginners and for advanced students, and Sohm's Institutes are accessible in Mr. Ledlie's scholarly translation. Professor Girard's "Manuel élémentaire de droit romain" (3rd ed., 1901) is, notwithstanding its modest title, one of the most learned and comprehensive, as well as the most recent, works on the subject. The reader of " Ancient Law " will understand that, as Maine was careful to explain in his first preface, the portions dealing with Roman law were never intended to take the place of a treatise on the subject. In fact, they assume the elementary knowledge which may be obtained from a good edition of Justinian's Institutes. It would therefore be idle to attempt a detailed commentary on them from a technical point of view which would not be appropriate; and any reader who thinks he can use Maine's work as a substitute for first-hand acquaintance with the texts and the best commentators, instead of a companion and aid, must do so wholly at his own peril. Still less can Maine be censured for having adopted, at the time, current views of the highest authorities in Roman legal history which have since been abandoned.

Germanic legal antiquities had been investigated to a considerable extent; but the Continental scholars who had done this were still hardly aware of the wealth or importance of the material awaiting scientific treatment in England. On the other hand, those who made their results known to English readers, John Mitchell Kemble the foremost, were not learned in the modern law of England,

and had not the means of connecting its later or even its mediæval history with the earliest monuments of English institutions. Thus no one had made any serious attempt to sift the mass of information collected by English professional writers and antiquaries of the sixteenth and seventeenth centuries, whose industrious labour assuredly deserves all praise, and whose judgment has in some cases been restored to credit which it had not deserved to lose. We need hardly say that Maine, not being a technical antiquary, did not attempt any such thing himself. Indeed, the work he actually did was needful to disclose the right lines of antiquarian research, and rescue it from the state of mere dilettante curiosity.

English legal history was very imperfectly known, and what was known was concealed under huge masses of comparatively modern formalism. There was much to be learnt (as there still is) from Blackstone, whose work was admirable in its day, notwithstanding conspicuous faults of method and arrangement mostly not his own; but Blackstone had ceased to be generally read with attention even by lawyers, and was not a safe guide for any period before the thirteenth century. Whatever was before the Great Charter (and I am taking the earliest possible date) lay under a cloud of thick darkness, pierced only in part by the brilliant lights of Kemble and Palgrave. These fell, moreover, chiefly on the political and constitutional aspects

of the common law, leaving in shadow those technical archaisms which we now know for landmarks.
Palgrave, again, was often exuberant and fanciful,
Kemble not seldom rash; and their work (though
its general merit can hardly be exaggerated) is by
no means free from positive mistakes, which, considering its novelty at the time, is in no way surprising. In every branch of the law scientific or
even well written and tolerably arranged text-
books were rare; in some they were wholly wanting. Constitutional law (and that from a political
more than a legal point of view) was the only department which could be said to have found an
adequate historian. On the whole, historical knowledge of English law before the twelfth century was
not to be found, and after the twelfth century was
pretty much what Blackstone had left it. In consequence of the general indifference to historical
study, besides the real difficulties then attending it,
lawyers and judges, even really learned ones, were
commonly prone to accept superficial explanations
which a little more research, not of a recondite kind,
would have proved to be erroneous. In particular
there was a strong tendency to exaggerate Roman
influence in the formation of English institutions,
by no means without plausible excuse. Perhaps
it was knowledge of Kemble's work that saved
Maine from this rife and dangerous error. Clearly
the English materials were not in a fit state, when
Maine was writing " Ancient Law," to be used

with effect for any purpose of historical generalisation or comparison; and he had no choice but to
leave them alone for the most part, and build on
other and at that time safer ground.

Asiatic systems of law were more or less known
to Orientalists, but only in so far as their texts
were documents of Arabic or Sanskrit literature.
On the other hand, it was the duty of a considerable number of British magistrates and officials in
India to have some acquaintance with so much of
Hindu and Mahometan law as was recognised and
applied by the civil courts; but this was only for the
necessities of judicial business. Few men, if any,
followed the splendid example of Sir William Jones
in combining literary with practical knowledge, as
indeed very few can at any one time reasonably be
supposed capable of it. As to the Mosaic law, it
was still the received opinion that there was an im-
passable or at least a highly perilous gulf between
sacred and profane history. Knowledge of the
text of the Old Testament, far more complete and
more generally diffused in English-speaking countries than anywhere else, had therefore produced
little result for secular learning. Neither the phil-
ological nor the official handling of Asiatic law-
books caused any appreciable number of scholars
to perceive the importance of Asiatic custom for
the general study of legal ideas and history.
Maine's pointed references to Hindu institutions,
at a time before he had or expected to have any-

thing to do with India, could have been made only by a man of quite extraordinary insight. It would be interesting to know from what quarter his attention was first directed that way.

It has been thought proper to reprint the text of " Ancient Law " as last revised by Maine not only without alteration, but without the interruption of editorial footnotes. Such comments as I have been able to add will be found collected in the Appendix at the end of the book. As "Ancient Law " touches on a greater variety of matters than almost any modern book of serious learning which is not of an encyclopædic nature, I have perforce omitted some topics, not because they might not have been considered with profit by a person competent in them, but because I was not competent. For the same reason I can by no means vouch for the accuracy in detail, according to the present state of knowledge, of everything I have passed over without remark. But my experience of the points I am qualified to test has led me to presume that such errors as may be discovered by specialists will seldom be found to affect the general course of the argument. I have purposely not dwelt on matters of elementary information which any student capable of profiting by Maine's work is equally capable of verifying for himself with little trouble. Maine did not write, for example, for readers who had never heard of Hobbes or Montesquieu. Such a name as Du Molin's, on the other

hand, may well be strange, not only to an educated
Englishman (as that of Bracton or Plowden might
be to an educated Frenchman), but to an English
lawyer who has not made a special study of the
Reformation controversies or the revival of classical Roman law; and in this case it would be vexatious to put off such readers with a bare reference
to the French biographical dictionaries.

I have to thank the owners and the editor of the
Edinburgh Review for permission to make free
use of an article entitled " Sir Henry Maine as a
Jurist," contributed by me in 1893.

F. P.

For general information about Maine's life and
works the following publications may be consulted:
" Sir Henry Maine: a brief memoir of his life," by
Sir M. E. Grant Duff, 1892; " Sir Henry Maine and
his Work," in " Oxford Lectures and other dis-
courses," 1890, by the present writer; and the articles in the Dictionary of National Biography
(1893), and the Supplement to the ninth edition of
the Encyclopædia Britannica (1902), by Leslie
(afterwards Sir L.) Stephen and the present writer
respectively.

PREFACE TO THE
BEACON PAPERBACK EDITION
by Raymond Firth

In the century that has passed since the first publication
of Maine's *Ancient Law* the reputation of this work and of
its author has steadily grown. Maine can be regarded as
the founder of comparative jurisprudence in the English-
speaking world. A lawyer, Carleton Kemp Allen, has said
of *Ancient Law*, "with the appearance of this book modern
historical jurisprudence was born." Maine was also an
eminent contributor to the study of the history of political
institutions. William Graham, a professor of jurisprudence
and political economy, has claimed him to be "the best
representative of the historical school of political studies."
In sociology, too, Maine's ideas have been apparent, and
Talcott Parsons has noted the influence of his views on contract in Tonnies' concept of *Gesellschaft*. His ideas have
played an increasingly important part in the development
of modern social anthropology. Robert Lowie has pointed
out that while in *Ancient Law* the anthropologist faces unfamiliar problems both of fact and of terminology and finds
much of the legal discussion beyond his competence, he still
derives from Maine's book a part of his most valuable intellectual equipment.

Who was this man who could contribute in a formative

way to so many disciplines? The details, as given by Leslie Stephen, by Pollock and by his biographer Grant-Duff, may be summarized as follows. Henry James Sumner Maine was born in 1822, was a very fine classical scholar at Cambridge, and in 1847 became Regius Professor of Civil Law at Cambridge. He was called to the Bar in 1850, and since at that time there was little scope for legal studies in Cambridge, he lived chiefly in London and devoted himself to writing, mainly articles for journals and newspapers. In 1852, when the Inns of Court developed their examination system, he became the first Reader in Roman Law and Jurisprudence, and is said to have been a very effective lecturer. Two years later he retired from his Chair at Cambridge. In 1861, the year in which he published *Ancient Law,* he was offered the appointment of legal member of the Viceroy's Council in India. He declined it on health grounds, but accepted a renewed offer in the following year. Despite his doctor's earlier prediction, he lived a vigorous and social life in India for seven years. Though he did not personally draft much legislation, he was very active in advice and undertook many public duties, including that of the Vice-Chancellorship of the University of Calcutta.

Retiring from India in 1869, he was appointed to the Corpus Professorship of Jurisprudence, just founded at Oxford. In 1871 he published his first course of lectures as *Village Communities in the East and West.* In 1878 he resigned his Professorship at Oxford and in 1887, like an academic chameleon, changed his coat once again to succeed Harcourt as Whewell Professor of International Law at Cambridge. With foresight, but with pathetic optimism, the founder of this Chair had laid it down that the professor should suggest measures tending toward the extinction of war. Maine does not seem to have suggested any such measures, though before going to India he had written a book on international law of which the manuscript had been lost. However, his time was short, and he died the following year.

Maine seems always to have suffered from poor health. In

a way this was of benefit to the development of his ideas
since, to save energy as well as from temperament, he generally wrote his books with very few references. His scholarship was such that there were few complaints when he gave
conclusions without giving the evidence on which they were
based; and generations of readers have benefited from the
clarity of his style and the uncluttered simplicity of his
page.

Something of Maine's personality comes through in his
writing. Without fully subscribing to Lowie's eulogy that
Maine "is the embodiment of serene wisdom coupled with
unusual subtlety," one can recognize his intellectual probity,
the balance of his judgment and his ability to look beyond
the intellectual fashion of the day. With this, at times, is a
delicate and attractive humor. In his examination of the
modern history of the law of nature, for instance, he dis-
cusses the value of a clear objective, even if it is an ideal,
and compares it to Benthamism. He writes, "English
lawyers of the last century were probably too acute to be
blinded by a paradoxical commonplace that English law was
the perfection of human reason. But they acted as if they
believed it, for want of any other principles to proceed
upon." In such contexts and in his refusal to assign current
denigratory moral values to unfamiliar institutions, Maine's
detachment shows itself. It is true that his admiration for
Roman jurisprudence and for the "elegance" of the harmony
for which Roman jurisconsults strove, at times did color
with enthusiasm his ordinarily placid prose. He could also
be moved to indignation, as when he describes the self-
immolation of a Hindu widow at her husband's funeral as a
"monstrous extension of family sacrifice."

But such moral judgment is rare with him. This detachment seems to have marked his personal life as well, and
Leslie Stephen is at some pains to point out that while
seemingly cold to the outside world, Maine could be warm
and sweet in his disposition to his friends. If at times his
style is a little Olympian for modern taste, it is a product

of intellectual sincerity, not arrogance. That the style of Maine has not been appreciated by all, however, despite his popularity as a source of jurisprudence, is shown by a brief summary of some of his leading ideas produced by a barrister of Lincoln's Inn shortly before the turn of the century. Pointing out that the works of Maine had to be studied for honors examinations of the Inns of Court and at universities at home and in the Colonies this man, Morgan O. Evans, complained that "in these works there was a great deal of writing that was absolutely useless to the student for examination purposes, and page after page has to be waded through in the search for a criticism or theory . . . This necessitates a great waste of time and mental energy on the part of the student, there being over two thousand pages in all." The resulting utilitarian compression of Maine's ideas from his six major works by this indignant Welshman is of sociological rather than scholarly interest, but it demonstrates the position in legal studies that Maine had attained within ten years of his death.

Where Maine's work differs so markedly from that of his predecessors is not only in the systematic penetration of his thought, but also in his use of a wide range of empirical material. Though when writing *Ancient Law* he had not yet visited India, he had already obtained enough familiarity with Hindu law to be able to compare it fruitfully with Roman law. Again, as Pollock has pointed out, Maine's use of Homeric poetry as evidence for archaic forms of legal ideas is a brilliant example of his insight. Throughout the book he emphasizes the importance of evidence as against speculation.

In this book Maine has succeeded in his principal objective in charting some of the early forms of legal institutions and indicating their relation to modern thought. If this historical treatment was not so complete as he at first supposed, he nevertheless illumined a number of most significant legal ideas and practices over a wide range of human society, and indicated with great plausibility their developmental characters. It is true that his treatment was of a mildly evolutionary kind which led occasionally to oversimplification, as when he permitted himself an incautious reflection on the universality of the patriarchal system. Moreover, his concept of all forms of status in early society — "the infancy of social brotherhood" — as being merged in common subjection to Paternal Power was ethnographically far too narrow. His evidence was defective in that he did not use any Oriental data except Indian — he regarded China as a stationary society. Nor did he draw upon the material already available from primitive societies in Africa and elsewhere. (The considerable evidence on primitive law accumulated and analyzed since his day — as by Post, Kohler, Barton, Malinowski, Radcliffe-Brown, Meek, Diamond, Huntington Cairns, Schapera, Hoebel, Ter Haar, Gluckman and Bohannan — has transformed our views in this field.) But his exploration of such concepts as agnation and cognation, legal fiction, corporation, patria potestas, crime and tort, and the definitions which he gave, have had a lasting value for jurists, anthropologists and sociologists alike.

For the earlier anthropologists, with their evolutionary preoccupations, it was Maine's views on the priority of father-right which attracted most attention, though L. H. Morgan paid tribute to his "brilliant researches" in the sources of ancient law and the early history of institutions. Later scholars have been more concerned with his analytical propositions. Many of the theoretical views expressed in *Ancient Law* are still continually being brought up for scrutiny afresh. His statement that in the history of political ideas kinship unity preceded recognition of the significance of local contiguity, has often been traversed, praised and qualified, as by Lowie, Radcliffe-Brown and Schapera. Hoebel has criticized his views on the rigidity of primitive law. Others have objected to the wholehearted way in which he saw early law as essentially compounded with religion and morality. Graham thought Maine was wrong in im-

plicitly denying the existence of a natural sense of justice
and other attributes of natural law. Allen saw Maine's
facility in phrase-making as having tempted him to the paradox that in primitive society judgments preceded custom,
and even held that Maine's account of the development of the
Roman law of contract, "leans a little toward the romantic."
Yet modern scholars have been able to ignore the dogmatic
aspect of Maine's ideas of development or opposition of
stages of society and have focused upon the enduring quality
of the basic social elements revealed by his subtle analyses.
In the field of African politics and law, for example, they
have found much to commend in Maine's arguments.
Schapera has demonstrated that the political communities
of primitive peoples are more complex than the classical
type set out by Maine, but he uses Maine's criteria as the
significant starting point of his analysis. Bohannan, following Maine, finds that the Tiv of Nigeria have precisely the
same difficulty as Maine described in distinguishing between
a wrong to a person and a wrong to the state. And Gluckman, on the basis of his examination of Lozi law, is even
inclined to regard as valid Maine's broad conception of an
historical trend in his familiar thesis of the movement of
progressive societies from status to contract.

Maine's significance in social anthropology is doubtless
largely due, as E. R. Leach has pointed out, to the view he
took of corporate institutions as imposing constraint upon
individuals. The emphasis which he laid upon the importance of studying history is another element in this popularity. His ideas of social development in terms of polar
opposites: family to individual, status to contract, penal
legislation to civil law, are too arbitrary and naive by modern
standards of analysis. But for all social scientists, as for
jurists, Maine's stress upon analysis in terms of power and
jurisdiction, and his continual concern to set his study of law
in relation to an examination of the structure of society, has
helped to provide some of the most important elements of
the theoretical frame for examining legal institutions.

Select Bibliographical References

Allen, Carleton Kemp, Introduction to Maine's *Ancient Law*, World's Classics, London, 1931.

Bohannan, Paul, *Justice and Judgement Among the Tiv*, London, 1957.

Duff, N. E. Grant, *Sir Henry Maine: A Brief Memoir of his Life*, London, 1892.

Evans, Morgan O., *Theories and Criticisms of Sir Henry Maine*, London, 1896.

Gluckman, Max, *The Judicial Process Among the Barotse of Northern Rhodesia*, Manchester, 1955.

Graham, William, *English Political Philosophy from Hobbes to Maine*, London, 1889.

*Hoebel, E. Adamson, *The Law of Primitive Man*, Cambridge, Mass., 1954.

Leach, E. R., *Pul Eliya: A Village in Ceylon*, Cambridge, 1961.

Lowie, Robert H., *Primitive Society*, New York, 1920.

────── *The History of Ethnological Theory*, London, 1937.

Parsons, Talcott, *The Structure of Social Action*, Glencoe, 1949.

Pollock, Frederick, Introduction and Notes to Sir Henry Maine's *Ancient Law*, London, 1906.

Schapera, I., *Government and Politics in Tribal Society*, London, 1956.

Stephen, Leslie, Article on Maine in *Dictionary of National Biography*, 1893.

────────

(* For other authors see bibliography in Hoebel.)

ANCIENT LAW.

CHAPTER I.

ANCIENT CODES.

THE most celebrated system of jurisprudence known to the world begins, as it ends, with a Code. From the commencement to the close of its history, the expositors of Roman Law consistently employed language which implied that the body of their system rested on the Twelve Decemviral Tables, and therefore on a basis of written law. Except in one particular, no institutions anterior to the Twelve Tables were recognised at Rome. The theoretical descent of Roman jurisprudence from a code, the theoretical ascription of English law to immemorial unwritten tradition, were the chief reasons why the development of their system differed from the development of ours. Neither theory corresponded exactly with the facts, but each produced consequences of the utmost importance.

I need hardly say that the publication of the

Twelve Tables is not the earliest point at which we can take up the history of law. The ancient Roman code belongs to a class of which almost every civil ised nation in the world can show a sample, and which, so far as the Roman and Hellenic worlds were concerned, were largely diffused over them at epochs not widely distant from one another. They appeared under exceedingly similar circumstances, and were produced, to our knowledge, by very similar causes. Unquestionably, many jural phenomena lie behind these codes and preceded them in point of time. Not a few documentary records exist which profess to give us information concerning the early phenomena of law; but, until philology has effected a complete analysis of the Sanskrit literature, our best sources of knowledge are undoubtedly the Greek Homeric poems, considered of course not as a history of actual occurrences, but as a description, not wholly idealised, of a state of society known to the writer. However the fancy of the poet may have exaggerated certain features of the heroic age, the prowess of warriors and the potency of gods, there is no reason to believe that it has tampered with moral or metaphysical conceptions which were not yet the subjects of conscious observation; and in this respect the Homeric literature is far more trustworthy than those relatively later documents which pretend to give an account of times similarly early, but which were compiled under philosophical or theological influences. If by any means we can determine the early forms of jural conceptions, they will be invaluable to us. These rudimentary ideas are to the jurist what the primary crusts of the earth are to the geologist. They contain, potentially, all the forms in which law has subsequently exhibited itself. The haste or the prejudice which has generally refused them all but the most superficial examination, must bear the blame of the unsatisfactory condition in which we find the science of jurisprudence. The inquiries of the jurist are in truth prosecuted much as inquiry in physics and physiology was prosecuted before observation had taken the place of assumption. Theories, plausible and comprehensive, but absolutely unverified, such as the Law of Nature or the Social Compact, enjoy a universal preference over sober research into the primitive history of society and law; and they obscure the truth not only by diverting attention from the only quarter in which it can be found, but by that most real and most important influence which, when once entertained and believed in, they are enabled to exercise on the later stages of jurisprudence.

The earliest notions connected with the conception, now so fully developed, of a law or rule of life, are those contained in the Homeric words "Themis" and "Themistes." "Themis," it is well known, appears in the later Greek pantheon as the Goddess of Justice, but this is a modern and much developed idea, and it is in a very different sense that Themis

is described in the Iliad as the assessor of Zeus. It
is now clearly seen by all trustworthy observers of
the primitive condition of mankind that, in the infancy of the race, men could only account for sustained or periodically recurring action by supposing
a personal agent. Thus, the wind blowing was a
person and of course a divine person; the sun
rising, culminating, and setting was a person and a
divine person; the earth yielding her increase was
a person and divine. As, then, in the physical
world, so in the moral. When a king decided a
dispute by a sentence, the judgment was assumed to
be the result of direct inspiration. The divine
agent, suggesting judicial awards to kings or to
gods, the greatest of kings, was *Themis*. The peculiarity of the conception is brought out by the use
of the plural. *Themistes*, Themiscs, the plural of
Themis, are the awards themselves, divinely dictated to the judge. Kings are spoken of as if they
had a store of "Themistes" ready to hand for use;
but it must be distinctly understood that they are
not laws, but judgments, or, to take the exact Teutonic equivalent, "dooms." "Zeus, or the human
king on earth," says Mr. Grote, in his History of
Greece, "is not a law-maker, but a judge." He is
provided with Themistes, but, consistently with
the belief in their emanation from above, they cannot be supposed to be connected by any thread of
principle; they are separate, isolated judgments.

Even in the Homeric poems, we can see that

these ideas are transient. Parities of circumstance
were probably commoner in the simple mechanism
of ancient society than they are now, and in the
succession of similar cases awards are likely to follow and resemble each other. Here we have the
germ or rudiment of a custom, a conception posterior to that of Themistes or judgments. However
strongly we, with our modern associations, may be
inclined to lay down à *priori* that the notion of a
Custom must precede that of a judicial sentence,
and that a judgment must affirm a Custom or pun
ish its breach, it seems quite certain that the his
torical order of the ideas is that in which I have
placed them. The Homeric word for a custom in
the embryo is sometimes "Themis" in the singular
—more often "Dike," the meaning of which visibly
fluctuates between a "judgment" and a "custom"
or "usage." $N\acute{o}\mu o\varsigma$, a Law, so great and famous a
term in the political vocabulary of the later Greek
society, does not occur in Homer.

The notion of a divine agency, suggesting the
Themistes, and itself impersonated in Themis, must
be kept apart from other primitive beliefs with
which a superficial inquirer might confound it. The
conception of the Deity dictating an entire code or
body of law as in the case of the Hindoo laws of
Menu, seems to belong to a range of ideas more recent and more advanced. "Themis" and "Themis
tes" are much less remotely linked with that per-
suasion which clung so long and so tenaciously to

the human mind, of a divine influence underlying
and supporting every relation of life, every social
institution.   In early law, and amid the rudiments
of political thought, symptoms of this belief meet
us on all sides.   A supernatural presidency is supposed to consecrate and keep together all the cardi-
nal institutions of those times, the State, the Race.
and the Family.   Men, grouped together in the different relations which those institutions imply, are
bound to celebrate periodically common rites and
to offer common sacrifices ; and every now and then
the same duty is even more significantly recognised
in the purifications and expiations which they perform, and which appear intended to deprecate punishment for involuntary or neglectful disrespect.
Everybody acquainted with ordinary classical literature will remember the *sacra gentilicia,* which
exercised so important an influence on the early
Roman law of adoption and of wills.   And to this
hour the Hindoo Customary Law, in which some of
the most curious features of primitive society are stereotyped, makes almost all the rights of persons and
all the rules of succession hinge on the due solemni-
sation of fixed ceremonies at the dead man's funeral,
that is, at every point where a breach occurs in the
continuity of the family.

Before we quit this stage of jurisprudence, a
caution may be usefully given to the English student.   Bentham, in his "Fragment on Government,'
and Austin, in his "Province of Jurisprudence De

termined," resolve every law into a *command* of
the lawgiver, an *obligation* imposed thereby on the
citizen, and a *sanction* threatened in the event of
disobedience; and it is further predicated of the
command, which is the first element in a law, that
it must prescribe, not a single act, but a series or
number of acts of the same class or kind. The
results of this separation of ingredients tally exactly
with the facts of mature jurisprudence; and, by a
little straining of language, they may be made to
correspond in form with all law, of all kinds, at all
epochs. It is not, however, asserted that the notion
of law entertained by the generality is even now
quite in conformity with this dissection; and it is
curious that, the farther we penetrate into the primitive history of thought, the farther we find ourselves from a conception of law which at all resembles a compound of the elements which Bentham
determined. It is certain that, in the infancy of
mankind, no sort of legislature, not even a distinct
author of law, is contemplated or conceived of.
Law has scarcely reached the footing of custom; it
is rather a habit. It is, to use a French phrase, " in
the air." The only authoritative statement of right
and wrong is a judicial sentence after the facts, not
one presupposing a law which has been violated,
but one which is breathed for the first time by a
higher power into the judge's mind at the moment
of adjudication. It is of course extremely difficult
for us to realise a view so far removed from us in

point both of time and of association, but it will be come more credible when we dwell more at length on the constitution of ancient society, in which every man, living during the greater part of his life under the patriarchal despotism, was practically controlled in all his actions by a regimen not of law but of caprice. I may add that an Englishman should be better able than a foreigner to appreciate the historical fact that the "Themistes" preceded any conception of law, because, amid the many inconsistent theories which prevail concerning the character of English jurisprudence, the most popular, or at all events the one which most affects practice, is certainly a theory which assumes that adjudged cases and precedents exist antecedently to rules, principles, and distinctions. The "Themistes" have too, it should be remarked, the characteristic which, in the view of Bentham and Austin, distinguishes single or mere commands from laws. A true law enjoins on all the citizens indifferently a number of acts similar in class or kind; and this is exactly the feature of a law which has most deeply impressed itself on the popular mind, causing the term "law" to be applied to mere uniformities, successions, and similitudes. A *command* prescribes only a single act, and it is to commands, therefore, that "Themistes" are more akin than to laws. They are simply adjudications on insulated states of fact, and do not necessarily follow each other in any orderly sequence.

The literature of the heroic age discloses to us law in the germ under the "Themistes" and a little more developed in the conception of "Dike." The next stage which we reach in the history of juris prudence is strongly marked and surrounded by the utmost interest. Mr. Grote, in the second part and ninth chapter of his History, has fully described the mode in which society gradually clothed itself with a different character from that delineated by Homer. Heroic kingship depended partly on divinely given prerogative, and partly on the possession of supereminent strength, courage, and wisdom. Gradually, as the impression of the monarch's sacredness became weakened, and feeble members occurred in the series of hereditary kings, the royal power decayed, and at last gave way to the dominion of aristocracies. If language so precise can be used of the revolution, we might say that the office of the king was usurped by that council of chiefs which Homer repeatedly alludes to and depicts. At all events from an epoch of kingly rule we come everywhere in Europe to an era of oligarchies; and even where the name of the monarchical functions does not absolutely disappear, the authority of the king is reduced to a mere shadow. He becomes a mere hereditary general, as in Lacedæmon, a mere functionary, as the King Archon at Athens, or a mere formal hierophant, like the *Rex Sacrificulus* at Rome. In Greece, Italy, and Asia Minor, the dominant orders seem to have universally consisted

of a number of families united by an assumed relationship in blood, and, though they all appear at
first to have laid claim to a quasi-sacred character,
their strength does not seem to have resided in
their pretended sanctity. Unless they were prema-
turely overthrown by the popular party, they all
ultimately approached very closely to what we
should now understand by a political aristocracy.
The changes which society underwent in the communities of the further Asia occurred of course at
periods long anterior in point of time to these revolutions of the Italian and Hellenic worlds; but their
relative place in civilisation appears to have been
the same, and they seem to have been exceedingly
similar in general character. There is some evidence
that the races which were subsequently united under
the Persian monarchy, and those which peopled the
peninsula of India, had all their heroic age and their
era of aristocracies; but a military and a religious
oligarchy appear to have grown up separately, nor
was the authority of the king generally superseded.
Contrary, too, to the course of events in the West,
the religious element in the East tended to get the
better of the military and political. Military and
civil aristocracies disappear, annihilated or crushed
into insignificance between the kings and the sacerdotal order; and the ultimate result at which we
arrive is, a monarch enjoying great power, but cir-
cumscribed by the privileges of a caste of priests.
With these differences, however, that in the East

aristocracies became religious, in the West civil or
political, the proposition that a historical era of aristocracies succeeded a historical era of heroic kings
may be considered as true, if not of all mankind, at
all events of all branches of the Indo-European
family of nations.

The important point for the jurist is that these
aristocracies were universally the depositaries and administrators of law. They seem to have succeeded
to the prerogatives of the king, with the important
difference, however, that they do not appear to have
pretended to direct inspiration for each sentence.
The connection of ideas which caused the judgments
of the patriarchal chieftain to be attributed to su-
perhuman dictation still shows itself here and there
in the claim of a divine origin for the entire body
of rules, or for certain parts of it, but the progress
of thought no longer permits the solution of particular disputes to be explained by supposing an extra-
human interposition. What the juristical oligarchy
now claims is to monopolise the *knowledge* of the
laws, to have the exclusive possession of the principles by which quarrels are decided. We have in
fact arrived at the epoch of Customary Law. Customs or Observances now exist as a substantive
aggregate, and are assumed to be precisely known
to the aristocratic order or caste. Our authorities
leave us no doubt that the trust lodged with the
oligarchy was sometimes abused, but it certainly
ought not to be regarded as a mere usurpation or

engine of tyranny. Before the invention of writing,
and during the infancy of the art, an aristocracy invested with judicial privileges formed the only ex
pedient by which accurate preservation of the customs of the race or tribe could be at all approximated to. Their genuineness was, so far as possible,
insured by confiding them to the recollection of a
limited portion of the community.

The epoch of Customary Law, and of its custody
by a privileged order, is a very remarkable one.
The condition of jurisprudence which it implies has
left traces which may still be detected in legal and
popular phraseology. The law, thus known exclusively to a privileged minority, whether a caste, an
aristocracy, a priestly tribe, or a sacerdotal college,
is true unwritten law. Except this, there is no such
thing as unwritten law in the world. English case-
law is sometimes spoken of as unwritten, and there
are some English theorists who assure us that if a
code of English jurisprudence were prepared, we
should be turning unwritten law into written—a
conversion, as they insist, if not of doubtful policy,
at all events of the greatest seriousness. Now, it is
quite true that there was once a period at which the
English common law might reasonably have been
termed unwritten. The elder English judges did
really pretend to knowledge of rules, principles, and
distinctions which were not entirely revealed to the
bar and to the lay-public. Whether all the law
which they claimed to monopolise was really un-

written is exceedingly questionable; but at all events, on the assumption that there was once a large mass of civil and criminal rules known exclusively to the judges, it presently ceased to be unwritten law. As soon as the Courts at Westminster Hall began to base their judgments on cases recorded, whether in the year books or elsewhere, the law which they administered became written law. At the present moment a rule of English law has first to be disentangled from the recorded facts of adjudged printed precedents, then thrown into a form of words, varying with the taste, precision, and knowledge of the particular judge, and then applied to the circumstances of the case for adjudication. But at no stage of this process has it any characteristic which distinguishes it from written law. It is written case-law, and only different from code-law because it is written in a different way.

From the period of Customary Law we come to another sharply defined epoch in the history of jurisprudence. We arrive at the era of Codes, those ancient codes of which the Twelve Tables of Rome were the most famous specimen. In Greece, in Italy, on the Hellenised sea-board of Western Asia, these codes all made their appearance at periods much the same everywhere, not, I mean, at periods identical in point of time, but similar in point of the relative progress of each community. Everywhere, in the countries I have named, laws engraven on tablets and published to the people take the place of usages

deposited with the recollection of a privileged oligarchy. It must not for a moment be supposed that
the refined considerations now urged in favour of
what is called codification had any part or place in
the change I have described. The ancient codes
were doubtless originally suggested by the discovery
and diffusion of the art of writing. It is true that
the aristocracies seem to have abused their monopoly
of legal knowledge; and at all events their exclusive
possession of the law was a formidable impediment to
the success of those popular movements which began
to be universal in the western world. But, though
democratic sentiment may have added to their popularity, the codes were certainly in the main a direct
result of the invention of writing. Inscribed tablets
were seen to be a better depositary of law, and a
better security for its accurate preservation, than
the memory of a number of persons however
strengthened by habitual exercise.

The Roman code belongs to the class of codes I
have been describing. Their value did not consist
in any approach to symmetrical classifications, or to
terseness and clearness of expression, but in their
publicity, and in the knowledge which they furnished to everybody, as to what he was to do, and
what not to do. It is indeed true that the Twelve
Tables of Rome do exhibit some traces of systematic
arrangement, but this is probably explained by the
tradition that the framers of that body of law called
in the assistance of Greeks who enjoyed the later

Greek experience in the art of law-making. The fragments of the Attic Code of Solon show, how ever, that it had but little order, and probably the laws of Draco had even less. Quite enough too remains of these collections, both in the East and in the West, to show that they mingled up religious civil, and merely moral ordinances, without any regard to differences in their essential character; and this is consistent with all we know of early thought from other sources, the severance of law from morality, and of religion from law, belonging very distinctly to the *later* stages of mental progress.

But, whatever to a modern eye are the singularities of these Codes, their importance to ancient societies was unspeakable. The question—and it was one which affected the whole future of each community—was not so much whether there should be a code at all, for the majority of ancient societies seem to have obtained them sooner or later, and, but for the great interruption in the history of jurisprudence created by feudalism, it is likely that all modern law would be distinctly traceable to one or more of those fountain-heads. But the point on which turned the history of the race was, at what period, at what stage of their social progress, they should have their laws put into writing. In the western world the plebeian or popular element in each State successfully assailed the oligarchical monopoly, and a code was nearly universally obtained *early* in the history of the Commonwealth. But, in

the East, as I have before mentioned, the ruling
aristocracies tended to become religious rather than
military or political, and gained, therefore, rather
than lost in power; while in some instances the
physical conformation of Asiatic countries had the
effect of making individual communities larger and
more numerous than in the West; and it is a known
social law that the larger the space over which a
particular set of institutions is diffused, the greater
is its tenacity and vitality. From whatever cause,
the codes obtained by Eastern societies were obtained, relatively, much later than by Western, and
wore a very different character. The religious
oligarchies of Asia, either for their own guidance, or
for the relief of their memory, or for the instruction
of their disciples, seem in all cases to have ultimately
embodied their legal learning in a code; but the
opportunity of increasing and consolidating their
influence was probably too tempting to be resisted
Their complete monopoly of legal knowledge ap
pears to have enabled them to put off on the world
collections, not so much of the rules actually observed
as of the rules which the priestly order considered
proper to be observed. The Hindoo Code, called the
Laws of Menu, which is certainly a Brahmin compilation, undoubtedly enshrines many genuine observances of the Hindoo race, but the opinion of the
best contemporary orientalists is, that it does not,
as a whole, represent a set of rules ever actually ad
ministered in Hindostan. It is, in great part, an

ideal picture of that which, in the view of the Brahmins, *ought* to be the law. It is consistent with human nature and with the special motives of their authors, that codes like that of Menu should pretend to the highest antiquity and claim to hav emanated in their complete form from the Deity Menu, according to Hindoo mythology, is an emanation from the supreme God; but the compilation which bears his name, though its exact date is not easily discovered, is, in point of the relative progress of Hindoo jurisprudence, a recent production.

Among the chief advantages which the Twelve Tables and similar codes conferred on the societies which obtained them, was the protection which they afforded against the frauds of the privileged oligar chy and also against the spontaneous depravation and debasement of the national institutions. The Roman Code was merely an enunciation in words of the existing customs of the Roman people. Rela tively to the progress of the Romans in civilization it was a remarkably early code, and it was published at a time when Roman society had barely emerged from that intellectual condition in which civi. obligation and religious duty are inevitably con· founded. Now a barbarous society practising a body of customs, is exposed to some especial dangers which may be absolutely fatal to its progress in civilisation. The usages which a particular community is found to have adopted in its infancy and in

its primitive seats are generally those which are on
the whole best suited to promote its physical and
moral well-being; and, if they are retained in their
integrity until new social wants have taught new
practices, the upward march of society is almost
certain. But unhappily there is a law of development which ever threatens to operate upon unwritten usage. The customs are of course obeyed by
multitudes who are incapable of understanding the
true ground of their expediency, and who are therefore left inevitably to invent superstitious reasons
for their permanence. A process then commences
which may be shortly described by saying that
usage which is reasonable generates usage which is
unreasonable. Analogy, the most valuable of instruments in the maturity of jurisprudence, is the
most dangerous of snares in its infancy. Prohibi-
tions and ordinances, originally confined, for good
reasons, to a simple description of acts, are made to
apply to all acts of the same class, because a man
menaced with the anger of the gods for doing one
thing, feels a natural terror in doing any other thing
which is remotely like it. After one kind of food
has been interdicted for sanitary reasons, the prohibition is extended to all food resembling it, though
the resemblance occasionally depends on analogies
the most fanciful. So, again, a wise provision for
insuring general cleanliness dictates in time long
routines of ceremonial ablution; and that division
into classes which at a particular crisis of social his

tory is necessary for the maintenance of the national existence degenerates into the most disastrous and blighting of all human institutions—Caste. The fate of the Hindoo law is, in fact, the measure of the value of the Roman Code. Ethnology shows us that the Romans and the Hindoos sprang from the same original stock, and there is indeed a striking resemblance between what appear to have been their original customs. Even now, Hindoo jurisprudence has a substratum of forethought and sound judgment, but irrational imitation has engrafted in it an immense apparatus of cruel absurdities. From these corruptions the Romans were protected by their code. It was compiled while usage was still wholesome, and a hundred years afterwards it might have been too late. The Hindoo law has been to a great extent embodied in writing, but ancient as in one sense are the compendia which still exist in Sanskrit, they contain ample evidence that they were drawn up after the mischief had been done. We are not of course entitled to say that if the Twelve Tables had not been published the Romans would have been condemned to a civilisation as feeble and perverted as that of the Hindoos, but thus much at least is certain, that *with* their code they were exempt from the very chance of so unhappy a destiny.

CHAPTER II.

LEGAL FICTIONS.

WHEN primitive law has once been embodied in a Code, there is an end to what may be called its spontaneous development. Henceforward the changes effected in it, if effected at all, are effected deliberately and from without. It is impossible to suppose that the customs of any race or tribe remained unaltered during the whole of the long—in some instances the immense—interval between their declaration by a patriarchal monarch and their publication in writing. It would be unsafe too to affirm that no part of the alteration was effected deliberately. But from the little we know of the progress of law during this period, we are justified in assuming that set purpose had the very smallest share in producing change. Such innovations on the earliest usages as disclose themselves appear to have been dictated by feelings and modes of thought which, under our present mental conditions, we are unable to comprehend. A new era begins, however, with the Codes. Wherever, after this epoch, we trace the course of legal modification we are able to attribute it to the conscious desire of improvement, or at all events of compassing objects other than those which were aimed at in the primitive times.

It may seem at first sight that no general propositions worth trusting can be elicited from the history of legal systems subsequent to the codes. The field is too vast. We cannot be sure that we have included a sufficient number of phenomena in our observations, or that we accurately understand those which we have observed. But the undertaking will be seen to be more feasible, if we consider that after the epoch of codes the distinction between stationary and progressive societies begins to make itself felt. It is only with the progressive societies that we are concerned, and nothing is more remarkable than their extreme fewness. In spite of overwhelming evidence, it is most difficult for a citizen of western Europe to bring thoroughly home to himself the truth that the civilisation which surrounds him is a rare exception in the history of the world. The tone of thought common among us, all our hopes, fears, and speculations, would be materially affected, if we had vividly before us the relation of the progressive races to the totality of human life. It is indisputable that much the greatest part of mankind has never shown a particle of desire that its civil institutions should be improved since the

moment when external completeness was first given
to them by their embodiment in some permanent
record. One set of usages has occasionally been
violently overthrown and superseded by another;
here and there a primitive code, pretending to a
supernatural origin, has been greatly extended, and
distorted into the most surprising forms, by the perversity of sacerdotal commentators; but, except in a
small section of the world, there has been nothing
like the gradual amelioration of a legal system.
There has been material civilisation, but, instead of
the civilisation expanding the law, the law has limited the civilisation. The study of races in their primitive condition affords us some clue to the point at
which the development of certain societies has
stopped. We can see that Brahminical India has
not passed beyond a stage which occurs in the history of all the families of mankind, the stage at
which a rule of law is not yet discriminated from a
rule of religion. The members of such a society
consider that the transgression of a religious ordinance should be punished by civil penalties, and that
the violation of a civil duty exposes the delinquent
to divine correction. In China this point has been
past, but progress seems to have been there arrested, because the civil laws are coextensive with all
the ideas of which the race is capable. The difference between the stationary and progressive societies is, however, one of the great secrets which
inquiry has yet to penetrate. Among partial ex-

planations of it I venture to place the considerations urged at the end of the last chapter. It may further be remarked that no one is likely to succeed in the investigation who does not clearly realise that the stationary condition of the human race is the rule, the progressive the exception. And another indispensable condition of success is an accurate knowledge of Roman law in all its principal stages. The Roman jurisprudence has the longest known history of any set of human institutions. The character of all the changes which it underwent is tolerably well ascertained. From its commencement to its close, it was progressively modified for the better, or for what the authors of the modification conceived to be the better, and the course of improvement was continued through periods at which all the rest of human thought and action materially slackened its space, and repeatedly threatened to settle down into stagnation.

I confine myself in what follows to the progressive societies. With respect to them it may be laid down that social necessities and social opinion are always more or less in advance of Law. We may come indefinitely near to the closing of the gap between them, but it has a perpetual tendency to reopen. Law is stable; the societies we are speaking of are progressive. The greater or less happiness of a people depends on the degree of promptitude with which the gulf is narrowed.

A general proposition of some value may be ad

vanced with respect to the agencies by which Law
is brought into harmony with society. These in
strumentalities seem to me to be three in number,
Legal Fictions, Equity, and Legislation. Their his
torical order is that in which I have placed them.
Sometimes two of them will be seen operating together, and there are legal systems which have escaped the influence of one or other of them. But
I know of no instance in which the order of their
appearance has been changed or inverted. The
early history of one of them, Equity, is universally
obscure, and hence it may be thought by some that
certain isolated statutes, reformatory of the civil
law, are older than any equitable jurisdiction. My
own belief is that remedial Equity is everywhere
older than remedial Legislation ; but, should this
be not strictly true, it would only be necessary to
limit the proposition respecting their order of sequence to the periods at which they exercise a sustained and substantial influence in transforming the
original law.

I employ the word "fiction" in a sense considerably wider than that in which English lawyers are
accustomed to use it, and with a meaning much more
extensive than that which belonged to the Roman
"fictiones." Fictio, in old Roman law, is properly a
term of pleading, and signifies a false averment on
the part of the plaintiff which the defendant was
not allowed to traverse ; such, for example, as an
averment that the plaintiff was a Roman citizen

when in truth he was a foreigner. The object of these " fictiones " was, of course, to give jurisdiction, and they therefore strongly resembled the allegations in the writs of the English Queen's Bench and Exchequer, by which those Courts contrived to usurp the jurisdiction of the Common Pleas:—the allegation that the defendant was in custody of the king's marshal, or that the plaintiff was the king's debtor, and could not pay his debt by reason of the defendant's default. But now I employ the expression " Legal Fiction " to signify any assumption which conceals, or affects to conceal, the fact that a rule of law has undergone alteration, its letter remaining unchanged, its operation being modified. The words, therefore, include the instances of fictions which I have cited from the English and Roman law, but they embrace much more, for I should speak both of the English Case-law and of the Roman Responsa Prudentum as resting on fictions. Both these examples will be examined presently. The *fact* is in both cases that the law has been wholly changed; the *fiction* is that it remains what it always was. It is not difficult to understand why fictions in all their forms are particularly congenial to the infancy of society. They satisfy the desire for improvement, which is not quite wanting, at the same time that they do not offend the superstitious disrelish for change which is always present. At a particular stage of social progress they are invaluable expedients for overcoming the rigidity of law

and, indeed, without one of them, the Fiction of
Adoption which permits the family tie to be artifi
cially created, it is difficult to understand how society would ever have escaped from its swaddling
clothes, and taken its first steps towards civilisation
We must, therefore, not suffer ourselves to be af
fected by the ridicule which Bentham pours on legal fictions wherever he meets them. To revile
them as merely fraudulent is to betray ignorance of
their peculiar office in the historical development of
law. But at the same time it would be equally
foolish to agree with those theorists who, discerning
that fictions have had their uses, argue that they
ought to be stereotyped in our system. There are
several Fictions still exercising powerful influence
on English jurisprudence which could not be discarded without a severe shock to the ideas, and considerable change in the language, of English practitioners; but there can be no doubt of the general
truth that it is unworthy of us to effect an admit-
tedly beneficial object by so rude a device as a
legal fiction. I cannot admit any anomaly to be innocent, which makes the law either more difficult to
understand or harder to arrange in harmonious
order. Now, among other disadvantages, legal fic
tions are the greatest of obstacles to symmetrical
classification. The rule of law remains sticking in
the system, but it is a mere shell. It has been long
ago undermined, and a new rule hides itself under
its cover. Hence there is at once a difficulty in

knowing whether the rule which is actually operative
should be classed in its true or in its apparent place,
and minds of different casts will differ as to the
branch of the alternative which ought to be se
lected.   If the English law is ever to assume an orderly distribution, it will be necessary to prune
away the legal fictions which, in spite of some
recent legislative improvements, are still abundant
in it.

The next instrumentality by which the adapta-
tion of law to social wants is carried on I call Equity, meaning by that word any body of rules existing by the side of the original civil law, founded on
distinct principles and claiming incidentally to supersede the civil law in virtue of a superior sanctity
inherent in those principles.   The Equity whether
of the Roman Prætors or of the English Chancellors,
differs from the Fictions which in each case preceded it, in that the interference with law is open and
avowed.   On the other hand, it differs from Legislation, the agent of legal improvement which comes
after it, in that its claim to authority is grounded,
not on the prerogative of any external person or
body, not even on that of the magistrate who enun-
ciates it, but on the special nature of its principles,
to which it is alleged that all law ought to conform.
The very conception of a set of principles, invested
with a higher sacredness than those of the original
law and demanding application independently of
the consent of any external body, belongs to a much

more advanced stage of thought than that to which legal fictions originally suggested themselves.

Legislation, the enactments of a legislature which, whether it take the form of an autocratic prince or of a parliamentary assembly, is the assumed organ of the entire society, is the last of the ameliorating instrumentalities. It differs from Legal Fictions just as Equity differs from them, and it is also distinguished from Equity, as deriving its authority from an external body or person. Its obligatory force is independent of its principles. The legislature, whatever be the actual restraints imposed on it by public opinion, is in theory empowered to impose what obligations it pleases on the members of the community. There is nothing to prevent its legislating in the wantonness of caprice. Legislation may be dictated by equity, if that last word be used to indicate some standard of right and wrong to which its enactments happen to be adjusted; but then these enactments are indebted for their binding force to the authority of the legislature, and not to that of the principles on which the legislature acted; and thus they differ from rules of Equity, in the technical sense of the word, which pretend to a paramount sacredness entitling them at once to the recognition of the courts even without the concurrence of prince or parliamentary assembly. It is the more necessary to note these differences because a student of Bentham would be apt to confound Fictions, Equity, and Statute law under the single

head of legislation. They all, he would say, involve
law-making ; they differ only in respect of the machinery by which the new law is produced. That
is perfectly true, and we must never forget it; but
it furnishes no reason why we should deprive our
selves of so convenient a term as Legislation in the
special sense. Legislation and Equity are disjoined
in the popular mind and in the minds of most lawyers; and it will never do to neglect the distinction
between them, however conventional, when important practical consequences follow from it.

It would be easy to select from almost any regularly developed body of rules examples of *legal fictions*, which at once betray their true character to
the modern observer. In the two instances which I
proceed to consider, the nature of the expedient
employed is not so readily detected. The first
authors of these fictions did not perhaps intend to
innovate, certainly did not wish to be suspected of
innovating. There are, moreover, and always have
been, persons who refuse to see any fiction in the
process, and conventional language bears out their
refusal. No examples, therefore, can be better calculated to illustrate the wide diffusion of legal fic
tions, and the efficiency with which they perform
their two-fold office of transforming a system of laws
and of concealing the transformation.

We in England are well accustomed to the extension, modification, and improvement of law by a
machinery which, in theory, is incapable of altering

one jot or one line of existing jurisprudence. The process by which this virtual legislation is effected is not so much insensible as unacknowledged. With respect to that great portion of our legal system which is enshrined in cases and recorded in law reports, we habitually employ a double language, and entertain, as it would appear, a double and inconsistent set of ideas. When a group of facts come before an English Court for adjudication, the whole course of the discussion between the judge and the advocate assumes that no question is, or can be, raised which will call for the application of any principles but old ones, or of any distinctions but such as have long since been allowed. It is taken absolutely for granted that there is somewhere a rule of known law which will cover the facts of the dispute now litigated, and that, if such a rule be not discovered, it is only that the necessary patience, knowledge or acumen, is not forthcoming to detect it. Yet the moment the judgment has been rendered and reported, we slide unconsciously or unavowedly into a new language and a new train of thought. We now admit that the new decision *has* modified the law. The rules applicable have, to use the very inaccurate expression sometimes employed, become more elastic. In fact they have been changed. A clear addition has been made to the precedents, and the canon of law elicited by comparing the precedents is not the same with that which would have been obtained if the series of cases had been

curtailed by a single example. The fact that the old
rule has been repealed, and that a new one has re-
placed it, eludes us, because we are not in the habit
of throwing into precise language the legal formulas
which we derive from the precedents, so that a
change in their tenor is not easily detected unless it
is violent and glaring. I shall not now pause to
consider at length the causes which have led English lawyers to acquiesce in these curious anomalies.
Probably it will be found that originally it·was the
received doctrine that somewhere, *in nubibus* or *in
gremio magistratuum*, there existed a complete, co-
herent, symmetrical body of English law, of an amplitude sufficient to furnish principles which would
apply to any conceivable combination of circumstances. The theory was at first much more
thoroughly believed in than it is now, and indeed it
may have had a better foundation. The judges of
the thirteenth century may have really had at their
command a mine of law unrevealed to the bar and
to the lay-public, for there is some reason for suspecting that in secret they borrowed freely, though
not always wisely, from current compendia of the
Roman and Canon laws. But that storehouse was
closed as soon as the points decided at Westminster
Hall became numerous enough to supply a basis for
a substantive system of jurisprudence; and now for
centuries English practitioners have so expressed
themselves as to convey the paradoxical proposition
that, except by Equity and Statute law, nothing has

been added to the basis since it was first constituted.
We do not admit that our tribunals legislate; we
imply that they have never legislated; and yet we
maintain that the rules of the English common law,
with some assistance from the Court of Chancery
and from Parliament, are coextensive with the complicated interests of modern society.

A body of law bearing a very close and very instructive resemblance to our case-law in those particulars which I have noticed, was known to the
Romans under the name of the Responsa Prudentum, the "answers of the learned in the law." The
form of these Responses varied a good deal at different periods of the Roman jurisprudence, but
throughout its whole course they consisted of ex-
planatory glosses on authoritative written documents, and at first they were exclusively collections
of opinions interpretative of the Twelve Tables. As
with us, all legal language adjusted itself to the assumption that the text of the old Code remained
unchanged. There was the express rule. It overrode all glosses and comments, and no one openly
admitted that any interpretation of it, however eminent the interpreter, was safe from revision on appeal to the venerable texts. Yet in point of fact,
Books of Responses bearing the names of leading
jurisconsults obtained an authority at least equal to
that of our reported cases, and constantly modified,
extended, limited or practically overruled the provisions of the Decemviral law. The authors of the

new jurisprudence during the whole progress of its
formation professed the most sedulous respect for
the letter of the Code. They were merely explaining it, deciphering it, bringing out its full meaning;
but then, in the result, by piecing texts together, by
adjusting the law to states of fact which actually presented themselves and by speculating on its possible
application to others which might occur, by introducing principles of interpretation derived from the
exegesis of other written documents which fell
under their observation, they educed a vast variety
of canons which had never been dreamed of by the
compilers of the Twelve Tables and which were in
truth rarely or never to be found there. All these
treatises of the jurisconsults claimed respect on the
ground of their assumed conformity with the Code,
but their comparative authority depended on the
reputation of the particular jurisconsults who gave
them to the world. Any name of universally acknowledged greatness clothed a Book of Responses
with a binding force hardly less than that which
belonged to enactments of the legislature; and such
a book in its turn constituted a new foundation on
which a further body of jurisprudence might rest.
The Responses of the early lawyers were not however published, in the modern sense, by their author. They were recorded and edited by his pupils,
and were not therefore in all probability arranged
according to any scheme of classification. The part
of the students in these publications must be care-

fully noted, because the service they rendered to
their teacher seems to have been generally repaid
by his sedulous attention to the pupils' education.
The educational treatises called Institutes or Commentaries, which are a later fruit of the duty then
recognised, are among the most remarkable features
of the Roman system. It was apparently in these
Institutional works, and not in the books intended
for trained lawyers, that the jurisconsults gave to
the public their classifications and their proposals
for modifying and improving the technical phraseology.

In comparing the Roman Responsa Prudentum
with their nearest English counterpart, it must be
carefully borne in mind that the authority by which
this part of the Roman jurisprudence was expounded
was not the *bench*, but the *bar*. The decision of a
Roman tribunal, though conclusive in the particular
case, had no ulterior authority except such as was
given by the professional repute of the magistrate
who happened to be in office for the time. Properly speaking, there was no institution at Rome
during the republic analogous to the English Bench,
the Chambers of Imperial Germany, or the Parlia-
ments of Monarchical France. There were magistrates indeed, invested with momentous judicial
functions in their several departments, but the ten
ure of the magistracies was but for a single year, so
that they are much less aptly compared to a permanent judicature than to a cycle of offices briskly cir-

culating among the leaders of the bar. Much might
be said on the origin of a condition of things which
looks to us like a startling anomaly, but which was
in fact much more congenial than our own system
to the spirit of ancient societies, tending, as they
always did, to split into distinct orders which, how
ever exclusive themselves, tolerated no professional
hierarchy above them.

It is remarkable that this system did not produce certain effects which might on the whole have
been expected from it. It did not, for example,
popularise the Roman law,—it did not, as in some
of the Greek republics, lessen the effort of intellect
required for the mastery of the science, although its
diffusion and authoritative exposition were opposed
by no artificial barriers. On the contrary, if it had
not been for the operation of a separate set of
causes, there were strong probabilities that the Roman jurisprudence would have become as minute,
technical, and difficult as any system which has since
prevailed. Again, a consequence which might still
more naturally have been looked for, does not appear at any time to have exhibited itself. The jurisconsults, until the liberties of Rome were overthrown, formed a class which was quite undefined
and must have fluctuated greatly in numbers; nevertheless, there does not seem to have existed a doubt
as to the particular individuals whose opinion, in
their generation, was conclusive on the cases submitted to them. The vivid pictures of a leading

jurisconsult's daily practice which abound in Latin literature—the clients from the country flocking to his antechamber in the early morning, and the students standing round with their note-books to record the great lawyer's replies—are seldom or never identified at any given period with more than one or two conspicuous names. Owing too to the direct contact of the client and the advocate, the Roman people itself seems to have been always alive to the rise and fall of professional reputation, and there is abundance of proof, more particularly in the well-known oration of Cicero, "Pro Muræna," that the reverence of the commons for forensic success was apt to be excessive rather than deficient.

We cannot doubt that the peculiarities which have been noticed in the instrumentality by which the development of the Roman law was first effected, were the source of its characteristic excellence, its early wealth in principles. The growth and exuberance of principle was fostered, in part, by the competition among the expositors of the law, an influence wholly unknown where there exists a Bench, the depositaries instrusted by king or commonwealth with the prerogative of justice. But the chief agency, no doubt, was the uncontrolled multiplication of cases for legal decision. The state of facts which caused genuine perplexity to a country client was not a whit more entitled to form the basis of the jurisconsult's Response, or legal decision, than a set of hypothetical circumstances propounded by an ingenious pupil. All combinations of fact were on precisely the same footing, whether they were real or imaginary. It was nothing to the jurisconsult that his opinion was overruled for the moment by the magistrate who adjudicated on his client's case, unless that magistrate happened to rank above him in legal knowledge or the esteem of his profession. I do not, indeed, mean it to be inferred that he would wholly omit to consider his client's advantage, for the client was in earlier times the great lawyer's constituent and at a later period his paymaster, but the main road to the rewards of ambition lay through the good opinion of his order, and it is obvious that under such a system as I have been describing this was much more likely to be secured by viewing each case as an illustration of a great principle, or an exemplification of a broad rule, than by merely shaping it for an insulated forensic triumph. It is evident that powerful influence must have been exercised by the want of any distinct check on the suggestion or invention of possible questions. Where the data can be multiplied at pleasure, the facilities for evolving a general rule are immensely increased. As the law is administered among ourselves, the judge cannot travel out of the sets of facts exhibited before him or before his predecessors. Accordingly each group of circumstances which is adjudicated upon receives, to employ a Gallicism, a sort of consecration. It acquires certain qualities which distinguish it from every other case genuine or hypothetical. But at Rome, as I have attempted to explain, there was nothing resembling a Bench or Chamber of judges; and therefore no combination of facts possessed any particular value more than another. When a difficulty came for opinion before the jurisconsult, there was nothing to prevent a person endowed with a nice perception of analogy from at once proceeding to adduce and consider an entire class of supposed questions with which a particular feature connected it. Whatever were the practical advice given to the client, the *responsum* treasured up in the note-books of listening pupils would doubtless contemplate the circumstances as governed by a great principle, or included in a sweeping rule. Nothing like this has ever been possible among ourselves, and it should be acknowledged that in many criticisms passed on the English law the manner in which it has been enunciated seems to have been lost sight of. The hesitation of our courts in declaring principles may be much more reasonably attributed to the comparative scantiness of our precedents, voluminous as they appear to him who is acquainted with no other system, than to the temper of our judges. It is true that in the wealth of legal principle we are considerably poorer than several modern European nations. But they, it must be remembered, took the Roman jurisprudence for the foundation of their civil institutions. They built the *débris* of the Roman law into their walls; but in the materials and workmanship of the residue there is not much which distinguishes it favourably from the structure erected by the English judicature.

The period of Roman freedom was the period during which the stamp of a distinctive character was impressed on the Roman jurisprudence; and through all the earlier part of it, it was by the Responses of the jurisconsults that the development of the law was mainly carried on. But as we approach the fall of the republic there are signs that the Responses are assuming a form which must have been fatal to their farther expansion. They are becoming systematised and reduced into compendia. Q. Mucius Scævola, the Pontifex, is said to have published a manual of the entire Civil Law, and there are traces in the writings of Cicero of growing disrelish for the old methods, as compared with the more active instruments of legal innovation. Other agencies had in fact by this time been brought to bear on the law. The Edict, or annual proclamation of the Prætor, had risen into credit as the principal engine of law reform, and L. Cornelius Sylla, by causing to be enacted the great group of statutes called the *Leges Corneliæ*, had shown what rapid and speedy improvements can be effected by direct legislation. The final blow to the Responses was dealt by Augustus, who limited to a few leading jurisconsults the right of giving binding opinions on cases submitted to them, a change which, though it brings us nearer the ideas of the modern world, must obviously have altered fundamentally the characteristics of the legal profession and the nature of its influence on Roman law. At a later period another school of jurisconsults arose, the great lights of jurisprudence for all time. But Ulpian and Paulus, Gaius and Papinian, were not authors of Responses. Their works were regular treatises on particular departments of the law, more especially on the Prætor's Edict.

The *Equity* of the Romans and the Prætorian Edict by which it was worked into their system, will be considered in the next chapter. Of the Statute Law it is only necessary to say that it was scanty during the republic, but became very voluminous under the empire. In the youth and infancy of a nation it is a rare thing for the legislature to be called into action for the general reform of private law. The cry of the people is not for change in the laws, which are usually valued above their real worth, but solely for their pure, complete and easy administration ; and recourse to the legislative body is generally directed to the removal of some great abuse, or the decision of some incurable quarrel between classes or dynasties. There seems in the minds of the Romans to have been some association between the enactment of a large body of statutes and the settlement of society after a great civil commotion. Sylla signalised his reconstitution of the republic by the Leges Corneliæ; Julius Cæsar contemplated vast additions to the Statute Law; Augustus caused

to be passed the all-important group of Leges Juliæ
nd among later emperors the most active promul
gators of constitutions are princes who, like Con
stantine, have the concerns of the world to readjust.
The true period of Roman Statute Law does not
begin till the establishment of the empire. The
enactments of the emperors, clothed at first in the
pretence of popular sanction, but afterwards ema·
nating undisguisedly from the imperial prerogative,
extend in increasing massiveness from the consolidation of Augustus's power to the publication of the
Code of Justinian. It will be seen that even in the
reign of the second emperor a considerable approximation is made to that condition of the law and
that mode of administering it with which we are all
familiar. A statute law and a limited board of expositors have arisen into being; a permanent court
of appeal and a collection of approved commentaries will very shortly be added; and thus we are
brought close on the ideas of our own day.

CHAPTER III.

LAW OF NATURE AND EQUITY.

THE theory of a set of legal principles entitled by their intrinsic superiority to supersede the older law, very early obtained currency both in the Roman State and in England. Such a body of principles, existing in any system, has in the foregoing chapters been denominated Equity, a term which, as will presently be seen, was one (though only one) of the designations by which this agent of legal change was known to the Roman jurisconsults. The jurisprudence of the Court of Chancery, which bears the name of Equity in England, could only be adequately discussed in a separate treatise. It is extremely complex in its texture, and derives its materials from several heterogeneous sources. The early ecclesiastical chancellors contributed to it, from the Canon Law, many of the principles which lie deepest in its structure. The Roman Law, more fertile than the Canon Law in rules applicable to secular disputes, was not seldom resorted to by a later gene ration of Chancery judges, amid whose recorded dicta we often find entire texts from the *Corpus Juris Civilis* imbedded, with their terms unaltered, though their origin is never acknowledged. Still more recently, and particularly at the middle and during the latter half of the eighteenth century, the mixed systems of jurisprudence and morals constructed by the publicists of the Low Countries appear to have been much studied by English lawyers, and from the chancellorship of Lord Talbot to the commencement of Lord Eldon's chancellorship these works had considerable effect on the rulings of the Court of Chancery. The system, which obtained its ingredients from these various quarters, was greatly controlled in its growth by the necessity imposed on it of conforming itself to the analogies of the common law, but it has always answered the description of a body of comparatively novel legal principles claiming to override the older jurisprudence of the country on the strength of an intrinsic ethical superiority.

The Equity of Rome was a much simpler struc ture, and its development from its first appearance can be much more easily traced. Both its character and its history deserve attentive examination. It is the root of several conceptions which have exercised profound influence on human thought, and through human thought have seriously affected the destinies of mankind.

The Romans described their legal system as consisting of two ingredients. "All nations," says the Institutional Treatise published under the authority of the Emperor Justinian, "who are ruled by laws and customs, are governed partly by their own particular laws, and partly by those laws which are common to all mankind. The law which a people enacts is called the Civil Law of that people, but that which natural reason appoints for all mankind is called the Law of Nations, because all nations use it." The part of the law "which natural reason appoints for all mankind" was the element which the Edict of the Prætor was supposed to have worked into Roman jurisprudence. Elsewhere it is styled more simply Jus Naturale, or the Law of Nature; and its ordinances are said to be dictated by Natural Equity (*naturalis æquitas*) as well as by natural reason. I shall attempt to discover the origin of these famous phrases, Law of Nations, Law of Nature, Equity, and to determine how the conceptions which they indicate are related to one another.

The most superficial student of Roman history must be struck by the extraordinary degree in which the fortunes of the republic were affected by the presence of foreigners, under different names, on her soil. The causes of this immigration are discernible enough at a later period, for we can readily understand why men of all races should flock to the mistress of the world; but the same phenomenon of a large population of foreigners and denizens meets us in the very earliest records of the Roman State. No doubt, the instability of society in ancient Italy, composed as it was in great measure of robber tribes, gave men considerable inducement to locate themselves in the territory of any community strong enough to protect itself and them from external attack, even though protection should be purchased at the cost of heavy taxation, political disfranchisement, and much social humiliation. It is probable, however, that this explanation is imperfect, and that it could only be completed by taking into account those active commercial relations which, though they are little reflected in the military traditions of the republic, Rome appears certainly to have had with Carthage and with the interior of Italy in pre-historic times. Whatever were the circumstances to which it was attributable, the foreign element in the commonwealth determined the whole course of its history, which, at all its stages, is little more than a narrative of conflicts between a stubborn nationality and an alien population. Nothing like this has been seen in modern times; on the one hand, because modern European communities have seldom or never received any accession of foreign immigrants which was large enough to make itself felt by the bulk of the native citizens, and on the other, because modern states, being held together by allegiance to a king or political superior, absorb considerable bodies of immigrant settlers with a quickness unknown to the ancient world, where the original citizens of a commonwealth always believed themselves to be

united by kinship in blood, and resented a claim to
equality of privilege as a usurpation of their birth
right.   In the early Roman republic the principle
of the absolute exclusion of foreigners pervaded the
Civil Law no less than the constitution.   The alien
or denizen could have no share in any institution
supposed to be coeval with the State.   He could not
have the benefit of Quiritarian law.   He could not
be a party to the *nexum* which was at once the
conveyance and the contract of the primitive Romans.   He could not sue by the Sacramental Action, a mode of litigation of which the origin mounts
up to the very infancy of civilisation.   Still, neither
the interest nor the security of Rome permitted
him to be quite outlawed.   All ancient communities ran the risk of being overthrown by a very
slight disturbance of equilibrium, and the mere instinct of self-preservation would force the Romans
to devise some method of adjusting the rights and
duties of foreigners, who might otherwise—and this
was a danger of real importance in the ancient
world—have decided their controversies by armed
strife.   Moreover, at no period of Roman history
was foreign trade entirely neglected.   It was therefore probably half as a measure of police and half
in furtherance of commerce that jurisdiction was first
assumed in disputes to which the parties were either
foreigners or a native and a foreigner.   The assumption of such a jurisdiction brought with it the im
mediate necessity of discovering some principles on

which the questions to be adjudicated upon could
be settled, and the principles applied to this object by the Roman lawyers were eminently characteristic of the time. They refused, as I have said
before, to decide the new cases by puro Roman
Civil Law. They refused, no doubt because it
seemed to involve some kind of degradation, to apply the law of the particular State from which the
foreign litigant came. The expedient to which they
resorted was that of selecting the rules of law common to Rome and to the different Italian communi
ties in which the immigrants were born. In other
words, they set themselves to form a system an-
swering to the primitive and literal meaning of Jus
Gentium, that is, Law common to all Nations. Jus
Gentium was, in fact, the sum of the common ingredients in the customs of the old Italian tribes, for
they were *all the nations* whom the Romans had
the means of observing, and who sent successive
swarms of immigrants to Roman soil. Whenever a
particular usage was seen to be practised by a large
number of separate races in common it was set
down as part of the Law common to all Nations, or
Jus Gentium. Thus, although the conveyance of
property was certainly accompanied by very different forms in the different commonwealths surrounding Rome, the actual transfer, tradition, or delivery
of the article intended to be conveyed was a part
of the ceremonial in all of them. It was, for instance, a part, though a subordinate part, in the

Mancipation or conveyance peculiar to Rome. Tradition, therefore, being in all probability the only
common ingredient in the modes of conveyance
which the jurisconsults had the means of observing
was set down as an institution Juris Gentium, or
rule of the Law common to all Nations. A vast
number of other observances were scrutinised with
the same result. Some common characteristic was
discovered in all of them, which had a common
object, and this characteristic was classed in the
Jus Gentium. The Jus Gentium was accordingly
a collection of rules and principles, determined by
observation to be common to the institutions which
prevailed among the various Italian tribes.

The circumstances of the origin of the Jus Gentium are probably a sufficient safeguard against the
mistake of supposing that the Roman lawyers had
any special respect for it. It was the fruit in part
of their disdain for all foreign law, and in part of
their disinclination to give the foreigner the advantage of their own indigenous Jus Civile. It is true
that we, at the present day, should probably take a
very different view of the Jus Gentium, if we were
performing the operation which was effected by the
Roman jurisconsults. We should attach some vague
superiority or precedence to the element which we
had thus discerned underlying and pervading so
great a variety of usage. We should have a sort of
respect for rules and principles so universal. Perhaps we should speak of the common ingredient as

being of the essence of the transaction into which it
entered, and should stigmatise the remaining apparatus of ceremony, which varied in different communities, as adventitious and accidental. Or it may
be, we should infer that the races which we were
comparing at once obeyed a great system of common institutions of which the Jus Gentium was the
reproduction, and that the complicated usages of
separate commonwealths were only corruptions and
depravations of the simpler ordinances which had
once regulated their primitive state. But the results
to which modern ideas conduct the observer are, as
nearly as possible, the reverse of those which were
instinctively brought home to the primitive Roman.
What we respect or admire, he disliked or regarded
with jealous dread. The parts of jurisprudence
which he looked upon with affection were exactly
those which a modern theorist leaves out of consideration as accidental and transitory; the solemn
gestures of the mancipation; the nicely adjusted
questions and answers of the verbal contract; the
endless formalities of pleading and procedure. The
Jus Gentium was merely a system forced on his attention by a political necessity. He loved it as little
as he loved the foreigners from whose institutions it
was derived and for whose benefit it was intended.
A complete revolution in his ideas was required before it could challenge his respect, but so complete
was it when it did occur, that the true reason why
our modern estimate of the Jus Gentium differs from

that which has just been described, is that both
modern jurisprudence and modern philosophy have
inherited the matured views of the later juriscon
sults on this subject. There did come a time when,
from an ignoble appendage of the Jus Civile, the
Jus Gentium came to be considered a great though
as yet imperfectly developed model to which all law
ought as far as possible to conform. This crisis ar·
rived when the Greek theory of a Law of Nature
was applied to the practical Roman administration
of the Law common to all Nations.

The Jus Naturale, or Law of Nature, is simply
the Jus Gentium or Law of Nations seen in the light
of a peculiar theory. An unfortunate attempt to
discriminate them was made by the jurisconsult
Ulpian, with the propensity to distinguish charac·
teristic of a lawyer, but the language of Gaius, a
much higher authority, and the passage quoted be·
fore from the Institutes, leave no room for doubt
that the expressions were practically convertible
The difference between them was entirely historical,
and no distinction in essence could ever be estab
lished between them. It is almost unnecessary to
add that the confusion between Jus Gentium, or Law
common to all nations, and *international law* is en·
tirely modern. The classical expression for inter·
national law is Jus Feciale, or the law of negotiation
and diplomacy. It is, however, unquestionable
that indistinct impressions as to the meaning of Jus
Gentium had considerable share in producing the

modern theory that the relations of independent states are governed by the Law of Nature.

It becomes necessary to investigate the Greek conceptions of Nature and her law. The word φύσις, which was rendered in the Latin *natura* and our *nature*, denoted beyond all doubt originally the material universe contemplated under an as- pect which—such is our intellectual distance from those times—it is not very easy to delineate in modern language. Nature signified the physical world regarded as the result of some primordial element or law. The oldest Greek philosophers have been accustomed to explain the fabric of crea- tion as the manifestation of some single principle which they variously asserted to be movement, *force*, fire, moisture, or generation. In its simplest and most ancient sense, Nature is precisely the physical universe looked upon in this way as the manifestation of a principle. Afterwards, the later Greek sects, returning to a path from which the greatest intellects of Greece had meanwhile strayed, added the *moral* to the *physical* world in the con- ception of Nature. They extended the term till it embraced not merely the visible creation, but the thoughts, observances, and aspirations of mankind. Still, as before, it was not solely the moral phe- nomena of human society which they understood by *Nature*, but these phenomena considered as re solvable into some general and simple laws.

Now, just as the oldest Greek theorists sup

posed that the sports of chance had changed the
material universe from its simple primitive form
into its present heterogeneous condition, so their
intellectual descendants imagined that but for un-
toward accident the human race would have conformed itself to simpler rules of conduct and a less
tempestuous life. To live according to *nature* came
to be considered as the end for which man was
created, and which the best men were bound to
compass. To live according to *nature* was to rise
above the disorderly habits and gross indulgences
of the vulgar to higher laws of action which nothing but self-denial and self-command would enable
the aspirant to observe. It is notorious that this
proposition—live according to nature—was the sum
of the tenets of the famous Stoic philosophy. Now
on the subjugation of Greece that philosophy made
instantaneous progress in Roman society. It possessed natural fascinations for the powerful class
who, in theory at least, adhered to the simple
habits of the ancient Italian race, and disdained to
surrender themselves to the innovations of foreign
fashion. Such persons began immediately to affect
the Stoic precepts of life according to nature—an
affectation all the more grateful, and, I may add, all
the more noble, from its contrast with the unbounded profligacy which was being diffused through the
imperial city by the pillage of the world and by the
example of its most luxurious races. In the front
of the disciples of the new Greek school, we might

be sure, even if we did not know it historically
that the Roman lawyers figured. We have abun
dant proof that, there being substantially but twc
professions in the Roman republic, the military men
were generally identified with the party of move
ment, but the lawyers were universally at the head
of the party of resistance.

The alliance of the lawyers with the Stoic phi
losophers lasted through many centuries. Some of
the earliest names in the series of renowned juris·
consults are associated with Stoicism, and ultimate·
ly we have the golden age of Roman jurisprudence
fixed by general consent at the era of the Antonine
Cæsars, the most famous disciples to whom that
philosophy has given a rule of life. The long
diffusion of these doctrines among the members of a
particular profession was sure to affect the art which
they practised and influenced. Several positions
which we find in the remains of the Roman jurisconsults are scarcely intelligible unless we use the
Stoic tenets as our key ; but at the same time it is
a serious, though a very common, error to measure
the influence of Stoicism on Roman law by counting
up the number of legal rules which can be confidently affiliated on Stoical dogmas. It has often
been observed that the strength of Stoicism resided
not in its canons of conduct, which were often re-
pulsive and ridiculous, but in the great though
vague principle which it inculcated of resistance to
passion. Just in the same way the influence on

jurisprudence of the Greek theories, which had their
most distinct expression in Stoicism, consisted not
in the number of specific positions which they contributed to Roman law, but in the single fundamental assumption which they lent to it. After
Nature had become a household word in the mouths
of the Romans, the belief gradually prevailed among
the Roman lawyers that the old Jus Gentium was
in fact the lost code of Nature, and that the Prætor
in framing an Edictal jurisprudence on the principles of the Jus Gentium was gradually restoring
a type from which law had only departed to de-
teriorate. The inference from this belief was immediate that it was the Prætor's duty to supersede the
Civil Law as much as possible by the Edict, to revive as far as might be the institutions by which
Nature had governed man in the primitive state.
Of course there were many impediments to the
amelioration of law by this agency. There may
have been prejudices to overcome even in the legal
profession itself, and Roman habits were far too
tenacious to give way at once to mere philosophical
theory. The indirect methods by which the Edict
combated certain technical anomalies, show the caution which its authors were compelled to observe,
and down to the very days of Justinian there was
some part of the old law which had obstinately resisted its influence. But on the whole, the progress
of the Romans in legal improvement was astonish-
ingly rapid as soon as stimulus was applied to it by

the theory of Natural Law. The ideas of simplification and generalization had always been associated with the conception of Nature; simplicity,
symmetry, and intelligibility came therefore to be
regarded as the characteristics of a good legal system, and the taste for involved language, multiplied
ceremonials, and useless difficulties disappeared altogether. The strong will and unusual opportunities of Justinian were needed to bring the Roman
law to its existing shape, but the ground plan of
the system had been sketched long before the imperial reforms were effected.

What was the exact point of contact between
the old Jus Gentium and the Law of Nature? I
think that they touch and blend through Æquitas,
or Equity in its original sense; and here we seem to
come to the first appearance in jurisprudence of this
famous term, Equity. In examining an expression
which has so remote an origin and so long a history
as this, it is always safest to penetrate, if possible,
to the simple metaphor or figure which at first
shadowed forth the conception. It has generally
been supposed that Æquitas is the equivalent of the
Greek ἰσότης, i. e. the principle of equal or propor-
tionate distribution. The equal division of numbers or physical magnitudes is doubtless closely entwined with our perceptions of justice; there are
few associations which keep their ground in the
mind so stubbornly or are dismissed from it with
such difficulty by the deepest thinkers. Yet in

tracing the history of this association, it certainly does not seem to have suggested itself to very early thought, but is rather the offspring of a compara tively late philosophy. It is remarkable too that the " equality " of laws on which the Greek democ- racies prided themselves—that equality which, in the beautiful drinking song of Callistratus, Harmo- dius and Aristogiton are said to have given to Athens—had little in common with the " equity " of the Romans. The first was an equal adminis- tration of civil laws among the citizens, however limited the class of citizens might be; the last im- plied the applicability of a law, which was not civil law, to a class which did not necessarily consist of citizens. The first excluded a despot; the last in- cluded foreigners, and for some purposes slaves. On the whole, I should be disposed to look in another direction for the germ of the Roman " Equity." The Latin word " æquus " carries with it more distinctly than the Greek " ἴσος " the sense of *levelling*. Now its levelling tendency was exact- ly the characteristic of the Jus Gentium, which would be most striking to a primitive Roman. The pure Quiritarian law recognised a multitude of ar- bitrary distinctions between classes of men and kinds of property; the Jus Gentium, generalised from a comparison of various customs, neglected the Quiritarian divisions. The old Roman law estab lished, for example, a fundamental difference be- tween "Agnatic " and " Cognatic " relationship, that is, between the Family considered as based upon common subjection to patriarchal authority and the Family considered (in conformity with modern ideas) as united through the mere fact of a common descent. This distinction disappears in the "law common to all nations," as also does the difference between the archaic forms of property, Things "Mancipi" and Things "nec Mancipi." The neglect of demarcations and boundaries seems to me, therefore, the feature of the Jus Gentium which was depicted in Æquitas. I imagine that the word was at first a mere description of that constant *levelling* or removal of irregularities which went on wherever the prætorian system was applied to the cases of foreign litigants. Probably no colour of ethical meaning belonged at first to the expression; nor is there any reason to believe that the process which it indicated was otherwise than extremely distasteful to the primitive Roman mind.

On the other hand, the feature of the Jus Gentium which was presented to the apprehension of a Roman by the word Equity, was exactly the first and most vividly realised characteristic of the hypothetical state of nature. Nature implied symmetrical order, first in the physical world, and next in the moral, and the earliest notion of order doubtless involved straight lines, even surfaces, and measured distances. The same sort of picture or figure would be unconsciously before the mind's eye, whether it strove to form the outlines of the sup-

posed natural state, or whether it took in at a glance
the actual administration of the "law common to
all nations;" and all we know of primitive thought
would lead us to conclude that this ideal similarity
would do much to encourage the belief in an identity of the two conceptions. But then, while the
Jus Gentium had little or no antecedent credit at
Rome, the theory of a Law of Nature came in surrounded with all the prestige of philosophical authority, and invested with the charms of association
with an elder and more blissful condition of the
race. It is easy to understand how the difference in
the point of view would affect the dignity of the
term which at once described the operation of the
old principles and the results of the new theory.
Even to modern ears it is not at all the same thing
to describe a process as one of "levelling" and to
call it the "correction of anomalies," though the
metaphor is precisely the same. Nor do I doubt
that, when once Æquitas was understood to convey an allusion to the Greek theory, associations
which grew out of the Greek notion of ἰσότης began
to cluster round it. The language of Cicero renders
it more than likely that this was so, and it was the
first stage of a transmutation of the conception of
Equity, which almost every ethical system which
has appeared since those days has more or less
helped to carry on.

Something must be said of the formal instrumentality by which the principles and distinctions

associated, first with the Law common to all Nations, and afterwards with the Law of Nature, were gradually incorporated with the Roman law. At the crisis of primitive Roman history which is marked by the expulsion of the Tarquins, a change occurred which has its parallel in the early annals of many ancient states, but which had little in common with those passages of political affairs which we now term revolutions. It may best be described by saying that the monarchy was put into commission. The powers heretofore accumulated in the hands of a single person were parcelled out among a number of elective functionaries, the very name of the kingly office being retained and imposed on a personage known subsequently as the Rex Sacrorum or Rex Sacrificulus. As part of the change, the settled duties of the supreme judicial office devolved on the Prætor, at the time the first functionary in the commonwealth, and together with these duties was transferred the undefined supremacy over law and legislation which always attached to ancient sovereigns, and which is not obscurely related to the patriarchal and heroic authority they had once enjoyed. The circumstances of Rome gave great importance to the more indefinite portion of the functions thus transferred, as with the establishment of the republic began that series of recurrent trials which overtook the state, in the difficulty of dealing with a multitude of persons who, not coming within the technical description of indigenous

Romans were nevertheless permanently located within Roman jurisdiction. Controversies between such persons, or between such persons and native born citizens, could have remained without the pale of the remedies provided by Roman law, if the Prætor had not undertaken to decide them, and he must soon have addressed himself to the more crit ical disputes which in the extension of commerce arose between Roman subjects and avowed foreigners. The great increase of such cases in the Roman Courts about the period of the first Punic War is marked by the appointment of a special Prætor, known subsequently as the Prætor Peregrinus, who gave them his undivided attention. Meantime, one precaution of the Roman people against the revival of oppression, had consisted in obliging every magistrate whose duties had any tendency to expand their sphere, to publish, on commencing his year of office, an Edict or proclamation, in which he declared the manner in which he intended to administer his department. The Prætor fell under the rule with other magistrates; but as it was necessarily impossible to construct each year a separate system of principles, he seems to have regularly republished his predecessor's Edict with such additions and changes as the exigency of the moment or his own views of the law compelled him to introduce. The Prætor's proclamation, thus lengthened by a new portion every year, obtained the name of the Edictum Perpetuum, that is, the *continuous* or *unbroken* edict. The immense length to which it extended, together perhaps with some distaste for its necessarily disorderly texture, caused the practice of increasing it to be stopped in the year of Salvius Julianus, who occupied the magistracy in the reign of the Emperor Hadrian. The edict of that Prætor embraced therefore the whole body of equity jurisprudence, which it probably disposed in new and symmetrical order, and the perpetual edict is therefore often cited in Roman law merely as the Edict of Julianus.

Perhaps the first inquiry which occurs to an Englishman who considers the peculiar mechanism of the Edict is, what were the limitations by which these extensive powers of the Prætor were restrained? How was authority so little definite to be reconciled with a settled condition of society and law? The answer can only be supplied by careful observation of the conditions under which our own English law is administered. The Prætor, it should be recollected, was a jurisconsult himself, or a person entirely in the hands of advisers who were jurisconsults, and it is probable that every Roman lawyer waited impatiently for the time when he should fill or control the great judicial magistracy. In the interval, his tastes, feelings, prejudices, and degree of enlightenment were inevitably those of his own order, and the qualifications which he ultimately brought to office were those which he had acquired in the practice and study of his profession.

An English Chancellor goes through precisely the
same training, and carries to the woolsack the same
qualifications. It is certain when he assumes office
that he will have, to some extent, modified the law
before he leaves it; but until he has quitted his
seat, and the series of his decisions in the Law Reports has been completed, we cannot discover how
far he has elucidated or added to the principles
which his predecessors bequeathed to him. The influence of the Prætor on Roman jurisprudence differed only in respect of the period at which its
amount was ascertained. As was before stated, he
was in office but for a year, and his decisions rendered during his year, though of course irreversible
as regarded the litigants, were of no ulterior value.
The most natural moment for declaring the changes
he proposed to effect, occurred therefore at his en-
trance on the prætorship; and hence, when commencing his duties, he did openly and avowedly
that which in the end his English representative
does insensibly and sometimes unconsciously. The
checks on his apparent liberty are precisely those
imposed on an English judge. Theoretically there
seems to be hardly any limit to the powers of either
of them, but practically the Roman Prætor, no less
than the English Chancellor, was kept within the
narrowest bounds by the prepossessions imbibed
from early training, and by the strong restraints of
professional opinion, restraints of which the stringency can only be appreciated by those who have

personally experienced them. It may be added that the lines within which movement is permitted, and beyond which there is to be no travelling were chalked with as much distinctness in the one case as in the other. In England the judge follows the analogies of reported decisions on insulated groups of facts. At Rome, as the intervention of the Prætor was at first dictated by simple concern for the safety of the state, it is likely that in the earliest times it was proportioned to the difficulty which it attempted to get rid of. Afterwards, when the taste for principle had been diffused by the Responses, he no doubt used the Edict as the means of giving a wider application to those fundamental principles which he and the other practising jurisconsults, his contemporaries, believed themselves to have detected underlying the law. Latterly he acted wholly under the influence of Greek philosophical theories, which at once tempted him to advance and confined him to a particular course of progress.

The nature of the measures attributed to Salvius Julianus has been much disputed. Whatever they were, their effects on the Edict are sufficiently plain. It ceased to be extended by annual additions, and henceforward the equity jurisprudence of Rome was developed by the labours of a succession of great jurisconsults who fill with their writings the interval between the reign of Hadrian and the reign of Alexander Severus. A fragment of the wonderful

system which they built up survives in the Pan
dects of Justinian, and supplies evidence that their
works took the form of treatises on all parts of Ro
man law, but chiefly that of commentaries on the
Edict. Indeed, whatever be the immediate subject
of a jurisconsult of this epoch, he may always be
called an expositor of Equity. The principles of
the Edict had, before the epoch of its cessation,
made their way into every part of Roman jurisprudence. The Equity of Rome, it should be understood, even when most distinct from the Civil Law,
was always administered by the same tribunals.
The Prætor was the chief equity judge as well as
the great common law magistrate, and as soon as
the Edict had evolved an equitable rule the Prætor's court began to apply it in place of or by the
side of the old rule of the Civil Law, which was
thus directly or indirectly repealed without any express enactment of the legislature. The result, of
course, fell considerably short of a complete fusion
of law and equity, which was not carried out till
the reforms of Justinian. The technical severance
of the two elements of jurisprudence entailed some
confusion and some inconvenience, and there were
certain of the stubborner doctrines of the Civil Law
with which neither the authors nor the expositors
of the Edict had ventured to interfere. But at the
same time there was no corner of the field of juris
prudence which was not more or less swept over by
the influence of Equity   It supplied the jurist with

all his materials for generalisation, with all his methods of interpretation, with his elucidations of first principles, and with that great mass of limiting rules which are rarely interfered with by the legis- lator, but which seriously control the application of every legislative act.

The period of jurists ends with Alexander Sev- erus. From Hadrian to that emperor the improve- ment of law was carried on, as it is at the present moment in most continental countries, partly by approved commentaries and partly by direct legis- lation. But in the reign of Alexander Severus the power of growth in Roman Equity seems to be ex hausted, and the succession of jurisconsults comes to a close. The remaining history of the Roman law is the history of the imperial constitutions, and, at the last, of attempts to codify what had now be- come the unwieldy body of Roman jurisprudence. We have the latest and most celebrated experiment of this kind in the *Corpus Juris* of Justinian.

It would be wearisome to enter on a detailed comparison or contrast of English and Roman Equity; but it may be worth while to mention two features which they have in common. The first may be stated as follows. Each of them tended, and all such systems tend, to exactly the same state in which the old common law was when Equity first interfered with it. A time always comes at which the moral principles originally adopted have been carried out to all their legitimate consequences

and then the system founded on them becomes as
rigid, as unexpansive, and as liable to fall behind
moral progress as the sternest code of rules avowedly legal. Such an epoch was reached at Rome in the
reign of Alexander Severus; after which, though
the whole Roman world was undergoing a moral
revolution, the Equity of Rome ceased to expand.
The same point of legal history was attained in
England under the chancellorship of Lord Eldon
the first of our equity judges who, instead of enlarging the jurisprudence of his court by indirect
legislation, devoted himself through life to explaining and harmonising it. If the philosophy of legal
history were better understood in England, Lord
Eldon's services would be less exaggerated on the
one hand and better appreciated on the other than
they appear to be among contemporary lawyers.
Other misapprehensions too, which bear some practical fruit, would perhaps be avoided. It is easily
seen by English lawyers that English Equity is a
system founded on moral rules; but it is forgotten
that these rules are the morality of past centuries—
not of the present—that they have received nearly
as much application as they are capable of, and
that, though of course they do not differ largely
from the ethical creed of our own day, they are not
necessarily on a level with it. The imperfect theories of the subject which are commonly adopted
have generated errors of opposite sorts. Many
writers of treatises on Equity, struck with the com-

pleteness of the system in its present state, commit themselves expressly or implicitly to the paradoxical assertion that the founders of the chancery jurisprudence contemplated its present fixity of form when they were settling its first bases. Others, again, complain—and this is a grievance frequently observed upon in forensic arguments—that the moral rules enforced by the Court of Chancery fall short of the ethical standard of the present day. They would have each Lord Chancellor perform precisely the same office for the jurisprudence which he finds ready to his hand, which was performed for the old common law by the fathers of English equity. But this is to invert the order of the agencies by which the improvement of the law is carried on. Equity has its place and its time; but I have pointed out that another instrumentality is ready to succeed it when its energies are spent.

Another remarkable characteristic of both English and Roman Equity is the falsehood of the assumptions upon which the claim of the equitable to superiority over the legal rule is originally defended. Nothing is more distasteful to men, either as individuals or as masses, than the admission of their moral progress as a substantive reality. This unwillingness shows itself, as regards individuals, in the exaggerated respect which is ordinarily paid to the doubtful virtue of consistency. The movement of the collective opinion of a whole society is too palpable to be ignored, and is generally too visibly

for the better to be decried ; but there is the great
est disinclination to accept it as a primary phenom.
enon, and it is commonly explained as the recovery of a lost perfection—the gradual return to a
state from which the race had lapsed. This tendency to look backward instead of forward for the
goal of moral progress produced anciently, as we
have seen, on Roman jurisprudence effects the most
serious and permanent. The Roman jurisconsults,
in order to account for the improvement of their
jurisprudence by the Prætor, borrowed from Greece
the doctrine of a Natural state of man—a Natural
society—anterior to the organization of commonwealths governed by positive laws. In England,
on the other hand, a range of ideas especially congenial to Englishmen of that day, explained the
claim of Equity to override the common law by supposing a general right to superintend the administration of justice which was assumed to be vested
in the king as a natural result of his paternal authority. The same view appears in a different and
quainter form in the old doctrine that Equity flowed
from the king's conscience—the improvement which
had in fact taken place in the moral standard of the
community being thus referred to an inherent elevation in the moral sense of the sovereign. The
growth of the English constitution rendered such a
theory unpalatable after a time ; but, as the juris,
diction of the Chancery was then firmly established-
it was not worth while to devise any formal sub-

stitute for it. The theories found in modern manuals of Equity are very various, but all alike in their untenability. Most of them are modifications of the Roman doctrine of a natural law, which is indeed adopted in terms by those writers who begin a discussion of the jurisdiction of the Court of Chancery by laying down a distinction between natural justice and civil.

CHAPTER IV.

Ir will be inferred from what has been said that the theory which transformed the Roman jurisprudence had no claim to philosophical precision. It involved, in fact, one of those "mixed modes of thought" which are now acknowledged to have characterized all but the highest minds during the infancy of speculation, and which are far from undiscoverable even in the mental efforts of our own day. The Law of Nature confused the Past and the Present. Logically, it implied a state of Nature which had once been regulated by natural law; yet the jurisconsults do not speak clearly or confidently of the existence of such a state, which indeed is little noticed by the ancients except where it finds a poetical expression in the fancy of a golden age. Natural law, for all practical purposes, was something belonging to the present, something entwined with existing institutions, something which could be distinguished from them by a competent observer. The test which separated the ordinances of Nature from the gross ingredients with which they were mingled was a sense of simplicity and harmony; yet it was not on account of their simplicity and harmony that these finer elements were primarily respected, but on the score of their descent from the aboriginal reign of Nature. This confusion has not been successfully explained away by the modern disciples of the jurisconsults, and in truth modern speculations on the Law of Nature betray much more indistinctness of perception and are vitiated by much more hopeless ambiguity of language than the Roman lawyers can be justly charged with. There are some writers on the subject who attempt to evade the fundamental difficulty by contending that the code of Nature exists in the future and is the goal to which all civil laws are moving, but this is to reverse the assumptions on which the old theory rested, or rather perhaps to mix together two inconsistent theories. The tendency to look not to the past but to the future for types of perfection was brought into the world by Christianity. Ancient literature gives few or no hints of a belief that the progress of society is necessarily from worse to better.

But the importance of this theory to mankind has been very much greater than its philosophical deficiencies would lead us to expect. Indeed, it is not easy to say what turn the history of thought, and therefore, of the human race, would have taken, if the belief in a law natural had not become universal in the ancient world.

There are two special dangers to which law and society which is held together by law, appear to be liable in their infancy. One of them is that law may be too rapidly developed. This occurred with the codes of the more progressive Greek communities, which disembarrassed themselves with astonishing facility from cumbrous forms of procedure and needless terms of art, and soon ceased to attach any superstitious value to rigid rules and prescriptions. It was not for the ultimate advantage of mankind that they did so, though the immediate benefit conferred on their citizens may have been considerable. One of the rarest qualities of national character is the capacity for applying and working out the law, as such, at the cost of constant miscarriages of abstract justice, without at the same time losing the hope or the wish that law may be conformed to a higher ideal. The Greek intellect, with all its nobility and elasticity, was quite unable to confine itself within the strait waistcoat of a legal formula ; and, if we may judge them by the popular courts of Athens, of whose working we possess accurate knowledge, the Greek tribunals exhibited the strongest tendency to confound law and fact. The remains of the Orators and the forensic commonplaces preserved by Aristotle in his Treatise on Rhetoric, show that ques tions of pure law were constantly argued on every consideration which could possibly influence the mind of the judges. No durable system of jurisprudence could be produced in this way. A community which never hesitated to relax rules of written law whenever they stood in the way of an ideally perfect decision on the facts of particular cases, would only, if it bequeathed any body of judicial principles to posterity, bequeath one consisting of the ideas of right and wrong which happened to be prevalent at the time. Such jurisprudence would contain no framework to which the more advanced conceptions of subsequent ages could be fitted. It would amount at best to a philosophy, marked with the imperfections of the civilisation under which it grew up.

Few national societies have had their jurisprudence menaced by this peculiar danger of precocious maturity and untimely disintegration. It is certainly doubtful whether the Romans were ever seriously threatened by it, but at any rate they had adequate protection in their theory of Natural Law. For the Natural Law of the jurisconsults was distinctly conceived by them as a system which ought gradually to absorb civil laws, without superseding them so long as they remained unrepealed. There was no such impression of its sanctity abroad, that an appeal to it would be likely to overpower the mind of a judge who was charged with the superintendence of a particular litigation   The value and

serviceableness of the conception arose from its
keeping before the mental vision a type of perfect
law, and from its inspiring the hope of an indefinite
approximation to it, at the same time that it never
tempted the practitioner or the citizen to deny the
obligation of existing laws which had not yet been
adjusted to the theory. It is important too to observe that this model system, unlike many of those
which have mocked men's hopes in later days, was
not entirely the product of imagination. It was
never thought of as founded on quite untested principles. The notion was that it underlay existing
law and must be looked for through it. Its functions were in short remedial, not revolutionary or
anarchical. And this, unfortunately, is the exact
point at which the modern view of a Law of Nature has often ceased to resemble the ancient.

The other liability to which the infancy of society is exposed has prevented or arrested the progress
of far the greater part of mankind. The rigidity of
primitive law, arising chiefly from its early associa
tion and identification with religion, has chained
down the mass of the human race to those views
of life and conduct which they entertained at the
time when their usages were first consolidated into
a systematic form. There were one or two races
exempted by a marvellous fate from this calamity,
and grafts from these stocks have fertilised a few
modern societies; but it is still true that, over the
larger part of the world, the perfection of law has

always been considered as consisting in adherence to
the ground plan supposed to have been marked out
by the original legislator. If intellect has in such
cases been exercised on jurisprudence, it has uniformly prided itself on the subtle perversity of the
conclusions it could build on ancient texts, without
discoverable departure from their literal tenor. I
know no reason why the law of the Romans should
be superior to the laws of the Hindoos, unless the
theory of Natural Law had given it a type of excellence different from the usual one. In this one exceptional instance, simplicity and symmetry were
kept before the eyes of a society whose influence on
mankind was destined to be prodigious from other
causes, as the characteristics of an ideal and absolutely perfect law. It is impossible to overrate the
importance to a nation or profession of having a distinct object to aim at in the pursuit of improvement.
The secret of Bentham's immense influence in England during the past thirty years is his success in
placing such an object before the country. He gave
us a clear rule of reform. English lawyers of the
last century were probably too acute to be blinded
by the paradoxical commonplace that English law
was the perfection of human reason, but they acted
as if they believed it, for want of any other principle to proceed upon. Bentham made the good of
the community take precedence of every other object, and thus gave escape to a current which had
long been trying to find its way outwards.

It is not an altogether fanciful comparison if we call the assumptions we have been describing the ancient counterpart of Benthamism. The Roman theory guided men's efforts in the same direction as the theory put into shape by the Englishman; its practical results were not widely different from those which would have been attained by a sect of law-reformers who maintained a steady pursuit of the general good of the community. It would be a mistake, however, to suppose it a conscious anticipation of Bentham's principles. The happiness of mankind is, no doubt, sometimes assigned both in the popular and in the legal literature of the Romans, as the proper object of remedial legislation, but it is very remarkable how few and faint are the testimonies to this principle compared with the tributes which are constantly offered to the overshadowing claims of the Law of Nature. It was not to anything resembling philanthropy, but to their sense of simplicity and harmony—of what they significantly termed "elegance"—that the Roman jurisconsults freely surrendered themselves. The coincidence of their labours with those which a more precise philosophy would have counselled has been part of the good fortune of mankind.

Turning to the modern history of the law of nature, we find it easier to convince ourselves of the vastness of its influence than to pronounce confidently whether that influence has been exerted for good or for evil. The doctrines and institutions which may be attributed to it are the material of some of the most violent controversies debated in our time, as will be seen when it is stated that the theory of Natural Law is the source of almost all the special ideas as to law, politics, and society which France during the last hundred years has been the instrument of diffusing over the western world. The part played by jurists in French history, and the sphere of jural conceptions in French thought, have always been remarkably large. It was not indeed in France, but in Italy, that the juridical science of modern Europe took its rise, but of the schools founded by emissaries of the Italian universities in all parts of the continent, and attempted (though vainly) to be set up in our island, that established in France produced the greatest effect on the fortunes of the country. The lawyers of France immediately formed a strict alliance with the kings of the houses of Capet and Valois, and it was as much through their assertions of royal prerogative, and through their interpretations of the rules of feudal succession, as by the power of the sword, that the French monarchy at last grew together out of the agglomeration of provinces and dependencies. The enormous advantage which their understanding with the lawyers conferred on the French kings in the prosecution of their struggle with the great feudatories, the aristocracy, and the church, can only be appreciated if we take into account the ideas which prevailed in Europe far down into the middle ages

There was, in the first place, a great enthusiasm for
generalisation and a curious admiration for all general propositions, and consequently, in the field of
law, an involuntary reverence for every general
formula which seemed to embrace and sum up a
number of the insulated rules which were practised
as usages in various localities. Such general formulas it was, of course, not difficult for practitioners
familiar with the Corpus Juris or the Glosses to
supply in almost any quantity. There was, however,
another cause which added yet more considerably
to the lawyers' power. At the period of which we
are speaking, there was universal vagueness of ideas
as to the degree and nature of the authority residing
in written texts of law. For the most part, the
peremptory preface, *Ita scriptum est*, seems to have
been sufficient to silence all objections. Where a
mind of our own day would jealously scrutinise the
formula which had been quoted, would inquire its
source, and would (if necessary) deny that the body
of law to which it belonged had any authority to
supersede local customs, the elder jurist would not
probably have ventured to do more than question
the applicability of the rule, or at best cite some
counter-proposition from the Pandects or the Canon
Law. It is extremely necessary to bear in mind the
uncertainty of men's notions on this most important
side of juridical controversies, not only because it
helps to explain the weight which the lawyers
threw into the monarchical scale, but on account of

the light which it sheds on several curious historical
problems. The motives of the author of the Forged
Decretals and his extraordinary success are rendered
more intelligible by it. And, to take a phenomenon
of smaller interest, it assists us, though only partially
to understand the plagiarisms of Bracton. That an
English writer of the time of Henry III. should have
been able to put off on his countrymen as a com-
pendium of pure English law a treatise of which the
entire form and a third of the contents were directly
borrowed from the Corpus Juris, and that he should
have ventured on this experiment in a country
where the systematic study of the Roman law was
formally proscribed, will always be among the most
hopeless enigmas in the history of jurisprudence;
but still it is something to lessen our surprise when
we comprehend the state of opinion at the period
as to the obligatory force of written texts, apart
from all consideration of the source whence they
were derived.

When the kings of France had brought their
long struggle for supremacy to a successful close, an
epoch which may be placed roughly at the accession
of the branch of Valois-Angoulême to the throne,
the situation of the French jurists was peculiar, and
continued to be so down to the outbreak of the
revolution. On the one hand, they formed the best
instructed and nearly the most powerful class in the
nation. They had made good their footing as a
privileged order by the side of the feudal aristoc

racy, and they had assured their influence by an
organisation which distributed their profession over
France in great chartered corporations possessing
large defined powers and still larger indefinite claims.
In all the qualities of the advocate, the judge, and the
legislator, they far excelled their compeers throughout Europe. Their juridical tact, their ease of expression, their fine sense of analogy and harmony,
and (if they may be judged by the highest names
among them) their passionate devotion to their
conceptions of justice, were as remarkable as the
singular variety of talent which they included, a
variety covering the whole ground between the opposite poles of Cujas and Montesquieu, of D'Agues-
seau and Dumoulin. But, on the other hand, the
system of laws which they had to administer stood
in striking contrast with the habits of mind which
they had cultivated. The France which had been
in great part constituted by their efforts was smitten
with the curse of an anomalous and dissonant jurisprudence beyond every other country in Europe.
One great division ran through the country and
separated it into *Pays du Droit Ecrit* and *Pays du
Droit Coutumier*, the first acknowledging the written Roman law as the basis of their jurisprudence,
the last admitting it only so far as it supplied general forms of expression, and courses of juridical
reasoning, which were reconcileable with the local
usages. The sections thus formed were again variously subdivided. In the *Pays du Droit Coutu*

mier province differed from province, county from county, municipality from municipality, in the nature of its customs. In the *Pays du Droit Ecrit* the stratum of feudal rules which overlay the Roman law was of the most miscellaneous composition. No such confusion as this ever existed in England. In Germany it did exist, but was too much in harmony with the deep political and religious divisions of the country to be lamented or even felt. It was the special peculiarity of France that an extraordinary diversity of laws continued without sensible alteration while the central authority of the monarchy was constantly strengthening itself, while rapid approaches were being made to complete administrative unity, and while a fervid national spirit had been developed among the people. The contrast was one which fructified in many serious results, and among them we must rank the effect which it produced on the minds of the French lawyers. Their speculative opinions and their intellectual bias were in the strongest opposition to their interests and professional habits. With the keenest sense and the fullest recognition of those perfections of jurisprudence which consist in simplicity and uniformity, they believed, or seemed to believe, that the vices which actually invested French law were ineradicable; and in practice they often resisted the reformation of abuses with an obstinacy which was not shown by many among their less enlightened countrymen. But there was a way to reconcile these

contradictions. They became passionate enthusiasts
for Natural Law. The Law of Nature overleapt all
provincial and municipal boundaries; it disregarded
all distinctions between noble and burgess, between
burgess and peasant; it gave the most exalted place
to lucidity, simplicity, and system; but it committed
its devotees to no specific improvement, and did not
directly threaten any venerable or lucrative techni-
cality. Natural law may be said to have become
the common law of France, or, at all events, the
admission of its dignity and claims was the one
tenet which all French practitioners alike subscribed to. The language of the præ-revolution
ary jurists in its eulogy is singularly unqualified,
and it is remarkable that the writers on the Customs, who often made it their duty to speak dis-
paragingly of the pure Roman law, speak even
more fervidly of Nature and her rules than the
civilians who professed an exclusive respect for the
Digest and the Code. Dumoulin, the highest of all
authorities on old French Customary Law, has some
extravagant passages on the Law of Nature; and
his panegyrics have a peculiar rhetorical turn which
indicates a considerable departure from the caution
of the Roman jurisconsults. The hypothesis of a
Natural Law had become not so much a theory
guiding practice as an article of speculative faith,
and accordingly we shall find that, in the transfor
mation which it more recently underwent, its weak

est parts rose to the level of its strongest in the esteem of its supporters.

The eighteenth century was half over when the most critical period in the history of Natural Law was reached. Had the discussion of the theory and of its consequences continued to be exclusively the employment of the legal profession, there would possibly have been an abatement of the respect which it commanded; for by this time the *Esprit des Lois* had appeared. Bearing in some exaggera-tions the marks of the excessive violence with which its author's mind had recoiled from assumptions usually suffered to pass without scrutiny, yet show-ing in some ambiguities the traces of a desire to compromise with existing prejudice, the book of Montesquieu, with all its defects, still proceeded on that Historical Method before which the Law of Nature has never maintained its footing for an in-stant. Its influence on thought ought to have been as great as its general popularity; but, in fact, it was never allowed time to put it forth, for the counter-hypothesis which it seemed destined to de stroy passed suddenly from the forum to the street, and became the key-note of controversies far more exciting than are ever agitated in the courts or the schools. The person who launched it on its new career was that remarkable man who, without learn-ing, with few virtues, and with no strength of char-acter, has nevertheless stamped himself ineffaceably on history by the force of a vivid imagination, and

by the help of a genuine and burning love for his fel-
low-men, for which much will always have to be for-
given him.   We have never seen in our own generation—indeed the world has not seen more than once
or twice in all the course of history—a literature
which has exercised such prodigious influence over
the minds of men, over every cast and shade of intellect, as that which emanated from Rousseau between 1749 and 1762.   It was the first attempt to
re-erect the edifice of human belief after the purely
iconoclastic efforts commenced by Bayle, and in part
by our own Locke, and consummated by Voltaire;
and besides the superiority which every constructive
effort will always enjoy over one that is merely de-
structive, it possessed the immense advantage of ap-
pearing amid an all but universal scepticism as to
the soundness of all foregone knowledge in matters
speculative.   Now, in all the speculations of Rousseau, the central figure, whether arrayed in an English dress as the signatary of a social compact, or
simply stripped naked of all historical qualities, is
uniformly Man, in a supposed state of nature.   Every
law or institution which would misbeseem this
imaginary being under these ideal circumstances is
to be condemned as having lapsed from an original
perfection; every transformation of society which
would give it a closer resemblance to the world
over which the creature of Nature reigned, is admirable and worthy to be effected at any apparent
cost.   The theory is still that of the Roman law-

yers, for in the phantasmagoria with which the
Natural Condition is peopled, every feature and
characteristic eludes the mind except the simplicity
and harmony which possessed such charms for the
jurisconsult; but the theory is, as it were, turned up-
side down. It is not the Law of Nature, but the
State of Nature, which is now the primary subject
of contemplation. The Roman had conceived that
by careful observation of existing institutions parts
of them could be singled out which either exhibited
already, or could by judicious purification be made
to exhibit, the vestiges of that reign of nature whose
reality he faintly affirmed. Rousseau's belief was
that a perfect social order could be evolved from
the unassisted consideration of the natural state, a
social order wholly irrespective of the actual condition of the world and wholly unlike it. The
great difference between the views is that one bit-
terly and broadly condemns the present for its un-
likeness to the ideal past; while the other, assuming
the present to be as necessary as the past, does not
affect to disregard or censure it. It is not worth
our while to analyse with any particularity that
philosophy of politics, art, education, ethics, and
social relation which was constructed on the basis
of a state of nature. It still possesses singular fascination for the looser thinkers of every country, and
is no doubt the parent, more or less remote, of almost all the prepossessions which impede the employment of the Historical Method of inquiry but

its discredit with the higher minds of our day is
deep enough to astonish those who are familiar with
the extraordinary vitality of speculative error.
Perhaps the question most frequently asked nowadays is not what is the value of these opinions, bu
what were the causes which gave them such over
shadowing prominence a hundred years ago. The
answer is, I conceive, a simple one. The study
which in the last century would best have corrected
the misapprehensions into which an exclusive attention to legal antiquities is apt to betray was the
study of religion. But Greek religion, as then understood, was dissipated in imaginative myths. The
Oriental religions, if noticed at all, appeared to be
lost in vain cosmogonies. There was but one body
of primitive records which was worth studying—
the early history of the Jews. But resort to this
was prevented by the prejudices of the time. One
of the few characteristics which the school of Rousseau had in common with the school of Voltaire
was an utter disdain of all religious antiquities; and,
more than all, of those of the Hebrew race. It is
well known that it was a point of honour with the
reasoners of that day to assume not merely that the
institutions called after Moses were not divinely dictated, nor even that they were codified at a later
date than that attributed to them, but that they and
the entire Pentateuch were a gratuitous forgery, executed after the return from the Captivity. Debar-
red, therefore, from one chief security against specu-

lative delusion, the philosophers of France, in their
eagerness to escape from what they deemed a superstition of the priests, flung themselves headlong into
a superstition of the lawyers.

But though the philosophy founded on the hypothesis of a state of nature has fallen low in general
esteem, in so far as it is looked upon under its coarser
and more palpable aspect, it does not follow that in
its subtler disguises it has lost plausibility, popularity, or power. I believe, as I have said, that it is
still the great antagonist of the Historical Method;
and whenever (religious objections apart) any mind
is seen to resist or contemn that mode of investigation, it will generally be found under the influence
of a prejudice or vicious bias traceable to a conscious
or unconscious reliance on a non-historic, natural,
condition of society or the individual. It is chiefly,
however, by allying themselves with political and
social tendencies that the doctrines of Nature and
her law have preserved their energy. Some of these
tendencies they have stimulated, others they have
actually created, to a great number they have given
expression and form. They visibly enter largely
into the ideas which constantly radiate from France
over the civilised world, and thus become part of the
general body of thought by which its civilisation is
modified. The value of the influence which they
thus exercise over the fortunes of the race is of
course one of the points which our age debates most
warmly, and it is beside the purpose of this treatise

to discuss it. Looking back, however, to the period at which the theory of the state of nature acquired the maximum of political importance, there are few who will deny that it helped most powerfully to bring about the grosser disappointments of which the first French revolution was fertile. It gave birth, or intense stimulus, to the vices of mental habit all but universal at the time, disdain of positive law, impatience of experience, and the preference of *à priori* to all other reasoning. In proportion too as this philosophy fixes its grasp on minds which have thought less than others and fortified themselves with smaller observation, its tendency is to become distinctly anarchical. It is surprising to note how many of the *Sophismes Anarchiques* which Dumont published for Bentham, and which embody Bentham's exposure of errors distinctively French, are derived from the Roman hypothesis in its French transformation, and are unintelligible unless referred to it. On this point too it is a curious exercise to consult the *Moniteur* during the principal eras of the Revolution. The appeals to the Law and State of Nature become thicker as the times grow darker.

There is a single example which very strikingly illustrates the effects of the theory of natural law on modern society, and indicates how very far are those effects from being exhausted. There cannot, I conceive, be any question that to the assumption of the Law Natural we owe the doctrine of the fundamental equality of human beings. That " all

men are equal" is one of a large number of legal
provisions which, in progress of time, have become
political. The Roman jurisconsults of the Antonine era lay down that "omnes homines naturâ
æquales sunt," but in their eyes this is a strictly juridical axiom. They intend to affirm that under
the hypothetical Law of Nature, and in so far as
positive law approximates to it, the arbitrary distinctions which the Roman Civil Law maintained
between classes of persons cease to have a legal existence. The rule was one of considerable importance to the Roman practitioner, who required to
be reminded that, wherever Roman jurisprudence
was assumed to conform itself exactly to the code
of Nature, there was no difference in the contemplation of the Roman tribunals between citizen
and foreigner, between freeman and slave, between
Agnate and Cognate. The jurisconsults who thus
expressed themselves most certainly never intended
to censure the social arrangements under which civil
law fell somewhat short of its speculative type; nor
did they apparently believe that the world would
ever see human society completely assimilated to the
economy of nature. But when the doctrine of human equality makes its appearance in a modern
dress it has evidently clothed itself with a new
shade of meaning. Where the Roman jurisconsult
had written "æquales sunt," meaning exactly what
he said, the modern civilian wrote "all men are
equal" in the sense of "all men ought to be equal."

The peculiar Roman idea that natural law coexisted
with civil law and gradually absorbed it, had evidently been lost sight of, or had become unintelligible,
and the words which had at most conveyed a theory
concerning the origin, composition and development of human institutions, were beginning to express the sense of a great standing wrong suffered
by mankind. As early as the beginning of the
fourteenth century, the current language concerning
the birth-state of men, though visibly intended to
be identical with that of Ulpian and his contemporaries has assumed an altogether different form and
meaning. The preamble to the celebrated ordinance of King Louis Hutin, enfranchising the serfs
of the royal domains, would have sounded strangely to Roman ears. " Whereas, according to natural law, everybody ought to be born free; and by
some usages and customs which, from long antiquity, have been introduced and kept until now in our
realm, and peradventure by reason of the misdeeds
of their predecessors, many persons of our common
people have fallen into servitude, therefore, We,"
&c. This is the enunciation not of a legal rule but
of a political dogma; and from this time the equality of men is spoken of by the French lawyers just
as if it were a political truth which happened to
have been preserved among the archives of their
science. Like all other deductions from the hypothesis of a Law Natural, and like the belief
itself in a Law of Nature, it was languidly as

sented to and suffered to have little influence on
opinion and practice until it passed out of the possession of the lawyers into that of the literary men
of the eighteenth century and of the public which
sat at their feet. With them it became the most
distinct tenet of their creed, and was even regarded
as a summary of all the others. It is probable,
however, that the power which it ultimately acquired over the events of 1789 was not entirely
owing to its popularity in France, for in the middle
of the century it passed over to America. The
American lawyers of the time, and particularly
those of Virginia, appear to have possessed a stock
of knowledge which differed chiefly from that of
their English contemporaries in including much
which could only have been derived from the legal
literature of continental Europe.   A very few
glances at the writings of Jefferson will show how
strongly his mind was affected by the semi-juridical,
semi-popular opinions which were fashionable in
France, and we cannot doubt that it was sympathy
with the peculiar ideas of the French jurists which
led him and the other colonial lawyers who guided
the course of events in America to join the specially
French assumption that " all men are born equal "
with the assumption, more familiar to Englishmen,
that all men are born free, in the very first lines of
their Declaration of Independence.   The passage
was one of great importance to the history of the
doctrine before us.   The American lawyers, in thus

prominently and emphatically affirming the funda
mental equality of human beings, gave an impulse
to political movements in their own country, and in
a less degree in Great Britain, which is far from
having yet spent itself; but beside this they re
turned the dogma they had adopted to its home in
France, endowed with vastly greater energy and
enjoying much greater claims on general reception
and respect. Even the more cautious politicians
of the first Constituent Assembly repeated Ulpian's
proposition as if it at once commended itself to the
instincts and intuitions of mankind; and of all the
" principles of 1789 " it is the one which has been
least strenuously assailed, which has most thoroughly leavened modern opinion, and which promises to modify most deeply the constitution of societies and the politics of states.

The grandest function of the Law of Nature was
discharged in giving birth to modern International
Law and to the modern Law of War, but this part
of its effects must here be dismissed with consideration very unequal to its importance.

Among the postulates which form the foundation of International Law, or of so much of it as retains the figure which it received from its original
architects, there are two or three of preeminent importance. The first of all is expressed in the position that there is a determinable Law of Nature
Grotius and his successors took the assumption
directly from the Romans, but they differed widely

from the Roman jurisconsults and from each other
in their ideas as to the mode of determination. The
ambition of almost every Publicist who has flourished since the revival of letters has been to provide
new and more manageable definitions of Nature
and of her law, and it is indisputable that the conception in passing through the long series of writers
on Public Law has gathered round it a large accre-
tion, consisting of fragments of ideas derived from
nearly every theory of ethics which has in its turn
taken possession of the schools. Yet it is a remarkable proof of the essentially historical character
of the conception that, after all the efforts which
have been made to evolve the code of nature from
the necessary characteristics of the natural state, so
much of the result is just what it would have been
if men had been satisfied to adopt the dicta of the
Roman lawyers without questioning or reviewing
them. Setting aside the Conventional or Treaty
Law of Nations, it is surprising how large a part
of the system is made up of pure Roman law.
Wherever there is a doctrine of the jurisconsults
affirmed by them to be in harmony with the Jus
Gentium, the Publicists have found a reason for
borrowing it, however plainly it may bear the
marks of a distinctively Roman origin. We may
observe too that the derivative theories are afflicted
with the weakness of the primary notion. In the
majority of the Publicists, the mode of thought is
still " mixed." In studying these writers, the great

difficulty is always to discover whether they are
discussing law or morality—whether the state of
international relations they describe is actual or
ideal—whether they lay down that which is, or
that which, in their opinion, ought to be.

The assumption that Natural Law is binding on
states *inter se* is the next in rank of those which
underlie International Law. A series of assertions
or admissions of this principle may be traced up to
the very infancy of modern juridical science, and at
first sight it seems a direct inference from the teaching of the Romans. The civil condition of society
being distinguished from the natural by the fact
that in the first there is a distinct author of law,
while in the last there is none, it appears as if the
moment a number of *units* were acknowledged to
obey no common sovereign or political superior
they were thrown back on the ulterior behests of
the Law Natural. States are such units ; the hypothesis of their independence excludes the notion
of a common lawgiver, and draws with it, therefore,
according to a certain range of ideas, the notion of
subjection to the primeval order of nature. The
alternative is to consider independent communities
as not related to each other by any law, but this
condition of lawlessness is exactly the vacuum which
the Nature of the jurisconsults abhorred. There is
certainly apparent reason for thinking that if the
mind of a Roman lawyer rested on any sphere from
which civil law was banished, it would instantly fill

the void with the ordinances of Nature. It is never safe, however, to assume that conclusions, however certain and immediate in our own eyes, were ac tually drawn at any period of history. No passage has ever been adduced from the remains of Roman law which, in my judgment, proves the jurisconsults to have believed natural law to have obligatory force between independent commonwealths; and we cannot but see that to citizens of the Roman empire, who regarded their sovereign's dominions as conterminous with civilization, the equal subjec tion of states to the Law of Nature, if contemplated at all, must have seemed at most an extreme result of curious speculation. The truth appears to be that modern International Law, undoubted as is its descent from Roman law, is only connected with it by an irregular filiation. The early modern inter preters of the jurisprudence of Rome, misconceiving the meaning of Jus Gentium, assumed without hesi tation that the Romans had bequeathed to them a system of rules for the adjustment of international transactions. This " Law of Nations " was at first an authority which had formidable competitors to strive with, and the condition of Europe was long such as to preclude its universal reception. Grad ually, however, the western world arranged itself in a form more favourable to the theory of the civilians; circumstances destroyed the credit of rival doctrines; and at last, at a peculiarly felici tous conjuncture, Ayala and Grotius were able to

obtain for it the enthusiastic assent of Europe, an
assent which has been over and over again renewed
in every variety of solemn engagement. The great
men to whom its triumph is chiefly owing attempted, it need scarcely be said, to place it on an entirely new basis, and it is unquestionable that in the
course of this displacement they altered much of its
structure, though far less of it than is commonly
supposed. Having adopted from the Antonine
jurisconsults the position that the Jus Gentium
and the Jus Naturæ were identical, Grotius, with
his immediate predecessors and his immediate successors, attributed to the Law of Nature an authority which would never perhaps have been claimed
for it, if " Law of Nations " had not in that age
been an ambiguous expression. They laid down
unreservedly that Natural Law is the code of states,
and thus put in operation a process which has continued almost down to our own day, the process of
engrafting on the international system rules which
are supposed to have been evolved from the unassisted contemplation of the conception of Nature.
There is too one consequence of immense practical
importance to mankind which, though not unknown
during the early modern history of Europe, was
never clearly or universally acknowledged till the
doctrines of the Grotian school had prevailed. If
the society of nations is governed by Natural Law
the atoms which compose it must be absolutely
equal. Men under the sceptre of Nature are all

equal, and accordingly commonwealths are equal if the international state be one of nature. The proposition that independent communities, however different in size and power, are all equal in the view of the law of nations, has largely contributed to the happiness of mankind, though it is constantly threatened by the political tendencies of each successive age. It is a doctrine which probably would never have obtained a secure footing at all if International Law had not been entirely derived from the majestic claims of Nature by the Publicists who wrote after the revival of letters.

On the whole, however, it is astonishing, as I have observed before, how small a proportion the additions made to International Law since Grotius's day bear to the ingredients which have been simply taken from the most ancient stratum of the Roman Jus Gentium. Acquisition of territory has always been the great spur of national ambition, and the rules which govern this acquisition, together with the rules which moderate the wars in which it too frequently results, are merely transcribed from the part of the Roman law which treats of the modes of acquiring property *jure gentium*. These modes of acquisition were obtained by the elder jurisconsults, as I have attempted to explain, by abstracting a common ingredient from the usages observed to prevail among the various tribes surrounding Rome ; and, having been classed on account of their origin in the " law common to all nations," they

were thought by the later lawyers to fit in, on the
score of their simplicity, with the more recent conception of a Law Natural. They thus made their
way into the modern Law of Nations, and the result is that those parts of the international system
which refer to *dominion*, its nature, its limitations,
the modes of acquiring and securing it, are pure
Roman Property Law—so much, that is to say, of
the Roman Law of Property as the Antonine jurisconsults imagined to exhibit a certain congruity
with the natural state. In order that these chapters of International Law may be capable of application, it is necessary that sovereigns should be related to each other like the members of a group of
Roman proprietors. This is another of the postulates which lie at the threshold of the International
Code, and it is also one which could not possibly
have been subscribed to during the first centuries
of modern European history. It is resolvable into
the double proposition that " sovereignty is territorial," *i. e.* that it is always associated with the
proprietorship of a limited portion of the earth's
surface, and that " sovereigns *inter se* are to be
deemed not *paramount*, but *absolute* owners of the
state's territory.

Many contemporary writers on Internationl Law
tacitly assume that the doctrines of their system,
founded on principles of equity and common sense,
were capable of being readily reasoned out in every
stage of modern civilisation. But this assumption,

while it conceals some real defects of the international theory, is altogether untenable so far as regards a large part of modern history. It is not true that the authority of the Jus Gentium in the concerns of nations was always uncontradicted; on the contrary, it had to struggle long against the claims of several competing systems. It is again not true that the territorial character of sovereignty was always recognised, for long after the dissolution of the Roman dominion the minds of men were under the empire of ideas irreconcileable with such a conception. An old order of things, and of views founded on it, had to decay—a new Europe, and an apparatus of new notions congenial to it, had to spring up—before two of the chiefest postulates of International Law could be universally conceded.

It is a consideration well worthy to be kept in view, that during a large part of what we usually term modern history no such conception was entertained as that of "*territorial sovereignty.*" Sovereignty was not associated with dominion over a portion or subdivision of the earth. The world had lain for so many centuries under the shadow of Imperial Rome as to have forgotten that distribution of the vast spaces comprised in the empire which had once parcelled them out into a number of independent commonwealths, claiming immunity from extrinsic interference, and pretending to equality of national rights. After the subsidence of the barbarian irruptions, the notion of sovereignty that prevailed seems to have been twofold. On the one hand it assumed the form of what may be called "*tribe*-sovereignty." The Franks, the Burgundians, the Vandals, the Lombards, and Visigoths were masters, of course, of the territories which they occupied, and to which some of them had given a geographical appellation; but they based no claim of right upon the fact of territorial possession, and indeed attached no importance to it whatever. They appear to have retained the traditions which they brought with them from the forest and the steppe, and to have still been in their own view a patriarchal society, a nomad horde, merely encamp- ed for the time upon the soil which afforded them sustenance. Part of Transalpine Gaul, with part of Germany, had now become the country *de facto* oc- cupied by the Franks—it was France; but the Mero- vingian line of chieftains, the descendants of Clovis, were not Kings of France, they were Kings of the Franks. Territorial titles were not unknown, but they seem at first to have come into use only as a convenient mode of designating the ruler of a *por- tion* of the tribe's possessions; the king of a *whole* tribe was king of his people, not of his people's lands. The alternative to this peculiar notion of sovereignty appears to have been—and this is the important point—the idea of universal dominion. When a monarch departed from the special relation of chief to clansmen, and became solicitous, for pur

poses of his own, to invest himself with a novel
form of sovereignty, the precedent which suggested
itself for his adoption was the domination of the
Emperors of Rome. To parody a common quota-
tion, he became " *aut Cæsar aut nullus.*" Either he
pretended to the full prerogative of the Byzantine
Emperor, or he had no political status. In our own
age, when a new dynasty is desirous of obliterating
the prescriptive title of a deposed line of sovereigns,
it takes its designation from the *people*, instead of
the *territory*. Thus we have Emperors and Kings of
the French, and a King of the Belgians. At the period of which we have been speaking, under similar
circumstances, a different alternative presented itself.
The chieftain who would no longer call himself
King of the tribe must claim to be Emperor of the
world. Thus, when the hereditary Mayors of the
Palace had ceased to compromise with the monarchs they had long since virtually dethroned, they
soon became unwilling to call themselves merely
Kings of the Franks, a title which belonged to the
displaced Merovings; but they could not style
themselves Kings of France, for such a designation,
though apparently not unknown, was not a title
of dignity. Accordingly they came forward as
aspirants to universal empire. Their motive has
been greatly misapprehended. It has been taken
for granted by recent French writers that Charlemagne was far before his age, quite as much in the
character of his designs as in the energy with

which he prosecuted them. Whether it be true or not that anybody is at any time before his age, it is certainly true that Charlemagne, in aiming at an unlimited dominion, was emphatically taking the only course which the characteristic idea of his age permitted him to follow. Of his intellectual eminence there cannot be a question, but it is proved by his acts and not by his theory.

The speculative universality of sovereignty long continued to be associated with the Imperial throne, and indeed was never thoroughly dissociated from it so long as the empire of Germany lasted. Territorial sovereignty—the view which connects sovereignty with the possession of a limited portion of the earth's surface—was distinctly an offshoot, though a tardy one, of *feudalism.* This might have been expected *à priori*, for it was feudalism which for the first time linked personal duties, and by consequence personal rights, to the ownership of land. Whatever be the proper view of its origin and legal nature, the best mode of vividly picturing to ourselves the feudal organisation is to begin with the basis; to consider the relation of the tenant to the patch of soil which created and limited his services —and then to mount up, through narrowing circles of superfeudation, till we approximate to the apex of the system. Where that summit exactly was during the later portion of the dark ages it is not easy to decide. Probably, wherever the conception of tribe sovereignty has really decayed, the topmost point

was always assigned to the supposed successor of
the Cæsars of the West. But before long, when
the actual sphere of imperial authority had immensely contracted, and when the emperors had
concentrated the scanty remains of their power
upon Germany and North Italy, the highest feudal
superiors in all the outlying portions of the former
Carlovingian empire found themselves practically
without a supreme head. Gradually they habituated themselves to the new situation, and the fact
of immunity put at last out of sight the theory of
dependence; but there are many symptoms that
this change was not quite easily accomplished;
and, indeed, to the impression that in the nature
of things there must necessarily be a culminating
domination somewhere, we may, no doubt, refer
the increasing tendency to attribute secular superiority to the See of Rome. The completion of the
first stage in the revolution of opinion is marked,
of course, by the accession of the Capetian dynasty
in France. Before that epoch arrived, several of
the holders of the great territorial fiefs into which
the Carlovingian empire was now split up, had
begun to call themselves Kings, instead of Dukes
or Counts; but the important change occurred
when the feudal prince of a limited territory surrounding Paris, usurped from the earlier house
their dynastic title, *Kings of the French.* Hugues
Capet and his descendants were kings in quite a
new sense, sovereigns standing in the same relation
to the soil of France as the baron to his estate, the

tenant to his freehold ; and the old tribal appella
tion, though long retained in the official Latin
style of the reigning house, passed rapidly, in the
vernacular, into *Kings of France.* The form of
the monarchy in France had visible effects in has
tening changes which were elsewhere proceeding
in the same direction. The kingship of our Anglo
Saxon regal houses was midway between the chieftainship of a tribe and a territorial supremacy ;
but the superiority of the Norman monarchs, imitated from that of the King of France, was dis
tinctly a territorial sovereignty. Every subsequent
dominion which was established or consolidated
was formed on the latter model. Spain, Naples,
and the principalities founded on the ruins of
municipal freedom in Italy, were all under rulers
whose sovereignty was territorial. Few things, I
may add, are more curious than the gradual lapse
of the *Venetians* from one view to the other. At
the commencement of its foreign conquests, the republic regarded itself as an antitype of the Roman
commonwealth, governing a number of subject
provinces. Move a century onwards, and you find
that it wishes to be looked upon as a corporate
sovereign, claiming the rights of a feudal suzerain
over its possessions in Italy and the Ægean.

During the period through which the popular
ideas on the subject of sovereignty were undergoing this remarkable change, the system which
stood in the place of what we now call International Law was heterogeneous in form and incon-

sistent in the principles to which it appealed.
Over so much of Europe as was comprised in the
Romano-German empire, the connection of the con-
federate states was regulated by the complex and
as yet incomplete mechanism of the Imperial constitution; and, surprising as it may seem to us, it
was a favorite notion of German lawyers that the
relations of commonwealths, whether inside or outside the empire, ought to be regulated not by the
Jus Gentium, but by the pure Roman jurisprudence, of which Cæsar was still the centre. This
doctrine was less confidently repudiated in the
outlying countries than we might have supposed
antecedently; but substantially, through the rest
of Europe feudal subordinations furnished a substitute for a public law; and when those were
undetermined or ambiguous, there lay behind, in
theory at least, a supreme regulating force in the
authority of the head of the Church. It is certain,
however, that both feudal and ecclesiastical influences were rapidly decaying during the fifteenth,
and even the fourteenth century; and if we closely
examine the current pretexts of wars, and the
avowed motives of alliances, it will be seen that,
step by step with the displacement of the old principles, the views afterwards harmonized and consolidated by Ayala and Grotius were making considerable progress, though it was silent and but
slow. Whether the fusion of all the sources of
authority would ultimately have evolved a system
of international relations, and whether that system

would have exhibited material differences from the fabric of Grotius, is not now possible to decide, for as a matter of fact the Reformation annihilated all its potential elements except one. Beginning in Germany, it divided the princes of the empire by a gulf too broad to be bridged over by the Imperial supremacy, even if the Imperial superior had stood neutral. He, however, was forced to take colour with the church against the reformers; the Pope was, as a matter of course, in the same predicament; and thus the two authorities to whom belonged the office of mediation between combatants became themselves the chiefs of one great faction in the schism of the nations. Feudalism, already enfeebled and discredited as a principle of public relations, furnished no bond whatever which was stable enough to countervail the alliances of religion. In a condition, therefore, of public law which was little less than chaotic, those views of a state system to which the Roman jurisconsults were supposed to have given their sanction alone remained standing. The shape, the symmetry, and the prominence which they assumed in the hands of Grotius are known to every educated man; but the great marvel of the Treatise "De Jure Belli et Pacis," was its rapid, complete, and universal success. The horrors of the Thirty Years' War, the boundless terror and pity which the unbridled license of the soldiery was exciting, must, no doubt, be taken to explain that success in some measure, but they do not wholly account for it.

Very little penetration into the ideas of that age is required to convince one that, if the ground plan of the international edifice which was sketched in the great book of Grotius had not appeared to be theoretically perfect, it would have been discarded by jurists and neglected by statesmen and soldiers.

It is obvious that the speculative perfection of the Grotian system is intimately connected with that conception of territorial sovereignty which we have been discussing. The theory of International Law assumes that commonwealths are, relatively to each other, in a state of nature; but the component atoms of a natural society must, by the fundamental assumption, be insulated and independent of each other. If there be a higher power connecting them, however slightly and occasionally, by the claim of common supremacy, the very conception of a common superior introduces the notion of positive law and excludes the idea of a law natural. It follows, therefore, that if the universal suzerainty of an Imperial head had been admitted even in bare theory, the labours of Grotius would have been idle. Nor is this the only point of junction between modern public law and those views of sovereignty of which I have endeavored to describe the development. I have said that there are entire departments of international jurisprudence which consist of the Roman Law of Property. What then is the inference? It is, that if there had been no such change as I have described in the estimate of sovereignty—if sovereignty had not been associated with the proprietorship of a limited portion of the earth, had not, in other words, become territorial—three parts of the Grotian theory would have been incapable of appli cation.

CHAPTER V.

PRIMITIVE SOCIETY AND ANCIENT LAW.

THE necessity of submitting the subject of jurisprudence to scientific treatment has never been entirely
lost sight of in modern times, and the essays which
the consciousness of this necessity has produced have
proceeded from minds of very various calibre, but
there is not much presumption, I think, in asserting
that what has hitherto stood in the place of a sci
ence has for the most part been a set of guesses,
those very guesses of the Roman lawyers which were
examined in the two preceding chapters. A series
of explicit statements, recognising and adopting these
conjectural theories of a natural state, and of a system of principles congenial to it, has been continued
with but brief interruption from the days of their
inventors to our own. They appear in the annota-
tions of the Glossators who founded modern jurisprudence, and in the writings of the scholastic jurists
who succeeded them. They are visible in the dog
mas of the canonists. They are thrust into promi-

nence by those civilians of marvellous erudition, who
flourished at the revival of ancient letters. Grotius
and his successors invested them not less with bril-
liancy and plausibility than with practical importance. They may be read in the introductory chapters of our own Blackstone, who has transcribed
them textually from Burlamaqui, and wherever the
manuals published in the present day for the guidance of the student or the practitioner begin with
any discussion of the first principles of law, it always resolves itself into a restatement of the Roman
hypothesis. It is however from the disguises with
which these conjectures sometimes clothe themselves, quite as much as from their native form,
that we gain an adequate idea of the subtlety with
which they mix themselves in human thought. The
Lockeian theory of the origin of Law in a Social
Compact scarcely conceals its Roman derivation,
and indeed is only the dress by which the ancient
views were rendered more attractive to a particular
generation of the moderns; but on the other hand
the theory of Hobbes on the same subject was purposely devised to repudiate the reality of a law of
nature as conceived by the Romans and their disciples. Yet these two theories, which long divided
the reflecting politicians of England into hostile
camps, resemble each other strictly in their fundamental assumption of a non-historic, unverifiable,
condition of the race. Their authors differed as to
the characteristics of the præ-social state, and as to

the nature of the abnormal action by which men lifted themselves out of it into that social organisa- tion with which alone we are acquainted, but they agreed in thinking that a great chasm separated man in his primitive condition from man in society and this notion we cannot doubt that they borrowed, consciously or unconsciously, from the Romans. If indeed the phenomena of law be regarded in the way in which these theorists regarded them—that is, as one vast complex whole—it is not surprising that the mind should often evade the task it has set to itself by falling back on some ingenious conjecture which (plausibly interpreted) will seem to reconcile everything, or else that it should sometimes abjure in despair the labour of systematization.

From the theories of jurisprudence which have the same speculative basis as the Roman doctrine two of much celebrity must be excepted. The first of them is that associated with the great name of Montesquieu. Though there are some ambiguous expressions in the early part of the *Esprit des Lois*, which seem to show its writer's unwillingness to break quite openly with the views hitherto popu- lar, the general drift of the book is certainly to in dicate a very different conception of its subject from any which had been entertained before. It has often been noticed that, amidst the vast variety of exam- ples which, in its immense width of survey, it sweeps together from supposed systems of jurispru- dence, there is an evident anxiety to thrust into

especial prominence those manners and institutions
which astonish the civilized reader by their uncouth
ness, strangeness, or indecency. The inference con
stantly suggested is, that laws are the creatures of
climate, local situation, accident, or imposture—the
fruit of any causes except those which appear to
operate with tolerable constancy. Montesquieu
seems, in fact, to have looked on the nature of man
as entirely plastic, as passively reproducing the impressions, and submitting implicitly to the impulses,
which it receives from without. And here no
doubt lies the error which vitiates his system as a
system. He greatly underrates the stability of human nature. He pays little or no regard to the
inherited qualities of the race, those qualities which
each generation receives from its predecessors, and
transmits but slightly altered to the generation
which follows it. It is quite true, indeed, that no
complete account can be given of social phenomena,
and consequently of laws, till due allowance has
been made for those modifying causes which are noticed in the *Esprit des Lois* ; but their number and
their force appear to have been overestimated by
Montesquieu. Many of the anomalies which he
parades have since been shown to rest on false reports or erroneous construction, and of those which
remain not a few prove the permanence rather than
the variableness of man's nature, since they are
relics of older stages of the race which have obsti
nately defied the influences that have elsewhere had

effect. The truth is that the stable part of our
mental, moral, and physical constitution is the
largest part of it, and the resistance it opposes to
change is such that, though the variations of human
society in a portion of the world are plain enough,
they are neither so rapid nor so extensive that their
amount, character, and general direction cannot be
ascertained. Approximation to truth may be all
that is attainable with our present knowledge, but
there is no reason for thinking that this is so remote, or (what is the same thing) that it requires
so much future correction, as to be entirely useless
and uninstructive.

The other theory which has been adverted to is,
the historical theory of Bentham. This theory
which is obscurely (and, it might even be said,
timidly) propounded in several parts of Bentham's
works is quite distinct from that analysis of the conception of law which he commenced in the " Frag
ment on Government," and which was more recently
completed by Mr. John Austin. The resolution of
a law into a command of a particular nature, imposed under special conditions, does not affect to
do more than protect us against a difficulty—a most
formidable one certainly—of language. The whole
question remains open as to the motives of societies
in imposing these commands on themselves, as to
the connexion of these commands with each other,
and the nature of their dependence on those which
preceded them, and which they have superseded.

Bentham suggests the answer that societies modify and have always modified, their laws according to modifications of their views of general expediency. It is difficult to say that this proposition is false, but it certainly appears to be unfruitful. For that which seems expedient to a society, or rather to the governing part of it, when it alters a rule of law is surely the same thing as the object, whatever it may be, which it has in view when it makes the change. Expediency and the greatest good are nothing more than different names for the impulse which prompts the modification; and when we lay down expediency as the rule of change in law or opinion, all we get by the proposition is the substitution of an express term for a term which is necessarily implied when we say that a change takes place.

There is such wide-spread dissatisfaction with existing theories of jurisprudence, and so general a conviction that they do not really solve the questions they pretend to dispose of, as to justify the suspicion that some line of inquiry, necessary to a perfect result, has been incompletely followed or altogether omitted by their authors. And indeed there is one remarkable omission with which all these speculations are chargeable, except perhaps those of Montesquieu. They take no account of what law has actually been at epochs remote from the particular period at which they made their appearance. Their originator carefully observed the

institutions of their own age and civilisation, and
those of other ages and civilisations with which they
had some degree of intellectual sympathy, but,
when they turned their attention to archaic states
of society which exhibited much superficial difference from their own, they uniformly ceased to observe and began guessing. The mistake which
they committed is therefore analogous to the error
of one who, in investigating the laws of the material universe, should commence by contemplating
the existing physical world as a whole, instead of
beginning with the particles which are its simplest
ingredients. One does not certainly see why such
a scientific solecism should be more defensible in
jurisprudence than in any other region of thought.
It would seem antecedently that we ought to commence with the simplest social forms in a state as
near as possible to their rudimentary condition. In
other words, if we followed the course usual in such
inquiries, we should penetrate as far up as we could
in the history of primitive societies. The phenomena which early societies present us with are
not easy at first to understand, but the difficulty of
grappling with them bears no proportion to the
perplexities which beset us in considering the baf-
fling entanglement of modern social organisation.
It is a difficulty arising from their strangeness and
uncouthness, not from their number and complexity. One does not readily get over the surprise
which they occasion when looked at from a modern

point of view; but when that is surmounted they are few enough and simple enough. But, even if they gave more trouble than they do, no pains would be wasted in ascertaining the germs out of which has assuredly been unfolded every form of moral restraint which controls our actions and shapes our conduct at the present moment.

The rudiments of the social state, so far as they are known to us at all, are known through testimony of three sorts—accounts by contemporary observers of civilisation less advanced than their own, the records which particular races have preserved concerning their primitive history, and ancient law. The first kind of evidence is the best we could have expected. As societies do not advance concurrently, but at different rates of progress, there have been epochs at which men trained to habits of methodical observation have really been in a position to watch and describe the infancy of mankind. Tacitus made the most of such an opportunity; but the *Germany*, unlike most celebrated classical books, has not induced others to follow the excellent example set by its author, and the amount of this sort of testimony which we possess is exceedingly small. The lofty contempt which a civilised people entertains for barbarous neighbours has caused a remarkable negligence in observing them, and this carelessness has been aggravated at times by fear, by religious prejudice, and even by the use of these very terms—civilisa-

tion and barbarism—which convey to most persons
the impression of a difference not merely in degree
but in kind.   Even the *Germany* has been suspected by some critics of sacrificing fidelity to poig-
nancy of contrast and picturesqueness of narrative
Other histories too, which have been handed down
to us among the archives of the people to whose infancy they relate, have been thought distorted by
the pride of race or by the religious sentiment of a
newer age.   It is important then to observe that
these suspicions, whether groundless or rational, do
not attach to a great deal of archaic law.   Much of
the old law which has descended to us was preserved merely because it was old.   Those who
practised and obeyed it did not pretend to understand it ; and in some cases they even ridiculed and
despised it.   They offered no account of it except
that it had come down to them from their ancestors.   If we confine our attention, then, to those
fragments of ancient institutions which cannot reasonably be supposed to have been tampered with,
we are able to gain a clear conception of certain
great characteristics of the society to which they
originally belonged.   Advancing a step further, we
can apply our knowledge to systems of law which,
like the Code of Menu, are as a whole of suspicious
authenticity ; and, using the key we have obtained,
we are in a position to discriminate those portions
of them which are truly archaic from those which
have been affected by the prejudices, interests, or

ignorance of the compiler.   It will at least be ac
knowledged that, if the materials for this process
are sufficient, and if the comparisons be accurately
executed, the methods followed are as little objec-
tionable as those which have led to such surprising
results in comparative philology.

The effect of the evidence derived from comparative jurisprudence is to establish that view of
the primeval condition of the human race which is
known as the Patriarchal Theory.   There is no
doubt, of course, that this theory was originally
based on the Scriptural history of the Hebrew
patriarchs in Lower Asia; but, as has been explained already, its connexion with Scripture rather
militated than otherwise against its reception as a
complete theory, since the majority of the inquirers
who till recently addressed themselves with most
earnestness to the colligation of social phenomena,
were either influenced by the strongest prejudice
against Hebrew antiquities or by the strongest desire to construct their system without the assistance of religious records.   Even now there is perhaps a disposition to undervalue these accounts, or
rather to decline generalising from them, as forming
part of the traditions of a Semitic people.   It is to
be noted, however, that the legal testimony comes
nearly exclusively from the institutions of societies
belonging to the Indo-European stock, the Romans
Hindoos, and Sclavonians, supplying the greater
part of it; and indeed the difficulty, at the present

stage of the inquiry, is to know where to stop, to
say of what races of men it is *not* allowable to lay
down that the society in which they are united was
originally organised on the patriarchal model. The
chief lineaments of such a society, as collected from
the early chapters in Genesis, I need not attempt to
depict with any minuteness, both because they are
familiar to most of us from our earliest childhood,
and because, from the interest once attaching to the
controversy which takes its name from the debate
between Locke and Filmer, they fill a whole chapter, though not a very profitable one, in English
literature. The points which lie on the surface
of the history are these:—The eldest male parent
—the eldest ascendant—is absolutely supreme in
his household. His dominion extends to life and
death, and is as unqualified over his children and
their houses as over his slaves ; indeed the relations
of sonship and serfdom appear to differ in little beyond the higher capacity which the child in blood
possesses of becoming one day the head of a family
himself. The flocks and herds of the children are
the flocks and herds of the father, and the possessions of the parent, which he holds in a representa
tive rather than in a proprietary character, are
equally divided at his death among his descendants
in the first degree, the eldest son sometimes receiving a double share under the name of birthright,
but more generally endowed with no hereditary advantage beyond an honorary precedence. A less

obvious inference from the Scriptural accounts is that they seem to plant us on the traces of the breach which is first effected in the empire of the parent. The families of Jacob and Esau separate and form two nations; but the families of Jacob's children hold together and become a people. This looks like the immature germ of a state or common-wealth, and of an order of rights superior to the claims of family relation.

If I were attempting, for the more special pur poses of the jurist, to express compendiously the characteristics of the situation in which mankind disclose themselves at the dawn of their history, I should be satisfied to quote a few verses from the *Odyssey* of Homer:

τοῖσιν δ' οὔτ' ἀγοραὶ βουληφόροι οὔτε θέμιστες.
.   .   .   θεμιστεύει δὲ ἕκαστος
παίδων ἠδ' ἀλόχων οὐδ' ἀλλήλων ἀλέγουσιν.

" They have neither assemblies for consultation nor *themistes*, but every one exercises jurisdiction over his wives and his children, and they pay no regard to one another." These lines are applied to the Cyclops, and it may not perhaps be an altogether fanciful idea when I suggest that the Cyclops is Homer's type of an alien and less advanced civilisa-tion; for the almost physical loathing which a primitive community feels for men of widely differ-ent manners from its own usually expresses itself by describing them as monsters, such as giants, or

even (which is almost always the case in Oriental
mythology) as demons. However that may be, the
verses condense in themselves the sum of the hints
which are given us by legal antiquities. Men are
first seen distributed in perfectly insulated groups
held together by obedience to the parent. Law is
the parent's word, but it is not yet in the condition
of those *themistes* which were analysed in the first
chapter of this work. When we go forward to the
state of society in which these early legal conceptions show themselves as formed, we find that they
still partake of the mystery and spontaneity which
must have seemed to characterise a despotic father's
commands, but that at the same time, inasmuch as
they proceed from a sovereign, they presuppose a
union of family groups in some wider organisation.
The next question is, what is the nature of this
union and the degree of intimacy which it involves?
It is just here that archaic law renders us one of
the greatest of its services and fills up a gap which
otherwise could only have been bridged by conjecture. It is full, in all its provinces, of the clearest
indications that society in primitive times was not
what it is assumed to be at present, a collection of
individuals. In fact, and in the view of the men
who composed it, it was *an aggregation of families*.
The contrast may be most forcibly expressed by
saying that the *unit* of an ancient society was the
Family, of a modern society the Individual. We
must be prepared to find in ancient law all the con-

sequences of this difference. It is so framed as to
be adjusted to a system of small independent corporations. It is therefore scanty, because it is supplemented by the despotic commands of the heads
of households. It is ceremonious, because the
transactions to which it pays regard resemble international concerns much more than the quick play
of intercourse between individuals. Above all it
has a peculiarity of which the full importance cannot be shown at present. It takes a view of *life*
wholly unlike any which appears in developed
jurisprudence. Corporations *never die*, and accordingly primitive law considers the entities with
which it deals, *i. e.* the patriarchal or family groups,
as perpetual and inextinguishable. This view is
closely allied to the peculiar aspect under which, in
very ancient times, moral attributes present themselves. The moral elevation and moral debasement
of the individual appear to be confounded with, or
postponed to, the merits and offences of the group
to which the individual belongs. If the community
sins, its guilt is much more than the sum of the
offences committed by its members ; the crime is
a corporate act, and extends in its consequences to
many more persons than have shared in its actual
perpetration. If, on the other hand, the individual
is conspicuously guilty, it is his children, his kinsfolk, his tribesmen, or his fellow-citizens, who suffer
with him, and sometimes for him. It thus happens
that the ideas of moral responsibility and retribu

tion often seem to be more clearly realised at very ancient than at more advanced periods, for, as the family group is immortal, and its liability to punishment indefinite, the primitive mind is not perplexed by the questions which become troublesome as soon as the individual is conceived as altogether separate from the group. One step in the transition from the ancient and simple view of the matter to the theological or metaphysical explanation of later days is marked by the early Greek notion of an inherited curse. The bequest received by his posterity from the original criminal was not a liability to punishment, but a liability to the commission of fresh offences which drew with them a condign retribution; and thus the responsibility of the family was reconciled with the newer phase of thought which limited the consequences of crime to the person of the actual delinquent.

It would be a very simple explanation of the origin of society if we could base a general conclusion on the hint furnished us by the Scriptural example already adverted to, and could suppose that communities began to exist wherever a family held together instead of separating at the death of its patriarchal chieftain. In most of the Greek states and in Rome there long remained the vestiges of an ascending series of groups out of which the State was at first constituted. The Family, House, and Tribe of the Romans may be taken as the type of them, and they are so described to us that we can

scarcely help conceiving them as a system of concen
tric circles which have gradually expanded from the
same point. The elementary group is the Family,
connected by common subjection to the highest male
ascendant. The aggregation of Families forms the
Gens or House. The aggregation of Houses makes
the Tribe. The aggregation of Tribes constitutes
the Commonwealth. Are we at liberty to follow
these indications, and to lay down that the commonwealth is a collection of persons united by
common descent from the progenitor of an original
family? Of this we may at least be certain, that all
ancient societies regarded themselves as having proceeded from one original stock, and even laboured
under an incapacity for comprehending any reason
except this for their holding together in political
union. The history of political ideas begins, in fact,
with the assumption that kinship in blood is the sole
possible ground of community in political functions
nor is there any of those subversions of feeling, which
we term emphatically revolutions, so startling and
so complete as the change which is accomplished
when some other principle—such as that, for instance of *local contiguity*—establishes itself for the
first time as the basis of common political action.
It may be affirmed then of early commonwealths
that their citizens considered all the groups in which
they claimed membership to be founded on common
lineage. What was obviously true of the Family
was believed to be true, first of the House, next of

the Tribe, lastly of the State. And yet we find that along with this belief, or, if we may use the word, this theory, each community preserved records or traditions which distinctly showed that the fundamental assumption was false. Whether we look to the Greek states, or to Rome, or to the Teutonic aristocracies in Ditmarsh which furnished Niebuhr with so many valuable illustrations, or to the Celtic clan associations, or to that strange social organisation of the Sclavonic Russians and Poles which has only lately attracted notice, everywhere we discover traces of passages in their history when men of alien descent were admitted to, and amalgamated with, the original brotherhood. Adverting to Rome singly, we perceive that the primary group, the Family, was being constantly adulterated by the practice of adoption, while stories seem to have been always current respecting the exotic extraction of one of the original Tribes and concerning a large addition to the Houses made by one of the early kings. The composition of the state uniformly assumed to be natural, was nevertheless known to be in great measure artificial. This conflict between belief or theory and notorious fact is at first sight extremely perplexing; but what it really illustrates is the efficiency with which Legal Fictions do their work in the infancy of society. The earliest and most extensively employed of legal fictions was that which permitted family relations to be created artificially, and there is none to which I conceive man kind to be more deeply indebted.   If it had never existed, I do not see how any one of the primitive groups, whatever were their nature, could have absorbed another, or on what terms any two of them could have combined, except those of absolute superiority on one side and absolute subjection on the other.   No doubt, when with our modern ideas we contemplate the union of independent communities, we can suggest a hundred modes of carrying it out, the simplest of all being that the individuals comprised in the coalescing groups shall vote or act together according to local propinquity; but the idea that a number of persons should exercise political rights in common simply because they happened to live within the same topographical limits was utterly strange and monstrous to primitive antiquity. The expedient which in those times commanded favour was that the incoming population should *feign themselves* to be descended from the same stock as the people on whom they were engrafted; and it is precisely the good faith of this fiction, and the closeness with which it seemed to imitate reality, that we cannot now hope to understand.   One circumstance, however, which it is important to recollect, is that the men who formed the various political groups were certainly in the habit of meeting together periodically, for the purpose of acknowledging and consecrating their association by common sacrifices.   Strangers amalgamated with the brotherhood were doubtless admitted to these sacri-

fices ; and when that was once done, we can believe
that it seemed equally easy, or not more difficult, to
conceive them as sharing in the common lineage.
The conclusion then which is suggested by the evidence is, not that all early societies were formed by
descent from the same ancestor, but that all of them
which had any permanence and solidity either were
so descended or assumed that they were. An indefinite number of causes may have shattered the
primitive groups, but wherever their ingredients
recombined, it was on the model or principle of an
association of kindred. Whatever were the fact, all
thought, language, and law adjusted themselves to
the assumption. But though all this seems to me to
be established with reference to the communities
with whose records we are acquainted, the remainder
of their history sustains the position before laid
down as to the essentially transient and terminable
influence of the most powerful Legal Fictions. At
some point of time—probably as soon as they felt
themselves strong enough to resist extrinsic pressure
—all these states ceased to recruit themselves by
factitious extensions of consanguinity. They necessarily, therefore, became Aristocracies, in all cases
where a fresh population from any cause collected
around them which could put in no claim to community of origin. Their sternness in maintaining
the central principle of a system under which po
litical rights were attainable on no terms whatever
except connexion in blood, real or artificial, taught

their inferiors another principle, which proved to
be endowed with a far higher measure of vitality.
This was the principle of *local contiguity*, now recognised everywhere as the condition of community in
political functions. A new set of political ideas
came at once into existence, which, being those of
ourselves, our contemporaries, and in great measure
of our ancestors, rather obscure our perception of
the older theory which they vanquished and dethroned.

The Family then is the type of an archaic society in all the modifications which it was capable of
assuming; but the family here spoken of is not exactly the family as understood by a modern. In
order to reach the ancient conception we must give
to our modern ideas an important extension and an
important limitation. We must look on the family
as constantly enlarged by the absorption of strangers within its circle, and we must try to regard the
fiction of adoption as so closely simulating the reality of kinship that neither law nor opinion makes the
slightest difference between a real and an adoptive
connexion. On the other hand, the persons theoretically amalgamated into a family by their common
descent are practically held together by common obedience to their highest living ascendant, the father,
grandfather, or great-grandfather. The patriarchal
authority of a chieftain is as necessary an ingredient
in the notion of the family group as the fact (or assumed fact) of its having sprung from his loins;

and hence we must understand that if there be any persons who, however truly included in the brotherhood by virtue of their blood-relationship, have nevertheless *de facto* withdrawn themselves from the empire of its ruler, they are always, in the beginnings of law, considered as lost to the family. It is this patriarchal aggregate—the modern family thus cut down on one side and extended on the other—which meets us on the threshold of primitive jurisprudence. Older probably than the State, the Tribe, and the House, it left traces of itself on private law long after the House and the Tribe had been forgotten, and long after consanguinity had ceased to be associated with the composition of States. It will be found to have stamped itself on all the great departments of jurisprudence, and may be detected, I think, as the true source of many of their most important and most durable characteristics. At the outset, the peculiarities of law in its most ancient state lead us irresistibly to the conclusion that it took precisely the same view of the family group which is taken of individual men by the systems of rights and duties now prevalent throughout Europe. There are societies open to our observation at this very moment whose laws and usages can scarcely be explained unless they are supposed never to have emerged from this primitive condition ; but in communities more fortunately circumstanced the fabric of jurisprudence fell gradually to pieces, and if we carefully observe the disin-

tegration we shall perceive that it took place prin
cipally in those portions of each system which were
most deeply affected by the primitive conception of
the family. In one all-important instance, that of
the Roman law, the change was effected so slowly
that from epoch to epoch we can observe the line and
direction which it followed, and can even give some
idea of the ultimate result to which it was tending.
And, in pursuing this last inquiry, we need not suffer ourselves to be stopped by the imaginary barrier
which separates the modern from the ancient world.
For one effect of that mixture of refined Roman law
with primitive barbaric usage, which is known to us
by the deceptive name of feudalism, was to revive
many features of archaic jurisprudence which had
died out of the Roman world, so that the decom-
position which had seemed to be over commenced
again, and to some extent is still proceeding.

On a few systems of law the family organisa
tion of the earliest society has left a plain and broad
mark in the life-long authority of the Father or
other ancestor over the person and property of his
descendants, an authority which we may conveniently call by its later Roman name of Patria Potestas. No feature of the rudimentary associations
of mankind is deposed to by a greater amount of
evidence than this, and yet none seems to have disappeared so generally and so rapidly from the
usages of advancing communities. Gaius, writing
under the Antonines, describes the institution as

distinctively Roman. It is true, that had he glanced across the Rhine or the Danube to those tribes of barbarians which were exciting the curiosity of some among his contemporaries, he would have seen examples of patriarchal power in its crudest form; and in the far East a branch of the same ethnical stock from which the Romans sprang was repeating their Patria Potestas in some of its most technical incidents. But among the races understood to be comprised within the Roman empire, Gaius could find none which exhibited an institution resembling the Roman " Power of the Father," except only the Asiatic Galatæ. There are reasons, indeed, as it seems to me, why the direct authority of the ancestor should, in the greater number of progressive societies, very shortly assume humbler proportions than belonged to it in their earliest state. The implicit obedience of rude men to their parent is doubtless a primary fact, which it would be absurd to explain away altogether by attributing to them any calculation of its advantages; but, at the same time, if it is natural in the sons to obey the father, it is equally natural that they should look to him for superior strength or superior wisdom. Hence, when societies are placed under circumstances which cause an especial value to be attached to bodily and mental vigour, there is an influence at work which tends to confine the Patria Potestas to the cases where its possessor is actually skilful and strong. When we obtain our first glimpse of organised

Hellenic society, it seems as if supereminent wisdom would keep alive the father's power in persons whose bodily strength had decayed; but the relations of Ulysses and Laertes in the *Odyssey* appear to show that, where extraordinary valour and sagacity were united in the son, the father in the decrepitude of age was deposed from the headship of the family. In the mature Greek jurisprudence, the rule advances a few steps on the practice hinted at in the Homeric literature; and though very many traces of stringent family obligation remain, the direct authority of the parent is limited, as in European codes, to the nonage or minority of the children, or, in other words, to the period during which their mental and physical inferiority may always be presumed. The Roman law, however, with its remarkable tendency to innovate on ancient usage only just so far as the exigency of the commonwealth may require, preserves both the primeval institution and the natural limitation to which I conceive it to have been subject. In every relation of life in which the collective community might have occasion to avail itself of his wisdom and strength, for all purposes of counsel or of war, the filius familias, or Son under Power, was as free as his father. It was a maxim of Roman jurisprudence that the Patria Potestas did not extend to the Jus Publicum. Father and son voted together in the city, and fought side by side in the field; indeed, the son, as general, might happen to com mand the father, or, as magistrate, decide on his contracts and punish his delinquencies. But in all the relations created by Private Law, the son lived under a domestic despotism which, considering the severity it retained to the last, and the number of centuries through which it endured, constitutes one of the strangest problems in legal history.

The Patria Potestas of the Romans, which is necessarily our type of the primeval paternal authority, is equally difficult to understand as an institution of civilized life, whether we consider its incidence on the person or its effects on property. It is to be regretted that a chasm which exists in its history cannot be more completely filled. So far as regards the person, the parent, when our information commences, has over his children the *jus vitæ necisque*, the power of life and death, and *à fortiori* of uncontrolled corporal chastisement; he can modify their personal condition at pleasure; he can give a wife to his son; he can give his daughter in marriage; he can divorce his children of either sex; he can transfer them to another family by adoption; and he can sell them. Late in the Imperial period we find vestiges of all these powers, but they are reduced within very narrow limits. The unqualified right of domestic chastisement has become a right of bringing domestic offences under the cognisance of the civil magistrate; the privilege of dictating marriage has declined into a conditional veto; the liberty of selling has been virtually

abolished, and adoption itself, destined to lose almost all its ancient importance in the reformed system of Justinian, can no longer be effected without
the assent of the child transferred to the adoptive
parentage. In short, we are bought very close to
the verge of the ideas which have at length prevailed in the modern world. But between these
widely distant epochs there is an interval of ob-
scurity, and we can only guess at the causes which
permitted the Patria Potestas to last as long as it
did by rendering it more tolerable than it appears.
The active discharge of the most important among
the duties which the son owed to the state must
have tempered the authority of his parent if they
did not annul it. We can readily persuade ourselves that the paternal despotism could not be
brought into play without great scandal against a
man of full age occupying a high civil office. During the earlier history, however, such cases of practical emancipation would be rare compared with
those which must have been created by the constant
wars of the Roman republic. The military tribune
and the private soldier who were in the field three
quarters of a year during the earlier contests, at a
later period the proconsul in charge of a province,
and the legionaries who occupied it, cannot have
had practical reason to regard themselves as the
slaves of a despotic master; and all these avenues
of escape tended constantly to multiply themselves
Victories led to conquests, conquests to occupations

the mode of occupation by colonies was exchanged
for the system of occupying provinces by standing
armies. Each step in advance was a call for the
expatriation of more Roman citizens and a fresh
draft on the blood of the failing Latin race. We
may infer, I think, that a strong sentiment in favour
of the relaxation of the Patria Potestas had become
fixed by the time that the pacification of the world
commenced on the establishment of the Empire.
The first serious blows at the ancient institution are
attributed to the earlier Cæsars, and some isolated
interferences of Trajan and Hadrian seem to have
prepared the ground for a series of express enactments which, though we cannot always determine
their dates, we know to have limited the father's
powers on the one hand, and on the other to have
multiplied facilities for their voluntary surrender.
The older mode of getting rid of the Potestas, by
effecting a triple sale of the son's person, is evidence, I may remark, of a very early feeling against
the unnecessary prolongation of the powers. The
rule which declared that the son should be free
after having been three times sold by his father
seems to have been originally meant to entail penal
consequences on a practice which revolted even the
imperfect morality of the primitive Roman. But
even before the publication of the Twelve Tables it
had been turned, by the ingenuity of the juriscon
sults, into an expedient for destroying the parental

authority wherever the father desired that it should cease.

Many of the causes which helped to mitigate the stringency of the father's power over the persons of his children are doubtless among those which do not lie upon the face of history. We cannot tell how far public opinion may have paralysed an authority which the law conferred, or how far natural affection may have rendered it endurable. But though the powers over the *person* may have been latterly nominal, the whole tenour of the extant Roman jurisprudence suggests that the father's rights over the son's *property* were always exercised without scruple to the full extent to which they were sanctioned by law. There is nothing to astonish us in the latitude of these rights when they first show themselves. The ancient law of Rome forbade the Children under Power to hold property apart from their parent, or (we should rather say) never contemplated the possibility of their claiming a separate ownership. The father was entitled to take the whole of the son's acquisitions, and to enjoy the benefit of his contracts without being entangled in any compensating liability. So much as this we should expect from the constitution of the earliest Roman society, for we can hardly form a notion of the primitive family group unless we suppose that its members brought their earnings of all kinds into the common stock while they were unable to bind it by improvident individual engagements. The true enigma of the Patria Potestas does not reside here, but in the slowness with which these proprietary privileges of the parent were curtailed, and in the circumstance that, before they were seriously diminished, the whole civilised world was brought within their sphere. No innovation of any kind was attempted till the first years of the Empire, when the acquisitions of soldiers on service were withdrawn from the operation of the Patria Potestas, doubtless as part of the reward of the armies which had overthrown the free commonwealth. Three centuries afterwards the same immunity was extended to the earnings of persons who were in the civil employment of the state. Both changes were obviously limited in their application, and they were so contrived in technical form as to interfere as little as possible with the principle of Patria Potestas. A certain qualified and dependent ownership had always been recognised by the Roman law in the perquisites and savings which slaves and sons under power were not compelled to include in the household accounts, and the special name of this permissive property, Peculium, was applied to the acquisitions newly relieved from Patria Potestas, which were called in the case of soldiers Castrense Peculium, and Quasi-castrense Peculium in the case of civil servants. Other modifications of the parental privileges followed, which showed a less studious outward respect for the ancient principle. Shortly after the introduction of the Quasi castrense Peculium, Constantine the Great took away the father's absolute control over property which his children had inherited from their mothers, and reduced it to a *usufruct*, or life-interest. A few more changes of slight importance followed in the Western Empire, but the furthest point reached was in the East, under Justinian, who enacted that unless the acquisitions of the child were derived from the parent's own property, the parent's rights over them should not extend beyond enjoying their produce for the period of his life. Even this, the utmost relaxation of the Roman Patria Potestas, left it far ampler and severer than any analogous institution of the modern world. The earliest modern writers on jurisprudence remark that it was only the fiercer and ruder of the conquerors of the empire, and notably the nations of Sclavonic origin, which exhibited a Patria Potestas at all resembling that which was described in the Pandects and the Code. All the Germanic immigrants seem to have recognised a corporate union of the family under the *mund*, or authority of a patriarchal chief; but his powers are obviously only the relics of a decayed Patria Potestas, and fell far short of those enjoyed by the Roman father. The Franks are particularly mentioned as not having the Roman institution, and accordingly the old French lawyers, even when most busily engaged in filling the interstices of barbarous custom with rules of Roman law, were obliged to protect themselves against the

intrusion of the Potestas by the express maxim,
Puyssance de père en France n'a lieu. The tenacity of the Romans in maintaining this relic of
their most ancient condition is in itself remarkable,
but it is less remarkable than the diffusion of the
Potestas over the whole of a civilisation from which
it had once disappeared. While the Castrense Peculium constituted as yet the sole exception to the
father's power over property, and while his power
over his children's persons was still extensive, the
Roman citizenship, and with it the Patria Potestas,
were spreading into every corner of the Empire.
Every African or Spaniard, every Gaul, Briton, or
Jew, who received this honour by gift, purchase, or
inheritance, placed himself under the Roman Law
of Persons, and, though our authorities intimate
that children born before the acquisition of citizenship could not be brought under Power against
their will, children born after it and all ulterior descendants were on the ordinary footing of a Roman
filius familias. It does not fall within the province
of this treatise to examine the mechanism of the
later Roman society, but I may be permitted to remark that there is little foundation for the opinion
which represents the constitution of Antoninus
Caracalla conferring Roman citizenship on the
whole of his subjects as a measure of small importance. However we may interpret it, it must have
enormously enlarged the sphere of the Patria Potestas, and it seems to me that the tightening of

family relations which it effected is an agency which
ought to be kept in view more than it has been
in accounting for the great moral revolution which
was transforming the world.

Before this branch of our subject is dismissed, it
should be observed that the Paterfamilias was an-
swerable for the delicts (or *torts*) of his Sons under
Power. He was similarly liable for the torts of his
slaves; but in both cases he originally possessed
the singular privilege of tendering the delinquent's
person in full satisfaction of the damage. The responsibility thus incurred on behalf of sons, coupled
with the mutual incapacity of Parent and Child
under Power to sue one another, has seemed to
some jurists to be best explained by the assumption of a "unity of person" between the Paterfamilias and the Filiusfamilias. In the Chapter on
Successions I shall attempt to show in what sense,
and to what extent, this "unity" can be accepted
as a reality. I can only say at present that these
responsibilities of the Paterfamilias, and other legal
phenomena which will be discussed hereafter, appear to me to point at certain *duties* of the primitive Patriarchal chieftain which balanced his *rights*
I conceive that, if he disposed absolutely of the
persons and fortune of his clansmen, this representa
tive ownership was coextensive with a liability to
provide for all members of the brotherhood out of
the common fund. The difficulty is to throw our
selves out of our habitual associations sufficiently

for conceiving the nature of his obligation. It was not a legal duty, for law had not yet penetrated into the precincts of the Family. To call it *moral* is perhaps to anticipate the ideas belonging to a later stage of mental development; but the expression "moral obligation" is significant enough for our purpose, if we understand by it a duty semiconsciously followed and enforced rather by instinct and habit than by definite sanctions.

The Patria Potestas, in its normal shape, has not been, and, as it seems to me, could not have been, a generally durable institution. The proof of its former universality is therefore incomplete so long as we consider it by itself ; but the demonstration may be carried much further by examining other departments of ancient law which depend on it ultimately, but not by a thread of connexion visible in all its parts or to all eyes. Let us turn for example to Kinship, or in other words, to the scale on which the proximity of relatives to each other is calculated in archaic jurisprudence. Here again it will be convenient to employ the Roman terms, Agnatic and Cognatic relationship. *Cognatic* relationship is simply the conception of kinship familiar to modern ideas; it is the relationship arising through common descent from the same pair of married persons, whether the descent be traced through males or females. *Agnatic* relationship is something very different: it excludes a number of persons whom we in our day should certainly consider of kin to

ourselves, and it includes many more whom we
should never reckon among our kindred. It is in
truth the connexion existing between the members
of the Family, conceived as it was in the most ancient times. The limits of this connexion are far
from conterminous with those of modern relationship.

Cognates then are all those persons who can
trace their blood to a single ancestor and ances-
tress ; or, if we take the strict technical meaning of
the word in Roman law, they are all who trace
their blood to the legitimate marriage of a common
pair. " Cognation " is therefore a relative term, and
the degree of connexion in blood which it indicates
depends on the particular marriage which is selected
as the commencement of the calculation. If we begin with the marriage of father and mother, Cognation will only express the relationship of brothers
and sisters ; if we take that of the grandfather and
grandmother, then uncles, aunts, and their descendants will also be included in the notion of Cognation, and following the same process a larger number of Cognates may be continually obtained by
choosing the starting point higher and higher up
in the line of ascent. All this is easily understood
by a modern ; but who are the Agnates ? In the
first place, they are all the Cognates who trace
their connexion exclusively through males. A
table of Cognates is, of course, formed by taking
each lineal ancestor in turn and including all his

descendants of both sexes in the tabular view; if then, in tracing the various branches of such a genealogical table or tree, we stop whenever we come to the name of a female and pursue that particular branch or ramification no further, all who remain after the descendants of women have been excluded are Agnates, and their connexion together is Agnatic Relationship. I dwell a little on the process which is practically followed in separating them from the Cognates, because it explains a memorable legal maxim, "Mulier est finis familiæ"— a woman is the terminus of the family. A female name closes the branch or twig of the genealogy in which it occurs. None of the descendants of a female are included in the primitive notion of family relationship.

If the system of archaic law at which we are looking be one which admits Adoption, we must add to the Agnates thus obtained all persons, male or female, who have been brought into the Family by the artificial extension of its boundaries. But the descendants of such persons will only be Agnates, if they satisfy the conditions which have just been described.

What then is the reason of this arbitrary inclusion and exclusion? Why should a conception of Kinship, so elastic as to include strangers brought into the family by adoption, be nevertheless so narrow as to shut out the descendants of a female member? To solve these questions, we must recur to the Patria Potestas. The foundation of Agnation is not the marriage of Father and Mother, but the authority of the Father. All persons are Agnatically connected together who are under the same Paternal Power, or who have been under it, or who might have been under it if their lineal ancestor had lived long enough to exercise his empire. In truth, in the primitive view, Relationship is exactly limited by Patria Potestas. Where the Potestas begins, Kinship begins; and therefore adoptive relatives are among the kindred. Where the Potestas ends, Kinship ends; so that a son emancipated by his father loses all rights of Agnation. And here we have the reason why the descendants of females are outside the limits of archaic kinship. If a woman died unmarried, she could have no legitimate descendants. If she married, her children fell under the Patria Potestas, not of her Father, but of her Husband, and thus were lost to her own family. It is obvious that the organisation of primitive societies would have been confounded, if men had called themselves relatives of their mother's relatives. The inference would have been that a person might be subject to two distinct Patriæ Potestates; but distinct Patriæ Potestates implied distinct jurisdictions, so that anybody amenable to two of them at the same time would have lived under two different dispensations. As long as the Family was an imperium in imperio, a community within the commonwealth, governed by its own institutions of which the parent was the source, the limitation of relationship to the Agnates was a necessary security against a conflict of laws in the domestic forum.

The Parental Powers proper are extinguished by the death of the Parent, but Agnation is as it were a mould which retains their imprint after they have ceased to exist. Hence comes the interest of Agnation for the inquirer into the history of jurisprudence. The powers themselves are discernible in comparatively few monuments of ancient law, but Agnatic Relationship, which implies their former existence, is discoverable almost everywhere. There are few indigenous bodies of law belonging to communities of the Indo-European stock, which do not exhibit peculiarities in the most ancient part of their structure which are clearly referable to Agnation. In Hindoo law, for example, which is saturated with the primitive notions of family dependency, kinship is entirely Agnatic, and I am informed that in Hindoo genealogies the names of women are generally omitted altogether. The same view of relationship pervades so much of the laws of the races who overran the Roman Empire as appears to have really formed part of their primitive usage, and we may suspect that it would have perpetuated itself even more than it has in modern European jurisprudence, if it had not been for the vast influence of the later Roman law on modern thought. The Prætors early laid hold on Cogna-

tion as the *natural* form of kinship, and spared no
pains in purifying their system from the older conception. Their ideas have descended to us, but still
traces of Agnation are to be seen in many of the
modern rules of succession after death. The exclusion of females and their children from govern-
mental functions, commonly attributed to the usage
of the Salian Franks, has certainly an agnatic origin,
being descended from the ancient German rule of
succession to allodial property. In Agnation too
is to be sought the explanation of that extraordinary rule of English Law, only recently repealed,
which prohibited brothers of the half-blood from
succeeding to one another's lands. In the Customs
of Normandy, the rule applies to *uterine* brothers
only, that is, to brothers by the same mother
but not by the same father; and, limited in this
way, it is a strict deduction from the system of Ag
nation, under which uterine brothers are no rela
tions at all to one another. When it was trans-
planted to England, the English judges, who had no
clue to its principle, interpreted it as a general prohibition against the succession of the half-blood,
and extended it to *consanguineous* brothers, that is
to sons of the same father by different wives. In
all the literature which enshrines the pretended
philosophy of law, there is nothing more curious
than the pages of elaborate sophistry in which
Blackstone attempts to explain and justify the exclusion of the half-blood.

It may be shown, I think, that the Family, as
held together by the Patria Potestas, is the nidus
out of which the entire Law of Persons has germi-
nated. Of all the chapters of that Law the most
important is that which is concerned with the
status of Females. It has just been stated that
Primitive Jurisprudence, though it does not allow
a Woman to communicate any rights of Agnation to
her descendants, includes herself nevertheless in the
Agnatic bond. Indeed, the relation of a female to
the family in which she was born is much stricter,
closer, and more durable than that which unites
her male kinsmen. We have several times laid
down that early law takes notice of Families only ;
this is the same thing as saying that it only takes
notice of persons exercising Patria Potestas, and accordingly the only principle on which it enfran-
chises a son or grandson at the death of his Parent,
is a consideration of the capacity inherent in such
son or grandson to become himself the head of a new
family and the root of a new set of Parental Powers.
But a woman, of course, has no capacity of the
kind, and no title accordingly to the liberation
which it confers. There is therefore a peculiar contrivance of archaic jurisprudence for retaining her
in the bondage of the Family for life. This is the
institution known to the oldest Roman law as the
Perpetual Tutelage of Women, under which a Female, though relieved from her Parent's authority
by his decease, continues subject through life to her

nearest male relations, or to her Father's nominees, as her Guardians. Perpetual Guardianship is obviously neither more nor less than an artificial prolongation of the Patria Potestas, when for other purposes it has been dissolved. In India, the system survives in absolute completeness, and its operation is so strict that a Hindoo Mother frequently becomes the ward of her own sons. Even in Europe, the laws of the Scandinavian nations respecting women preserved it until quite recently. The invaders of the Western Empire had it universally among their indigenous usages, and indeed their ideas on the subject of Guardianship, in all its forms, were among the most retrogressive of those which they introduced into the Western world. But from the mature Roman jurisprudence it had entirely disappeared. We should know almost nothing about it, if we had only the compilations of Justinian to consult; but the discovery of the manuscript of Gaius discloses it to us at a most interesting epoch, just when it had fallen into complete discredit and was verging on extinction. The great jurisconsult himself scouts the popular apology offered for it in the mental inferiority of the female sex, and a considerable part of his volume is taken up with descriptions of the numerous expedients, some of them displaying extraordinary ingenuity, which the Roman lawyers had devised for enabling Women to defeat the ancient rules. Led by their theory of Natural Law, the jurisconsults

had evidently at this time assumed the equality of
the sexes as a principle of their code of equity.
The restrictions which they attacked were, it is to
be observed, restrictions on the disposition of property, for which the assent of the woman's guardians
was still formally required. Control of her person was apparently quite obsolete.

Ancient law subordinates the woman to her
blood-relations, while a prime phenomenon of modern jurisprudence has been her subordination to her
husband. The history of the change is remarkable.
It begins far back in the annals of Rome. Anciently, there were three modes in which marriage
might be contracted according to Roman usage, one
involving a religious solemnity, the other two the
observance of certain secular formalities. By the
religious marriage or *Confarreation* ; by the higher
form of civil marriage, which was called *Coemption* ;
and by the lower form, which was termed *Usus*,
the Husband acquired a number of rights over the
person and property of his wife, which were on the
whole in excess of such as are conferred on him in
any system of modern jurisprudence. But in what
capacity did he acquire them ? Not as *Husband*, but
as *Father*. By the Confarreation, Coemption, and
Usus, the woman passed *in manum viri*, that is,
in law she became the *Daughter* of her husband.
She was included in his Patria Potestas. She incurred all the liabilities springing out of it while it
subsisted, and surviving it when it had expired.

All her property became absolutely his, and she was retained in tutelage after his death to the guardian whom he had appointed by will. These three ancient forms of marriage fell, however, gradually into disuse, so that, at the most splendid period of Roman greatness, they had almost entirely given place to a fashion of wedlock—old apparently, but not hitherto considered reputable—which was founded on a modification of the lower form of civil marriage. Without explaining the technical mechanism of the institution now generally popular, I may describe it as amounting in law to little more than a temporary deposit of the woman by her family. The rights of the family remained unimpaired, and the lady continued in the tutelage of guardians whom her parents had appointed and whose privileges of control overrode, in many material respects, the inferior authority of her husband. The consequence was that the situation of the Roman female, whether married or unmarried became one of great personal and proprietary independence, for the tendency of the later law, as I have already hinted, was to reduce the power of the guardian to a nullity, while the form of marriage in fashion conferred on the husband no compensating superiority. But Christianity tended somewhat from the very first to narrow this remarkable liberty. Led at first by justifiable disrelish for the loose practice of the decaying heathen world, but afterwards hurried on by a passion of

asceticism, the professors of the new faith looked
with disfavour on a marital tie which was in fact
the laxest the Western world has seen. The latest
Roman law, so far as it is touched by the Constitutions of the Christian Emperors, bears some
marks of a reaction against the liberal doctrines of
the great Antonine jurisconsults. And the prevalent state of religious sentiment may explain why
it is that modern jurisprudence, forged in the fur-
nace of barbarian conquest, and formed by the fusion of Roman jurisprudence with patriarchal usage,
has absorbed, among its rudiments, much more than
usual of those rules concerning the position of
women which belong peculiarly to an imperfect
civilisation. During the troubled era which begins
modern history, and while the laws of the Germanic and Sclavonic immigrants remained super-
posed like a separate layer above the Roman jurisprudence of their provincial subjects, the women
of the dominant races are seen everywhere under
various forms of archaic guardianship, and the husband who takes a wife from any family except his
own pays a money-price to her relations for the
tutelage which they surrender to him. When we
move onwards, and the code of the middle ages has
been formed by the amalgamation of the two systems, the law relating to women carries the stamp
of its double origin. The principle of the Roman
jurisprudence is so far triumphant that unmarried
females are generally (though there are local excep-

tions to the rule) relieved from the bondage of the
family ; but the archaic principle of the barbarians
has fixed the position of married women, and the
husband has drawn to himself in his marital character the powers which had once belonged to his
wife's male kindred, the only difference being that
he no longer purchases his privileges. At this
point therefore the modern law of Western and
Southern Europe begins to be distinguished by one
of its chief characteristics, the comparative freedom
it allows to unmarried women and widows, the
heavy disabilities it imposes on wives. It was very
long before the subordination entailed on the other
sex by marriage was sensibly diminished. The
principal and most powerful solvent of the revived
barbarism of Europe was always the codified jurisprudence of Justinian, wherever it was studied with
that passionate enthusiasm which it seldom failed to
awaken. It covertly but most efficaciously undermined the customs which it pretended merely to interpret. But the Chapter of law relating to married women was for the most part read by the light,
not of Roman, but of Canon Law, which in no one
particular departs so widely from the spirit of the
secular jurisprudence as in the view it takes of the
relations created by marriage. This was in part
inevitable, since no society which preserves any
tincture of Christian institution is likely to restore
to married women the personal liberty conferred on
them by the middle Roman law, but the proprie-

tary disabilities of married females stand on quite a
different basis from their personal incapacities, and
it is by the tendency of their doctrines to keep alive
and consolidate the former, that the expositors of
the Canon Law have deeply injured civilisation
There are many vestiges of a struggle between the
secular and ecclesiastical principles, but the Canon
Law nearly everywhere prevailed.   In some of the
French provinces, married women, of a rank below
nobility, obtained all the powers of dealing with
property which Roman jurisprudence had allowed,
and this local law has been largely followed by the
Code Napoleon; but the state of the Scottish law
shows that scrupulous deference to the doctrines of
the Roman jurisconsults did not always extend to
mitigating the disabilities of wives.   The systems
however which are least indulgent to married
women are invariably those which have followed
the Canon Law exclusively, or those which, from
the lateness of their contact with European civilisation, have never had their archaisms weeded out.
The Danish and Swedish laws, harsh for many centuries to all females, are still much less favourable
to wives than the generality of Continental codes
And yet more stringent in the proprietary incapacities it imposes is the English Common Law,
which borrows far the greatest number of its fundamental principles from the jurisprudence of the
Canonists.   Indeed, the part of the Common Law
which prescribes the legal situation of married

women may serve to give an Englishman clear notions of the great institution which has been the
principal subject of this chapter. I do not know
how the operation and nature of the ancient Patria
Potestas can be brought so vividly before the mind
as by reflecting on the prerogatives attached to the
husband by the pure English Common Law, and by
recalling the rigorous consistency with which the
view of a complete legal subjection on the part of
the wife is carried by it, where it is untouched by
equity or statutes, through every department of
rights, duties and remedies. The distance between
the eldest and latest Roman law on the subject of
Children under Power may be considered as equivalent to the difference between the Common Law
and the jurisprudence of the Court of Chancery in
the rules which they respectively apply to wives.

If we were to lose sight of the true origin of
Guardianship in both its forms, and were to employ
the common language on these topics, we should
find ourselves remarking that, while the Tutelage
of Women is an instance in which systems of archaic law push to an extravagant length the fiction
of suspended rights, the rules which they lay down
for the Guardianship of Male Orphans are an ex
ample of a fault in precisely the opposite direction.
Such systems terminate the Tutelage of Males at
an extraordinary early period. Under the ancient
Roman law, which may be taken as their type, the
son who was delivered from Patria Potestas by the

death of his Father or Grandfather remained under
guardianship till an epoch which for general pur
poses may be described as arriving with his fifteenth
year; but the arrival of that epoch placed him at
once in the full enjoyment of personal and proprietary independence. The period of minority appears therefore to have been as unreasonably short
as the duration of the disabilities of women was
preposterously long. But, in point of fact, there
was no element either of excess or of shortcoming
in the circumstances which gave their original form
to the two kinds of guardianship. Neither the one
nor the other of them was based on the slightest
consideration of public or private convenience. The
guardianship of male orphans was no more designed originally to shield them till the arrival of
years of discretion than the tutelage of women was
intended to protect the other sex against its own
feebleness. The reason why the death of the father
delivered the son from the bondage of the family
was the son's capacity for becoming himself the
head of a new family and the founder of a new
Patria Potestas; no such capacity was possessed by
the woman, and therefore she was *never* enfranchised.
Accordingly the Guardianship of Male Orphans
was a contrivance for keeping alive the semblance
of subordination to the family of the Parent, up to
the time when the child was supposed capable of
becoming a parent himself. It was a prolongation
of the Patria Potestas up to the period of bare

physical manhood. It ended with puberty, for the rigour of the theory demanded that it should be so. Inasmuch, however, as it did not profess to con- duct the orphan ward to the age of intellectual maturity or fitness for affairs, it was quite unequal to the purposes of general convenience; and this the Romans seem to have discovered at a very early stage of their social progress. One of the very oldest monuments of Roman legislation is the *Lex Lœtoria* or *Plœtoria*, which placed all free males who were of full years and rights under the temporary control of a new class of guardians, called *Curatores*, whose sanction was required to validate their acts or contracts. The twenty-sixth year of the young man's age was the limit of this statutory supervision; and it is exclusively with reference to the age of twenty-five that the terms "majority" and "minority" are employed in Roman law. *Pu- pilage* or *wardship* in modern jurisprudence has adjusted itself with tolerable regularity to the sim- ple principle of protection to the immaturity of youth both bodily and mental. It has its natural termination with years of discretion. But for pro- tection against physical weakness and for protection against intellectual incapacity, the Romans looked to two different institutions, distinct both in theory and design. The ideas attendant on both are com bined in the modern idea of guardianship.

The Law of Persons contains but one other chapter which can be usefully cited for our present

purpose. The legal rules by which systems of mature jurisprudence regulate the connexion of *Master
and Slave*, present no very distinct traces of the
original condition common to ancient societies. But
there are reasons for this exception. There seems
to be something in the institution of Slavery which
has at all times either shocked or perplexed mankind, however little habituated to reflection, and
however slightly advanced in the cultivation of its
moral instincts. The compunction which ancient
communities almost unconsciously experienced appears to have always resulted in the adoption of
some imaginary principle upon which a defence, or
at least a rationale, of slavery could be plausibly
founded. Very early in their history the Greeks
explained the institution as grounded on the intellectual inferiority of certain races and their conse-
quent natural aptitude for the servile condition.
The Romans, in a spirit equally characteristic, derived it from a supposed agreement between the
victor and the vanquished in which the first stipulated for the perpetual services of his foe ; and the
other gained in consideration the life which he had
legitimately forfeited. Such theories were not only
unsound but plainly unequal to the case for which
they affected to account. Still they exercised powerful influence in many ways. They satisfied the
conscience of the Master. They perpetuated and
probably increased the debasement of the Slave.
And they naturally tended to put out of sight the

relation in which servitude had originally stood to the rest of the domestic system. The relation, though not clearly exhibited, is casually indicated in many parts of the primitive law, and more particularly in the typical system—that of ancient Rome.

Much industry and much learning have been bestowed in the United States of America on the question whether the Slave was in the early stages of society a recognised member of the Family. There is a sense in which an affirmative answer must certainly be given. It is clear, from the testimony both of ancient law and of many primeval histories, that the Slave might under certain conditions be made the Heir, or Universal Successor, of the Master, and this significant faculty, as I shall explain in the Chapter on Succession, implies that the government and representation of the Family might, in a particular state of circumstances, devolve on the bondman. It seems, however, to be assumed in the American arguments on the subject that, if we allow Slavery to have been a primitive Family institution, the acknowledgment is pregnant with an admission of the moral defensibility of Negro-servitude at the present moment. What then is meant by saying that the Slave was originally included in the Family? Not that his situation may not have been the fruit of the coarsest motives which can actuate man. The simple wish to use the bodily powers of another person as a

means of ministering to one's own ease or pleasure
is doubtless the foundation of Slavery, and as old
as human nature. When we speak of the Slave as
anciently included in the Family, we intend to assert nothing as to the motives of those who brought
him into it or kept him there; we merely imply
that the tie which bound him to his master was regarded as one of the same general character with
that which united every other member of the group
to his chieftain. This consequence is, in fact, carried
in the general assertion already made that the
primitive ideas of mankind were unequal to comprehending any basis of the connexion *inter se* of
individuals, apart from the relations of family. The
Family consisted primarily of those who belonged
to it by consanguinity, and next of those who had
been engrafted on it by adoption; but there was
still a third class of persons who were only joined
to it by common subjection to its head, and these
were the Slaves. The born and the adopted subjects of the chief were raised above the Slave by
the certainty that in the ordinary course of events
they would be relieved from bondage and entitled
to exercise powers of their own; but that the inferiority of the Slave was not such as to place him
outside the pale of the Family, or such as to de-
grade him to the footing of inanimate property, is
clearly proved, I think, by the many traces which
remain of his ancient capacity for inheritance in the
last resort. It would, of course, be unsafe in the

highest degree to hazard conjectures how far the lot
of the Slave was mitigated, in the beginnings of society, by having a definite place reserved to him in
the empire of the Father. It is, perhaps, more
probable that the son was practically assimilated
to the Slave, than that the Slave shared any of the
tenderness which in later times was shown to the
son. But it may be asserted with some confidence
of advanced and matured codes that, wherever
servitude is sanctioned, the slave has uniformly
greater advantages under systems which preserve
some memento of his earlier condition than under
those which have adopted some other theory of his
civil degradation. The point of view from which
jurisprudence regards the Slave is always of great
importance to him. The Roman law was arrested
in its growing tendency to look upon him more and
more as an article of property by the theory of the
Law of Nature; and hence it is that, wherever
servitude is sanctioned by institutions which have
been deeply affected by Roman jurisprudence, the
servile condition is never intolerably wretched.
There is a great deal of evidence that in those
American States which have taken the highly Ro
manised code of Louisiana as the basis of their ju
risprudence, the lot and prospects of the Negro-pop
ulation were better in many material respects, until
the letter of the fundamental law was overlaid by
recent statutory enactments passed under the influence of panic, than under institutions founded on

the English Common Law, which, as recently interpreted, has no true place for the Slave, and can only
therefore regard him as a chattel.

We have now examined all parts of the ancient
Law of Persons which fall within the scope of this
treatise, and the result of the inquiry is, I trust, to
give additional definiteness and precision to our
view of the infancy of jurisprudence. The Civil
laws of States first make their appearance as the
Themistes of a patriarchal sovereign, and we can
now see that these Themistes are probably only
a developed form of the irresponsible commands
which, in a still earlier condition of the race, the
head of each isolated household may have addressed
to his wives, his children, and his slaves. But,
even after the State has been organised, the laws
have still an extremely limited application. Whether they retain their primitive character as Themistes, or whether they advance to the condition of
Customs or Codified Texts, they are binding not on
individuals, but on Families. Ancient jurisprudence, if a perhaps deceptive comparison may be
employed, may be likened to International Law,
filling nothing, as it were, except the interstices between the great groups which are the atoms of society. In a community so situated, the legislation
of assemblies and the jurisdiction of Courts reach
only to the heads of families, and to every other individual the rule of conduct is the law of his home,
of which his Parent is the legislator. But the

sphere of civil law, small at first, tends steadily to
enlarge itself. The agents of legal change, Fictions,
Equity, and Legislation, are brought in turn to
bear on the primeval institutions, and at every point
of the progress, a greater number of personal rights
and a larger amount of property are removed from
the domestic forum to the cognizance of the public
tribunals. The ordinances of the government ob
tain gradually the same efficacy in private concerns
as in matters of state, and are no longer liable to be
overridden by the behests of a despot enthroned by
each hearthstone. We have in the annals of Roman law a nearly complete history of the crumbling
away of an archaic system, and of the formation of
new institutions from the re-combined materials, institutions some of which descended unimpaired to
the modern world, while others, destroyed or cor-
rupted by contact with barbarism in the dark ages,
had again to be recovered by mankind. When we
leave this jurisprudence at the epoch of its final reconstruction by Justinian, few traces of archaism
can be discovered in any part of it except in the
single article of the extensive powers still reserved
to the living Parent. Everywhere else principles
of convenience, or of symmetry, or of simplification
—new principles at any rate—have usurped the
authority of the jejune considerations which satisfied the conscience of ancient times. Everywhere
a new morality has displaced the canons of conduct
and the reasons of acquiescence which were in unison

with the ancient usages, because in fact they were born of them.

The movement of the progressive societies has been uniform in one respect. Through all its course it has been distinguished by the gradual dissolution of family dependency and the growth of individual obligation in its place. The individual is steadily substituted for the Family, as the unit of which civil laws take account. The advance has been accom plished at varying rates of celerity, and there are societies not absolutely stationary in which the col- lapse of the ancient organisation can only be perceiv- ed by careful study of the phenomena they present. But, whatever its pace, the change has not been subject to reaction or recoil, and apparent retarda- tions will be found to have been occasioned through the absorption of archaic ideas and customs from some entirely foreign source. Nor is it difficult to see what is the tie between man and man which replaces by degrees those forms of reciprocity in rights and duties which have their origin in the Family. It is Contract. Starting, as from one terminus of history, from a condition of society in which all the relations of Persons are summed up in the relations of Fami- ly, we seem to have steadily moved towards a phase of social order in which all these relations arise from the free agreement of individuals. In Western Europe the progress achieved in this direction has been considerable. Thus the status of the Slave has disappeared—it has been superseded by the con-

tractual relation of the servant to his master.   The
status of the Female under Tutelage, if the tutelage
be understood of persons other than her husband,
has also ceased to exist ; from her coming of age to
her marriage all the relations she may form are relations of contract.   So too the status of the Son
under Power has no true place in the law of modern European societies.   If any civil obligation
binds together the Parent and the child of full age,
it is one to which only contract gives its legal validity.   The apparent exceptions are exceptions of that
stamp which illustrate the rule.   The child before
years of discretion, the orphan under guardianship,
the adjudged lunatic, have all their capacities and
incapacities regulated by the Law of Persons.   But
why ?   The reason is differently expressed in the
conventional language of different systems, but in
substance it is stated to the same effect by all.
The great majority of Jurists are constant to the
principle that the classes of persons just mentioned
are subject to extrinsic control on the single ground
that they do not possess the faculty of forming a
judgment on their own interests ; in other words,
that they are wanting in the first essential of an engagement by Contract.

The word Status may be usefully employed to
construct a formula expressing the law of progress
thus indicated, which, whatever be its value, seems
to me to be sufficiently ascertained.   All the forms
of Status taken notice of in the Law of Persons were

derived from, and to some extent are still coloured by, the powers and privileges anciently residing in the Family. If then we employ Status, agreeably with the usage of the best writers, to signify these personal conditions only, and avoid applying the term to such conditions as are the immediate or remote result of agreement, we may say that the movement of the progressive societies has hitherto been a movement *from Status to Contract.*

CHAPTER VI.

THE EARLY HISTORY OF TESTAMENTARY SUCCESSION.

IF an attempt were made to demonstrate in England
the superiority of the historical method of investigation to the modes of inquiry concerning Jurisprudence which are in fashion among us, no department
of Law would better serve as an example than Testaments or Wills. Its capabilities it owes to its
great length and great continuity. At the beginning
of its history we find ourselves in the very infancy
of the social state, surrounded by conceptions which
it requires some effort of mind to realise in their
ancient form ; while here, at the other extremity of
its line of progress, we are in the midst of legal notions which are nothing more than those same conceptions disguised by the phraseology and by the
habits of thought which belong to modern times,
and exhibiting therefore a difficulty of another kind,
the difficulty of believing that ideas which form
part of our every-day mental stock can really stand
in need of analysis and examination. The growth

of the Law of Wills between these extreme points
can be traced with remarkable distinctness. It was
much less interrupted at the epoch of the birth of
feudalism, than the history of most other branches
of Law. It is, indeed, true that as regards all provinces of jurisprudence, the break caused by the
division between ancient and modern history, or in
other words by the dissolution of the Roman empire,
has been very greatly exaggerated. Indolence has
disinclined many writers to be at the pains of looking for threads of connexion entangled and obscured by the confusions of six troubled centuries,
while other inquirers, not naturally deficient in patience and industry, have been misled by idle pride
in the legal system of their country, and by conse-
quent unwillingness to confess its obligations to the
jurisprudence of Rome. But these unfavourable
influences have had comparatively little effect on the
province of Testamentary Law. The barbarians
were confessedly strangers to any such conception
as that of a Will. The best authorities agree that
there is no trace of it in those parts of their written
codes which comprise the customs practised by them
in their original seats and in their subsequent settlements on the edge of the Roman Empire. But
soon after they became mixed with the population
of the Roman provinces they appropriated from the
Imperial jurisprudence the conception of a Will, at
first in part, and afterwards in all its integrity.
The influence of the Church had much to do with

this rapid assimilation.   The ecclesiastical power
had very early succeeded to those privileges of custody and registration of Testaments which several
of the heathen temples had enjoyed; and even thus
early it was almost exclusively to private bequests
that the religious foundations owed their temporal
possessions.   Hence it is that the decrees of the
earliest Provincial Councils perpetually contain ana-
themas against those who deny the sanctity of Wills.
Here, in England, Church influence was certainly
chief among the causes which by universal acknowledgment have prevented that discontinuity in the
history of Testamentary Law which is sometimes
believed to exist in the history of other provinces
of Jurisprudence.   The jurisdiction over one class
of Wills was delegated to the Ecclesiastical Courts,
which applied to them, though not always intelli-
gently, the principles of Roman jurisprudence; and,
though neither the Courts of Common Law nor the
Court of Chancery owned any positive obligation to
follow the Ecclesiastical tribunals, they could not
escape the potent influence of a system of settled
rules in course of application by their side.   The
English law of testamentary succession to personalty has become a modified form of the dispensation
under which the inheritances of Roman citizens
were administered.

It is not difficult to point out the extreme difference of the conclusions forced on us by the historical treatment of the subject, from those to which

we are conducted when, without the help of history, we merely strive to analyse our *primâ facie* impres sions. I suppose there is nobody who, starting from the popular or even the legal conception of a Will, would not imagine that certain qualities are necessa- rily attached to it. He would say, for example, that a Will necessarily takes effect *at death only*,—that it is *secret*, not known as a matter of course to persons taking interests under its provisions,—that it is *revo cable*, i. e. always capable of being superseded by a new act of testation. Yet I shall be able to show that there was a time when none of these characteris- tics belonged to a Will. The Testaments from which our Wills are directly descended at first took effect immediately on their execution ; they were not se- cret ; they were not revocable. Few legal agencies are, in fact, the fruit of more complex historical agencies than that by which a man's written in tentions control the posthumous disposition of his goods. Testaments very slowly and gradually ga- thered around them the qualities I have mentioned ; and they did this from causes and under pressure of events which may be called casual, or which at any rate have no interest for us at present, except so far as they have affected the history of law.

At a time when legal theories were more abund- ant than at present,—theories which, it is true, were for the most part gratuitous and premature enough, but which nevertheless rescued jurisprudence from that worse and more ignoble condition, not unknown to ourselves, in which nothing like a generalisation is aspired to, and law is regarded as a mere empirical pursuit—it was the fashion to explain the ready and apparently intuitive perception which we have of certain qualities in a Will, by saying that they were natural to it, or, as the phrase would run in full, attached to it by the Law of Nature. Nobody, I imagine, would affect to maintain such a doctrine, when once it was ascertained that all these characteristics had their origin within historical memory ; at the same time, vestiges of the theory of which the doctrine is an offshoot, linger in forms of expression which we all of us use and perhaps scarcely know how to dispense with. I may illustrate this by mentioning a position common in the legal literature of the seventeenth century. The jurists of that period very commonly assert that the power of Testation itself is of Natural Law, that it is a right conferred by the Law of Nature. Their teaching, though all persons may not at once see the connexion, is in substance followed by those who affirm that the right of dictating or controlling the posthumous disposal of property is a necessary or natural consequence of the proprietary rights themselves. And every student of technical jurisprudence must have come across the same view, clothed in the language of a rather different school, which, in its rationale of this department of law, treats succession *ex testamento* as the mode of devolution which the property of deceased persons ought primarily to follow, and then

proceeds to account for succession *ab intestato* as the
incidental provision of the lawgiver for the discharge of a function which was only left unperform-
ed through the neglect or misfortune of the deceased
proprietor. These opinions are only expanded forms
of the more compendious doctrine that Testamentary disposition is an institution of the Law of Nature. It is certainly never quite safe to pronounce
dogmatically as to the range of association embraced
by modern minds, when they reflect on Nature and
her Law; but I believe that most persons, who affirm that the Testamentary Power is of Natural
Law, may be taken to imply either that, as a matter
of fact, it is universal, or that nations are prompted
to sanction it by an original instinct and impulse.
With respect to the first of these positions, I think
that, when explicitly set forth, it can never be seriously contended for in an age which has seen the
severe restraints imposed on the Testamentary Power by the *Code Napoléon,* and has witnessed the
steady multiplication of systems for which the
French codes have served as a model. To the second assertion we must object that it is contrary to
the best-ascertained facts in the early history of law,
and I venture to affirm generally that, in all indigenous societies, a condition of jurisprudence in
which Testamentary privileges are *not* allowed, or
rather not contemplated, has preceded that later
stage of legal development in which the mere will
of the proprietor is permitted under more or less of

restriction to override the claims of his kindred in blood.

The conception of a Will or Testament cannot be considered by itself. It is a member, and not the first, of a series of conceptions. In itself a Will is simply the instrument by which the intention of the testator is declared. It must be clear, I think, that before such an instrument takes its turn for discussion, there are several preliminary points to be examined—as for example, what is it, what sort of right or interest, which passes from a dead man on his decease? to whom and in what form does it pass? and how came it that the dead were allowed to control the posthumous disposition of their property? Thrown into technical language, the dependence of the various conceptions which contribute to the notion of a Will is thus expressed. A Will or Testament is an instrument by which the devolution of an inheritance is prescribed. Inheritance is a form of universal succession. A universal succession is a succession to a *universitas juris*, or university of rights and duties. Inverting this order we have therefore to inquire what is a *universitas juris*; what is a universal succession; what is the form of universal succession which is called an inheritance? And there are also two further questions, independent to some extent of the points I have mooted, but demanding solution before the subject of Wills can be exhausted. These are, how came an inheri tance to be controlled in any case by the testator's volition, and what is the nature of the instrument by which it came to be controlled?

The first question relates to the *universitas juris;* that is, a university (or bundle) of rights and duties. A *universitas juris* is a collection of rights and duties united by the single circumstance of their having belonged at one time to some one person. It is, as it were, the legal clothing of some given individual. It is not formed by grouping together *any* rights and *any* duties. It can only be constituted by taking all the rights and all the duties of a particular person. The tie which connects a number of rights of property, rights of way, rights to legacies, duties of specific performance, debts, obligations to compensate wrongs—which so connects all these legal privileges and duties together as to constitute them a *universitas juris*, is the *fact* of their having attached to some individual capable of exercising them. Without this *fact* there is no university of rights and duties. The expression *universitas juris* is not classical, but for the notion jurisprudence is exclusively indebted to Roman law; nor is it at all difficult to seize. We must endeavour to collect under one conception the whole set of legal relations in which each one of us stands to the rest of the world. These, whatever be their character and composition, make up together a *universitas juris;* and there is but little danger of mistake in forming the notion, if we are only careful to remember that duties enter into it quite as much as rights. Our duties may overbalance our rights. A man may owe more than he is worth, and therefore if a money value is set on his collective legal relations he may be what is called insolvent. But for all that, the entire group of rights and duties which centres in him is not the less a "juris universitas."

We come next to a "universal succession." A universal succession is a succession to a *universitas juris*. It occurs when one man is invested with the legal clothing of another, becoming at the same moment subject to all his liabilities and entitled to all his rights. In order that the universal succession may be true and perfect, the devolution must take place *uno ictu*, as the jurists phrase it. It is of course possible to conceive one man acquiring the whole of the rights and duties of another at different periods, as for example by successive purchases; or he might acquire them in different capacities, part as heir, part as purchaser, part as legatee. But though the group of rights and duties thus made up should in fact amount to the whole legal personality of a particular individual, the acquisition would not be a universal succession. In order that there may be a true universal succession, the transmission must be such as to pass the whole aggregate of rights and duties at the *same* moment and in virtue of the *same* legal capacity in the recipient. The notion of a universal succession, like that of a juris universitas, is permanent in jurisprudence, though in the English legal system it is obscured by the great variety of

capacities in which rights are acquired, and, above
all, by the distinction between the two great provinces of English property, "realty " and "personalty." The succession of an assignee in bankruptcy
to the entire property of the bankrupt is, however,
a universal succession, though as the assignee only
pays debts to the extent of the assets this is only a
modified form of the primary notion. Were it common among us for persons to take assignments of
all a man's property on condition of paying *all* his
debts, such transfers would exactly resemble the universal successions known to the oldest Roman Law.
When a Roman citizen *adrogated* a son, i. e. took a
man, not already under Patria Potestas, as his adoptive child, he succeeded *universally* to the adoptive
child's estate, i. e. he took all the property and became liable for all the obligations. Several other
forms of universal succession appear in the primitive
Roman Law, but infinitely the most important and
the most durable of all was that one with which we
are more immediately concerned, Hæreditas or Inheritance. Inheritance was a universal succession
occurring at a death. The universal successor was
Hæres or Heir. He stepped at once into all the
rights and all the duties of the dead man. He was
instantly clothed with his entire legal person, and I
need scarcely add that the special character of the
Hæres remained the same, whether he was named
by a Will or whether he took on an Intestacy. The
term Hæres is no more emphatically used of the

Intestate than of the Testamentary Heir, for the
manner in which a man became Hæres had nothing
to do with the legal character he sustained. The
dead man's universal successor, however he became
so, whether by Will or by Intestacy, was his Heir.
But the heir was not necessarily a single person.
A group of persons, considered in law as a single unit, might succeed as *co-heirs* to the Inheritance.

Let me now quote the usual Roman definition
of an Inheritance. The reader will be in a position
to appreciate the full force of the separate terms.
*Hæreditas est successio in universum jus quod de-
functus habuit* (" an inheritance is a succession to
the entire legal position of a deceased man "). The
notion was that though the physical person of the
deceased had perished, his legal personality survived
and descended unimpaired on his Heir or Co-heirs,
in whom his identity (so far as the law was con
cerned) was continued. Our own law, in constituting the Executor or Administrator the representative of the deceased to the extent of his personal
assets, may serve as an illustration of the theory
from which it emanated ; but, although it illustrates,
it does not explain it. The view of even the later
Roman Law required a closeness of correspondence
between the position of the deceased and of his
Heir which is no feature of an English representa
tion ; and in the primitive jurisprudence everything
turned on the continuity of succession. Unless

provision was made in the will for the instant devolution of the testator's rights and duties on the
Heir or Co-heirs, the testament lost all its effect.

In modern Testamentary jurisprudence, as in the
later Roman law, the object of first importance is
the execution of the testator's intentions. In the
ancient law of Rome the subject of corresponding
carefulness was the bestowal of the Universal Succession. One of these rules seems to our eyes a
principle dictated by common sense, while the other
looks very much like an idle crotchet. Yet that
without the second of them the first would never
have come into being is as certain as any proposition of the kind can be.

In order to solve this apparent paradox, and to
bring into greater clearness the train of ideas which
I have been endeavouring to indicate, I must borrow the results of the inquiry which was attempted
in the earlier portion of the preceding chapter.
We saw one peculiarity invariably distinguishing
the infancy of society. Men are regarded and
treated, not as individuals, but always as members
of a particular group. Everybody is first a citizen,
and then, as a citizen, he is a member of his order
—of an aristocracy or a democracy, of an order of
patricians or plebeians; or in those societies which
an unhappy fate has afflicted with a special perversion in their course of development, of a caste.
Next, he is a member of a gens, house, or clan; and
lastly, he is a member of his *family*. This last was

the narrowest and most personal relation in which he stood; nor, paradoxical as it may seem, was he ever regarded as *himself*, as a distinct individual. His individuality was swallowed up in his family. I repeat the definition of a primitive society given before. It has for its units, not individuals, but groups of men united by the reality or the fiction of blood-relationship.

It is in the peculiarities of an undeveloped society that we seize the first trace of a universal succession. Contrasted with the organisation of a modern state, the commonwealths of primitive times may be fairly described as consisting of a number of little despotic governments, each perfectly distinct from the rest, each absolutely controlled by the prerogative of a single monarch. But though the Patriarch, for we must not yet call him the Pater-familias, had rights thus extensive, it is impossible to doubt that he lay under an equal amplitude of obligations. If he governed the family, it was for its behoof. If he was lord of its possessions, he held them as trustee for his children and kindred. He had no privilege or position distinct from that conferred on him by his relation to the petty commonwealth which he governed. The Family, in fact, was a Corporation; and he was its representative or, we might almost say, its Public officer. He enjoyed rights and stood under duties, but the rights and duties were, in the contemplation of his fellow-citizens and in the eye of the law, quite as much those of the collective body as his own.   Let us consider for a moment, the effect which would be produced by the death of such a representative.   In the eye of the law, in the view of the civil magistrate, the demise of the domestic authority would be a perfectly immaterial event. The person representing the collective body of the family and primarily responsible to municipal juris- diction would bear a different name; and that would be all.   The rights and obligations which attached to the deceased head of the house would attach, without breach of continuity, to his succes- sor; for, in point of fact, they would be the rights and obligations of the family, and the family had the distinctive characteristic of a corporation—that it never died.   Creditors would have the same remedies against the new chieftain as against the old, for the liability being that of the still existing family would be absolutely unchanged.   All rights available to the family would be as available after the demise of the headship as before it—except that the Corporation would be obliged—if indeed lan- guage so precise and technical can be properly used of these early times—would be obliged to *sue* under slightly modified name.

The history of jurisprudence must be followed in its whole course, if we are to understand how gradually and tardily society dissolved itself into the component atoms of which it is now constituted —by what insensible gradations the relation of man

to man substituted itself for the relation of the individual to his family and of families to each other.
The point now to be attended to is that even when
the revolution had apparently quite accomplished
itself, even when the magistrate had in great measure assumed the place of the Pater-familias, and the
civil tribunal substituted itself for the domestic
forum, nevertheless the whole scheme of rights and
duties administered by the judicial authorities remained shaped by the influence of the obsolete
privileges and coloured in every part by their reflection. There seems little question that the devolution of the Universitas Juris, so strenuously insisted upon by the Roman Law as the first condition of a testamentary or intestate succession, was a
feature of the older form of society which men's
minds had been unable to dissociate from the new,
though with that newer phase it had no true or
proper connection. It seems, in truth, that the prolongation of a man's legal existence in his heir, or
in a group of co-heirs, is neither more nor less than
a characteristic of *the family* transferred by a fiction
to *the individual*. Succession in corporations is
necessarily universal, and the family was a corpora
tion. Corporations never die. The decease of individual members makes no difference to the collective existence of the aggregate body, and does not
in any way affect its legal incidents, its faculties or
liabilities. Now in the idea of a Roman universal
succession all these qualities of a corporation seem

to have been transferred to the individual citizen.
His physical death is allowed to exercise no effect
on the legal position which he filled, apparently on
the principle that that position is to be adjusted as
closely as possible to the analogies of a family,
which in its corporate character was not of course
liable to physical extinction.

I observe that not a few continental jurists have
much difficulty in comprehending the nature of the
connection between the conceptions blended in a
universal succession, and there is perhaps no topic
in the philosophy of jurisprudence on which their
speculations, as a general rule, possess so little
value.   But the student of English law ought to be
in no danger of stumbling at the analysis of the
idea which we are examining.   Much light is cast
upon it by a fiction in our own system with which
all lawyers are familiar.   English lawyers classify
corporations as Corporations aggregate and Corporations sole.   A Corporation aggregate is a true corporation, but a Corporation sole is an individual,
being a member of a series of individuals, who is
invested by a fiction with the qualities of a Corporation.   I need hardly cite the King or the Parson of a Parish as instances of Corporations sole.
The capacity or office is here considered apart from
the particular person who from time to time may
occupy it, and, this capacity being perpetual, the
series of individuals who fill it are clothed with
the leading attribute of Corporations—Perpetuity.

Now in the older theory of Roman Law the indi
vidual bore to the family precisely the same relation
which in the rationale of English jurisprudence a
Corporation sole bears to a Corporation aggregate.
The derivation and association of ideas are exactly
the same. In fact, if we say to ourselves that for
purposes of Roman Testamentary Jurisprudence
each individual citizen was a Corporation sole, we
shall not only realize the full conception of an inheritance, but have constantly at command the clue
to the assumption in which it originated. It is an
axiom with us that the King never dies, being
a Corporation sole. His capacities are instantly
filled by his successor, and the continuity of dominion is not deemed to have been interrupted. With
the Romans it seemed an equally simple and natural
process, to eliminate the fact of death from the devolution of rights and obligations. The testator lived
on in his heir or in the group of his co-heirs. He
was in law the same person with them, and if any
one in his testamentary dispositions had even con-
structively violated the principle which united his
actual and his posthumous existence, the law re-
jected the defective instrument, and gave the inheritance to the kindred in blood, whose capacity to
fulfil the conditions of heirship was conferred on
them by the law itself, and not by any document
which by possibility might be erroneously framed.

When a Roman citizen died intestate or leaving
no valid Will, his descendants or kindred became

his heirs according to a scale which will be presently described. The person or class of persons who
succeeded did not simply *represent* the deceased,
but, in conformity with the theory just delineated,
they *continued* his civil life, his legal existence.
The same results followed when the order of succession was determined by a Will, but the theory
of the identity between the dead man and his heirs
was certainly much older than any form of Testament or phase of Testamentary jurisprudence. This
indeed is the proper moment for suggesting a doubt
which will press on us with greater force the further
we plumb the depths of this subject—whether *wills*
would ever have come into being at all if it had not
been for these remarkable ideas connected with universal succession. Testamentary law is the application of a principle which may be explained on a variety of philosophical hypotheses as plausible as
they are gratuitous; it is interwoven with every
part of modern society, and it is defensible on the
broadest grounds of general expediency. But the
warning can never be too often repeated, that the
grand source of mistake in questions of jurisprudence is the impression that those reasons which
actuate us at the present moment, in the maintenance of an existing institution, have necessarily
anything in common with the sentiment in which
the institution originated. It is certain that, in the
old Roman Law of Inheritance, the notion of a will
or testament is inextricably mixed up, I might

almost say confounded, with the theory of a man's posthumous existence in the person of his heir.

The conception of a universal succession, firmly as it has taken root in jurisprudence, has not occurred spontaneously to the framers of every body of laws. Wherever it is now found, it may be shown to have descended from Roman law; and with it have come down a host of legal rules on the subject of Testaments and Testamentary gifts, which modern practitioners apply without discerning their relation to the parent theory. But, in the pure Roman jurisprudence, the principle that a man lives on in his Heir—the elimination, if we may so speak, of the fact of death—is too obviously for mistake the centre round which the whole Law of Testamentary and Intestate succession is circling. The unflinching sternness of the Roman law in enforcing compliance with the governing theory would in itself suggest that the theory grew out of something in the primitive constitution of Roman society; but we may push the proof a good way beyond the presumption. It happens that several technical expressions, dating from the earliest institutions of Wills at Rome, have been accidentally preserved to us. We have in Gaius the formula of investiture by which the universal successor was created. We have the ancient name by which the person afterwards called Heir was at first designated. We have further the text of the celebrated clause in the Twelve Tables by which the Testamentary power was expressly recognised, and the clauses regulating Intestate Succession have also been preserved. All these archaic phrases have one salient peculiarity. They indicate that what passed from the Testator to the Heir was the *Family*, that is the aggregate of rights and duties contained in the Patria Potestas and growing out of it. The material property is in three instances not mentioned at all; in two others, it is visibly named as an adjunct or appendage of the Family. The original Will or Testament was therefore an instrument, or (for it was probably not at first in writing) a proceeding by which the devolution of the *Family* was regulated. It was a mode of declaring who was to have the chieftainship, in succession to the Testator. When Wills are understood to have this for their original object, we see at once how it is that they came to be connected with one of the most curious relics of ancient religion and law, the *sacra*, or Family Rites. These *sacra* were the Roman form of an institution which shows itself wherever society has not wholly shaken itself free from its primitive clothing. They are the sacrifices and ceremonies by which the brotherhood of the family is commemorated, the pledge and the witness of its perpetuity. Whatever be their nature,—whether it be true or not that in all cases they are the worship of some mythical ancestor,—they are everywhere employed to attest the sacredness of the family relation; and therefore they acquire prominent significance and

importance, whenever the continuous existence of
the Family is endangered by a change in the person
of its chief. Accordingly, we hear most about them
in connection with demises of domestic sovereignty.
Among the Hindoos, the right to inherit a dead
man's property is exactly co-extensive with the duty
of performing his obsequies. If the rites are not
properly performed or not performed by the proper
person, no relation is considered as established between the deceased and anybody surviving him;
the Law of Succession does not apply, and nobody
can inherit the property. Every great event in the
life of a Hindoo seems to be regarded as leading up
to and bearing upon these solemnities. If he mar-
ries, it is to have children who may celebrate them
after his death; if he has no children, he lies under
the strongest obligation to adopt them from another
family, "with a view," writes the Hindoo doctor,
"to the funeral cake, the water, and the solemn
sacrifice." The sphere preserved to the Roman
sacra in the time of Cicero, was not less in extent.
It embraced Inheritances and Adoptions. No
Adoption was allowed to take place without due
provision for the *sacra* of the family from which the
adoptive son was transferred, and no Testament was
allowed to distribute an Inheritance without a strict
apportionment of the expenses of these ceremonies
among the different co-heirs. The differences between the Roman law at this epoch, when we obtain
our last glimpse of the *sacra*, and the existing Hin-

doo system, are most instructive.   Among the Hindoos, the religious element in law has acquired a complete predominance.   Family sacrifices have become the keystone of all the Law of Persons and much of the Law of Things.   They have even received a monstrous extension, for it is a plausible opinion that the self-immolation of the widow at her husband's funeral, a practice continued to historical times by the Hindoos, and commemorated in the traditions of several Indo-European races, was an addition grafted on the primitive *sacra* under the influence of the impression, which always accompanies the idea of sacrifice, that human blood is the most precious of all oblations.   With the Romans, on the contrary, the legal obligation and the religious duty have ceased to be blended.   The necessity of solemnising the *sacra* forms no part of the theory of civil law, but they are under the separate jurisdiction of the College of Pontiffs.   The letters of Cicero to Atticus, which are full of allusions to them, leave no doubt that they constituted an intolerable burden on Inheritances ; but the point of development at which law breaks away from religion has been passed, and we are prepared for their entire disappearance from the later jurisprudence.

In Hindoo law there is no such thing as a true Will.   The place filled by Wills is occupied by Adoptions.   We can now see the relation of the Testamentary Power to the Faculty of Adoption, and the reason why the exercise of either of them

could call up a peculiar solicitude for the perform
ance of the *sacra*. Both a Will and an Adoption
threaten a distortion of the ordinary course of Family descent, but they are obviously contrivances for
preventing the descent being wholly interrupted
when there is no succession of kindred to carry it
on. Of the two expedients Adoption, the factitious
creation of blood-relationship, is the only one which
has suggested itself to the greater part of archaic
societies. The Hindoos have indeed advanced one
point on what was doubtless the antique practice,
by allowing the widow to adopt when the father
has neglected to do so, and there are in the local
customs of Bengal some faint traces of the Testamentary powers. But to the Romans belongs pre-
eminently the credit of inventing the Will, the institution which, next to the Contract, has exercised
the greatest influence in transforming human society. We must be careful not to attribute to it in
its earliest shape the functions which have attended
it in more recent times. It was at first not a mode
of distributing a dead man's goods, but one among
several ways of transferring the representation of
the household to a new chief. The goods descend
no doubt to the Heir, but that is only because the
government of the family carries with it in its devo
lution the power of disposing of the common stock
We are very far as yet from that stage in the his
tory of Wills, in which they become powerful instru
ments in modifying society through the stimulus

they give to the circulation of property and the
plasticity they produce in proprietary rights. No
such consequences as these appear in fact to have
been associated with the Testamentary power even
by the latest Roman lawyers. It will be found
that Wills were never looked upon in the Roman
community as a contrivance for parting Property
and the Family, or for creating a variety of miscellaneous interests, but rather as a means of making a
better provision for the members of a household
than could be secured through the rules of Intestate
succession. We may suspect indeed that the associations of a Roman with the practice of will-making were extremely different from those familiar to
us nowadays. The habit of regarding Adoption
and Testation as modes of continuing the Family
cannot but have had something to do with the
singular laxity of Roman notions as to the inheritance of sovereignty. It is impossible not to see
that the succession of the early Roman Emperors to
each other was considered reasonably regular, and
that, in spite of all that had occurred, no absurdity
attached to the pretension of such Princes as Theo-
dosius or Justinian to style themselves Cæsar and
Augustus.

When the phenomena of primitive societies
emerge into light, it seems impossible to dispute a
proposition which the jurists of the seventeenth
century considered doubtful, that Intestate Inheritance is a more ancient institution than Testamen-

tary Succession. As soon as this is settled, a question of much interest suggests itself, how and under what conditions were the directions of a will first allowed to regulate the devolution of authority over the household, and consequently the posthumous distribution of property. The difficulty of deciding the point arises from the rarity of Testamentary power in archaic communities. It is doubtful whether a true power of testation was known to any original society except the Roman. Rudimentary forms of it occur here and there, but most of them are not exempt from the suspicion of a Roman origin. The Athenian Will was, no doubt, indigenous, but then, as will appear presently, it was only an inchoate Testament. As to the Wills which are sanctioned by the bodies of law which have descended to us as the codes of the barbarian conquerors of imperial Rome, they are almost certainly Roman. The most penetrating German criticism has recently been directed to these *leges Barbarorum*, the great object of investigation being to detach those portions of each system which formed the customs of the tribe in its original home from the adventitious ingredients which were borrowed from the laws of the Romans. In the course of this process, one result has invariably disclosed itself, that the ancient nucleus of the code contains no trace of a Will. Whatever testamentary law exists, has been taken from Roman jurisprudence. Similarly, the rudimentary Testament which (as I am inform ed) the Rabbinical Jewish law provides for, has been attributed to contact with the Romans. The only form of testament, not belonging to a Roman or Hellenic society, which can reasonably be sup-posed indigenous, is that recognised by the usages of the province of Bengal; and the testament of Bengal, which some have even supposed to be an invention of Anglo-Indian lawyers, is at most only a rudimentary Will.

The evidence, however, such as it is, seems to point to the conclusion that Testaments are at first only allowed to take effect on failure of the persons entitled to have the inheritance by right of blood genuine or fictitious.   Thus, when Athenian citi-zens were empowered for the first time by the Laws of Solon to execute Testaments, they were forbidden to disinherit their direct male descen-dants.   So, too, the Will of Bengal is only per-mitted to govern the succession so far as it is con-sistent with certain overriding claims of the family. Again, the original institutions of the Jews having provided nowhere for the privileges of Testator-ship, the later Rabbinical jurisprudence, which pre-tends to suply the *casus omissi* of the Mosaic law, allows the power of Testation to attach when all the kindred entitled under the Mosaic system to succeed have failed or are undiscoverable.   The limitations by which the ancient German codes hedge in the testamentary jurisprudence which has been incorporated with them are also significant,

and point in the same direction. It is the peculiar
ity of most of these German laws, in the only shape
in which we know them, that, besides the *allod* or
domain of each household, they recognise several
subordinate kinds or orders of property, each of
which probably represents a separate transfusion
of Roman principles into the primitive body of
Teutonic usage. The primitive German or allodial
property is strictly reserved to the kindred. Not
only is it incapable of being disposed of by testament, but it is scarcely capable of being alienated
by conveyance *inter vivos*. The ancient German
law, like the Hindoo jurisprudence, makes the male
children co-proprietors with their father, and the
endowment of the family cannot be parted with except by the consent of all its members. But the
other sorts of property, of more modern origin and
lower dignity than the allodial possessions, are
much more easily alienated than they, and follow
much more lenient rules of devolution. Women
and the descendants of women succeed to them, obviously on the principle that they lie outside the
sacred precinct of the Agnatic brotherhood. Now,
it is on these last descriptions of property, and on
these only, that the Testaments borrowed from
Rome were at first allowed to operate.

These few indications may serve to lend additional plausibility to that which in itself appears to
be the most probable explanation of an ascertained
fact in the early history of Roman wills. We have

it stated on abundant·authority that Testaments during the primitive period of the Roman State, were executed in the Comitia Calata, that is, in the Comitia Curiata, or Parliament of the Patrician Burghers of Rome, when assembled for Private Business. This mode of execution has been the source of the assertion, handed down by one generation of civilians to another, that every Will at one era of Roman history was a solemn legislative enactment. But there is no necessity whatever for resorting to an explanation which has the defect of attributing far too much precision to the proceedings of the ancient assembly. The proper key to the story concerning the execution of Wills in the Comitia Calata must no doubt be sought in the oldest Roman Law of *intestate* succession. The canons of primitive Roman jurisprudence regulating the inheritance of relations from each other were, so long as they remained unmodified by the Edictal Law of the Prætor, to the following effect :—First, the *sui* or direct descendants who had never been emancipated succeeded. On the failure of the *sui*, the Nearest Agnate came into their place, that is, the nearest person or class of the kindred who was or might have been under the same Patria Potestas with the deceased. The third and last degree came next, in which the inheritance devolved on the *gentiles*, that is, on the collective members of the dead man's *gens* or *House*. The House, I have explained already, was a fictitious extension of the family,

consisting of all Roman Patrician citizens who bore
the same name, and who on the ground of bearing
the same name, were supposed to be descended
from a common ancestor. Now the Patrician Assembly called the Comitia Curiata was a Legislature in which Gentes or Houses were exclusively
represented. It was a representative assembly of
the Roman people, constituted on the assumption
that the constituent unit of the state was the Gens.
This being so, the inference seems inevitable, that
the cognisance of Wills by the Comitia was connected with the rights of the Gentiles, and was intended to secure them in their privilege of ultimate
inheritance. The whole apparent anomaly is removed, if we suppose that a Testament could only
be made when the testator had no *gentiles* discov
erable, or when they waived their claims, and that
every Testament was submitted to the General Assembly of the Roman Gentes, in order that those
aggrieved by its dispositions might put their veto
upon it if they pleased, or by allowing it to pass
might be presumed to have renounced their reversion. It is possible that on the eve of the publication of the Twelve Tables this vetoing power may
have been greatly curtailed or only occasionally and
capriciously exercised. It is much easier, however
to indicate the meaning and origin of the jurisdiction confided to the Comitia Calata, than to trace
its gradual development or progressive decay.

The Testament to which the pedigree of all

modern Wills may be traced is not, however, the Testament executed in the Calata Comitia, but another Testament designed to compete with it and destined to supersede it. The historical importance of this early Roman Will, and the light it casts on much of ancient thought, will excuse me for describing it at some length.

When the Testamentary power first discloses itself to us in legal history, there are signs that, like almost all the great Roman institutions, it was the subject of contention between the Patricians and the Plebeians. The effect of the political maxim, *Plebs Gentem non habet,* " a Plebeian cannot be a member of a house," was entirely to exclude the Plebeians from the Comitia Curiata. Some critics have accordingly supposed that a Plebeian could not have his Will read or recited to the Patrician Assembly, and was thus deprived of Testamentary privileges altogether. Others have been satisfied to point out the hardships of having to submit a proposed Will to the unfriendly jurisdiction of an assembly in which the Testator was not represented. Whatever be the true view, a form of Testament came into use, which has all the characteristics of a contrivance intended to evade some distasteful obligation. The Will in question was a conveyance *inter vivos,* a complete and irrevocable alienation of the Testator's family and substance to the person whom he meant to be his heir. The strict rules of Roman law must always have permitted such an alienation, but when the transaction was intended to have a posthumous effect, there may have been disputes whether it was valid for Testamentary purposes without the formal assent of the Patrician Parliament. If a difference of opinion existed on the point between the two classes of the Roman population, it was extinguished, with many other sources of heartburning, by the great Decemviral compromise. The text of the Twelve Tables is still extant which says, *"Pater familias uti de pecuniá tutelâve rei suæ legássit, ita jus esto"*—a law which can hardly have had any other object than the legalisation of the Plebeian Will.

It is well known to scholars that, centuries after the Patrician Assembly had ceased to be the legislature of the Roman State, it still continued to hold formal sittings for the convenience of private business. Consequently, at a period long subsequent to the publication of the Decemviral Law, there is reason to believe that the Comitia Calata still assembled for the validation of Testaments. Its probable functions may be best indicated by saying that it was a Court of Registration, with the understanding, however, that the Wills exhibited were not *enrolled*, but simply recited to the members, who were supposed to take note of their tenor and to commit them to memory. It is very likely that this form of Testament was never reduced to writing at all, but at all events if the Will had been originally written, the office of the Comitia was certainly confined to hearing it read aloud, the document being retained afterwards in the custody of the Testator, or deposited under the safeguard of some religious corporation. This publicity may have been one of the incidents of the Testament executed in the Comitia Calata which brought it into popular disfavour. In the early years of the Empire the Comitia still held its meetings, but they seem to have lapsed into the merest form, and few Wills, or none, were probably presented at the periodical sitting.

It is the ancient Plebeian Will—the alternative of the Testament just described—which in its remote effects has deeply modified the civilisation of the modern world. It acquired at Rome all the popularity which the Testament submitted to the Calata Comitia appears to have lost. The key to all its characteristics lies in its descent from the *mancipium*, or ancient Roman conveyance, a proceeding to which we may unhesitatingly assign the parentage of two great institutions without which modern society can scarcely be supposed capable of holding together, the Contract and the Will. The *mancipium*, or, as the word would exhibit itself in later Latinity, the Mancipation, carries us back by its incidents to the infancy of civil society. As it sprang from times long anterior, if not to the invention, at all events to the popularisation, of the art of writing, gestures, symbolical acts, and solemn phrases take the place of documentary forms, and

a lengthy and intricate ceremonial is intended to
call the attention of the parties to the importance
of the transaction, and to impress it on the memory
of the witnesses. The imperfection, too, of oral, as
compared with written, testimony necessitates the
multiplication of the witnesses and assistants beyond what in later times would be reasonable or
intelligible limits.

The Roman Mancipation required the presence
first of all the parties, the vendor and vendee,
or we should perhaps rather say, if we are to use
modern legal language, the grantor and grantee.
There were also no less than *five* witnesses; and
an anomalous personage, the Libripens, who brought
with him a pair of scales to weigh the uncoined
copper money of ancient Rome. The Testament
we are considering—the Testament *per æs et libram*,
" with the copper and the scales," as it long continued to be technically called—was an ordinary Mancipation with no change in the form and hardly
any in words. The Testator was the grantor; the
five witnesses and the libripens were present; and
the place of grantee was taken by a person known
technically as the *familiæ emptor*, the Purchaser
of the Family. The ordinary ceremony of a Mancipation was then proceeded with. Certain formal
gestures were made and sentences pronounced.
The *Emptor familiæ* simulated the payment of a
price by striking the scales with a piece of money,
and finally the Testator ratified what had been done

in a set form of words called the " Nuncupatio " or
publication of the transaction, a phrase which, I
need scarcely remind the lawyer, has had a long
history in Testamentary jurisprudence.   It is necessary to attend particularly to the character of the
person called *familiæ emptor*.   There is no douht
that at first he was the Heir himself.   The Testator
conveyed to him outright his whole " familia," that
is, all the rights he enjoyed over and through the
family ; his property, his slaves, and all his an-
cestral privileges, together, on the other hand, with
all his duties and obligations.

With these data before us, we are able to note
several remarkable points in which the Mancipatory
Testament, as it may be called, differed in its primitive form from a modern will.   As it amounted to
a conveyance *out-and-out* of the Testator's estate, it
was not *revocable*.   There could be no new exercise
of a power which had been exhausted.

Again, it was not secret.   The Familiæ Emptor,
being himself the Heir, knew exactly what his
rights were, and was aware that he was irreversibly
entitled to the inheritance ; a knowledge which the
violences inseparable from the best-ordered ancient
society rendered extremely dangerous.   But perhaps the most surprising consequence of this relation of Testaments to Conveyances was the immediate vesting of the inheritance in the Heir.   This
has seemed so incredible to not a few civilians, that
they have spoken of the Testator's estate as vesting

conditionally on the Testator's death, or as granted
to him from a time uncertain, i. e. the death of the
grantor. But down to the latest period of Roman
jurisprudence there were a certain class of transac
tions which never admitted of being directly modified by a condition, or of being limited to or from a
point of time. In technical language they did not
admit *conditio* or *dies*. Mancipation was one of
them, and therefore, strange as it may seem, we are
forced to conclude that the primitive Roman Will
took effect at once, even though the Testator survived his act of Testation. It is indeed likely that
Roman citizens originally made their Wills only in
the article of death, and that a provision for the
continuance of the Family effected by a man in the
flower of life would take the form rather of an
Adoption than of a Will. Still we must believe
that, if the Testator did recover, he could only continue to govern his household by the sufferance of
his Heir.

Two or three remarks should be made before I
explain how these inconveniences were remedied,
and how Testaments came to be invested with the
characteristics now universally associated with them.
The Testament was not necessarily written : at
first, it seems to have been invariably oral, and even
in later times, the instrument declaratory of the bequests was only incidentally connected with the Will
and formed no essential part of it. It bore in fact
exactly the same relation to the Testament, which

the deed leading the uses bore to the Fines and Recoveries of old English law, or which the charter of
feoffment bore to the feoffment itself. Previously,
indeed, to the Twelve Tables, no writing would
have been of the slightest use, for the Testator had
no power of giving legacies, and the only persons
who could be advantaged by a will were the Heir
or Co-Heirs. But the extreme generality of the
clause in the Twelve Tables soon produced the doctrine that the Heir must take the inheritance burdened by any directions which the Testator might
give him, or in other words, take it subject to legacies. Written testamentary instruments assumed
thereupon a new value, as a security against the
fraudulent refusal of the heir to satisfy the legatees;
but to the last it was at the Testator's pleasure to
rely exclusively on the testimony of the witnesses,
and to declare by word of mouth the legacies which
the *familiæ emptor* was commissioned to pay.

The terms of the expression *Emptor familiæ* demand notice. " Emptor " indicates that the Will
was literally a sale, and the word " familiæ, " when
compared with the phraseology in the Testamentary
clause in the Twelve Tables, leads us to some instructive conclusions. " Familia, " in classical Latinity,
means always a man's slaves. Here, however, and
generally in the language of ancient Roman law, it
includes all persons under his Potestas, and the Testator's material property or substance is understood
to pass as an adjunct or appendage of his household.

Turning to the law of the Twelve Tables, it will be
seen that it speaks of *tutela rei suæ* "the guardianship of his substance," a form of expression which
is the exact reverse of the phrase just examined.
There does not therefore appear to be any mode of
escaping from the conclusion, that even at an era so
comparatively recent as that of the Decemviral compromise, terms denoting "household" and "property" were blended in the current phraseology.   If a
man's household had been spoken of as his property
we might have explained the expression as pointing
to the extent of the Patria Potestas, but, as the inter-
change is reciprocal, we must allow that the form of
speech carries us back to that primeval period in
which property is owned by the family, and the family is governed by the citizen, so that the members
of the community do not own their property *and*
their family, but rather own their property *through*
their family.

At an epoch not easy to settle with precision, the
Roman Prætors fell into the habit of acting upon
Testaments solemnized in closer conformity with the
spirit than the letter of the law.   Casual dispensations became insensibly the established practice till
at length a wholly new form of Will was matured
and regularly engrafted on the Edictal Jurisprudence.   The new or *Prætorian* Testament derived
the whole of its impregnability from the *Jus Hono-
rarium* or Equity of Rome.   The Prætor of some
particular year must have inserted a clause in his

Inaugural Proclamation declaratory of his intention
to sustain all Testaments which should have been
executed with such and such solemnities ; and, the
reform having been found advantageous, the article
relating to it must have been again introduced by
the Prætor's successor, and repeated by the next in
office, till at length it formed a recognised portion
of that body of jurisprudence which from these successive incorporations was styled the Perpetual or
Continuous Edict.   On examining the conditions of
a valid Prætorian Will they will be plainly seen to
have been determined by the requirements of the
Mancipatory Testament, the innovating Prætor having obviously prescribed to himself the retention of
the old formalities just so far as they were warrants
of genuineness or securities against fraud.   At the
execution of the Mancipatory Testament seven persons had been present besides the Testator.   Seven
witnesses were accordingly essential to the Prætorian
Will : two of them corresponding to the *libripens*
and *familiæ emptor*, who were now stripped of their
symbolical character, and were merely present for
the purpose of supplying their testimony.   No em-
blematic ceremony was gone through ; the Will was
merely recited ; but then it is probable (though
not absolutely certain) that a written instrument was
necessary to perpetuate the evidence of the Testator's dispositions.   At all events, whenever a writing was read or exhibited as a person's last Will, we
know certainly that the Prætorian Court would not

sustain it by special intervention, unless each of
the seven witnesses had severally affixed his seal to
the outside.   This is the first appearance of *seal-
ing* in the history of jurisprudence, considered as a
mode of authentication.   The use of seals, however,
as mere fastenings, is doubtless of much higher antiquity; and it appears to have been known to the
Hebrews. We may observe, that the seals of Roman
Wills, and other documents of importance, did not
only serve as the index of the presence or assent of
the signatary, but were also literally fastenings which
had to be broken before the writing could be in-
spected.

The Edictal Law would therefore enforce the
dispositions of a Testator, when, instead of being
symbolised through the forms of mancipation, they
were simply evidenced by the seals of seven witnesses.   But it may be laid down as a general
proposition, that the principal qualities of Roman
property were incommunicable except through processes which were supposed to be coëval with the
origin of the Civil Law.   The Prætor therefore
could not confer an *Inheritance* on anybody.   He
could not place the Heir or Co-heirs in that very relation in which the Testator had himself stood to his
own rights and obligations.   All he could do was
to confer on the person designated as Heir the practical enjoyment of the property bequeathed, and to
give the force of legal acquittances to his payments
of the Testator's debts.   When he exerted his

powers to these ends, the Prætor was technically
said to communicate the *Bonorum Possessio*. The
Heir specially inducted under these circumstances
or *Bonorum Possessor*, had every proprietary priv
ilege of the Heir by the Civil Law. He took the
profits and he could alienate, but then, for all his
remedies for redress against wrong, he must go, as
we should phrase it, not to the Common Law, but
to the Equity side of the Prætorian Court. No
great chance of error would be incurred by describing him as having an *equitable* estate in the inheritance; but then, to secure ourselves against being
deluded by the analogy, we must always recollect
that in one year the *Bonorum Possessio* was operated upon by a principle of Roman Law known as
Usucapion, and the Possessor became Quiritarian
owner of all the property comprised in the inheritance.

We know too little of the older law of Civil
Process to be able to strike the balance of advantage and disadvantage between the different classes
of remedies supplied by the Prætorian Tribunal. It
is certain, however, that, in spite of its many defects,
the Mancipatory Testament by which the *universitas juris* devolved at once and unimpaired was never
entirely superseded by the new Will; and at a period less bigoted to antiquarian forms, and perhaps
not quite alive to their significance, all the ingenuity
of the Jurisconsults seems to have been expended
on the improvement of the more venerable instru-

ment. At the era of Gaius, which is that of the Antonine Cæsars, the great blemishes of the Mancipatory Will had been removed. Originally, as we have seen, the essential character of the formalities had required that the Heir himself should be the Purchaser of the Family, and the consequence was that he not only instantly acquired a vested interest in the Testator's Property, but was formally made aware of his rights. But the age of Gaius permitted some unconcerned person to officiate as Purchaser of the Family. The Heir, therefore, was not necessarily informed of the succession to which he was destined; and Wills thenceforward acquired the property of *secrecy*. The substitution of a stranger for the actual Heir in the functions of " Familiæ Emptor " had other ulterior consequences. As soon as it was legalised, a Roman Testament came to consist of two parts or stages,—a Conveyance, which was a pure form, and a Nuncupatio, or Publication. In this latter passage of the proceeding, the Testator either orally declared to the assistants the wishes which were to be executed after his death, or produced a written document in which his wishes were embodied. It was not probably till attention had been quite drawn off from the imaginary Conveyance, and concentrated on the Nuncupation as the essential part of the transaction, that Wills were allowed to become *revocable*.

I have thus carried the pedigree of Wills some way down in legal history. The root of it is the old Testament " with the copper and the scales," founded on a Mancipation or Conveyance. This ancient Will has, however, manifold defects, which are remedied, though only indirectly, by the Prætorian law. Meantime the ingenuity of the Jurisconsults effects, in the Common-Law Will or Mancipatory Testament, the very improvements which the Prætor may have concurrently carried out in Equity. These last ameliorations depend, however, on more legal dexterity, and we see accordingly that the Testamentary Law of the day of Gaius or Ulpian is only transitional. What changes next ensued we know not; but at length just before the reconstruction of the jurisprudence by Justinian, we find the subjects of the Eastern Roman Empire employing a form of Will of which the pedigree is traceable to the Prætoriar Testament on one side, and to the Testament " with the copper and the scales," on the other. Like the Testament of the Prætor, it required no Mancipation, and was invalid unless sealed by seven witnesses. Like the Mancipatory Will, it passed the Inheritance and not merely a *Bonorum Possessio*. Several, however, of its most important features were annexed by positive enactments, and it is out of regard to this threefold derivation from the Prætorian Edict, from the Civil Law, and from the Imperial Constitutions, that Justinian speaks of the Law of Wills in his own days as *Jus Tripertitum*. The New Testament thus described is the one generally known as the Roman Will. But it was the

Will of the Eastern Empire only ; and the researches
of Savigny have shown that in Western Europe the
old Mancipatory Testament, with all its apparatus
of conveyance, copper, and scales, continued to be
the form in use far down in the Middle Ages.

CHAPTER VII.

ANCIENT AND MODERN IDEAS RESPECTING WILLS AND SUCCESSIONS.

ALTHOUGH there is much in the modern European Law of Wills which is intimately connected with the oldest rules of Testamentary disposition practised among men, there are nevertheless some important differences between ancient and modern ideas on the subject of Wills and Successions. Some of the points of difference I shall endeavor to illustrate in this chapter.

At a period, removed several centuries from the era of the Twelve Tables, we find a variety of rules engrafted on the Roman Civil Law with the view of limiting the disinherison of children ; we have the jurisdiction of the Prætor very actively exerted in the same interest ; and we are also presented with a new remedy, very anomalous in character and of uncertain origin, called the Querela Inofficiosi Testamenti, " the Plaint of an Unduteous Will," directed to the reinstatement of the issue in inheritances from which they had been unjustifiably excluded by a father's Testament. Comparing this condition of the law with the text of the Twelve Tables which concedes in terms the utmost liberty of Testation, several writers have been tempted to interweave a good deal of dramatic incident into their history of the Law Testamentary. They tell us of the boundless license of disinherison in which the heads of families instantly began to indulge, of the scandal and injury to public morals which the new practices engendered, and of the applause of all good men which hailed the courage of the Prætor in arresting the progress of paternal depravity. This story, which is not without some foundation for the principal fact it relates, is often so told as to disclose very serious misconceptions of the principles of legal history. The Law of the Twelve Tables is to be explained by the character of the age in which it was enacted. It does not license a tendency which a later era thought itself bound to counteract, but it proceeds on the assumption that no such tendency exists, or, perhaps we should say, in ignorance of the possibility of its existence. There is no likelihood that Roman citizens began immediately to avail themselves freely of the power to disinherit. It is against all reason and sound appreciation of history to suppose that the yoke of family bondage, still patiently submitted to, as we know, where its pressure galled most cruelly, would be cast off in the very particular in which its incidence in our own

day is not otherwise than welcome. The Law of
the Twelve Tables permitted the execution of Testa
ments in the only case in which it was thought pos
sible that they could be executed, viz.: on failure of
children and proximate kindred. It did not forbid
the disinherison of direct descendants, inasmuch as
it did not legislate against a contingency which no
Roman lawgiver of that era could have contemplated. No doubt, as the offices of family affection
progressively lost the aspect of primary personal
duties, the disinherison of children was occasionally
attempted. But the interference of the Prætor, so
far from being called for by the universality of the
abuse, was doubtless first prompted by the fact that
such instances of unnatural caprice were few and
exceptional, and at conflict with the current morality.

The indications furnished by this part of Roman
Testamentary Law are of a very different kind. It
is remarkable that a Will never seems to have been
regarded by the Romans as a means of *disinheriting*
a Family, or of effecting the unequal distribution of
a patrimony. The rules of law preventing its being
turned to such a purpose, increase in number and
stringency as the jurisprudence unfolds itself; and
these rules correspond doubtless with the abiding
sentiment of Roman society, as distinguished from
occasional variations of feeling in individuals. It
would rather seem as if the Testamentary Power
were chiefly valued for the assistance it gave in

making provision for a Family, and in dividing the inheritance more evenly and fairly than the Law of Intestate Succession would have divided it.   If this be the true reading of the general sentiment on the point, it explains to some extent the singular horror of Intestacy which always characterised the Roman No evil seems to have been considered a heavier visitation than the forfeiture of Testamentary privileges ; no curse appears to have been bitterer than that which imprecated on an enemy that he might die without a Will.   The feeling has no counterpart, or none that is easily recognisable, in the forms of opinion which exist at the present day.   All men at all times will doubtless prefer chalking out the destination of their substance to having that office performed for them by the law ; but the Roman passion for Testacy is distinguished from the mere desire to indulge caprice by its intensity ; and it has, of course, nothing whatever in common with that pride of family, exclusively the creation of feudalism, which accumulates one description of property in the hands of a single representative.   It is probable, *à priori*, that it was something in the rules of Intestate Succession which caused this verement preference for the distribution of property under a Testament over its distribution by law.   The difficulty, however, is, that on glancing at the Roman law of Intestate Succession, in the form which it wore for many centuries before Justinian shaped it into that scheme of inheritance which has been almost universally

adopted by modern lawgivers, it by no means strikes
one as remarkably unreasonable or inequitable.   On
the contrary, the distribution it prescribes is so fair
and rational, and differs so little from that with
which modern society has been generally contented,
that no reason suggests itself why it should have
been regarded with extraordinary distaste, especially
under a jurisprudence which pared down to a narrow compass the testamentary privileges of persons
who had children to provide for.   We should rather
have expected that, as in France at this moment,
the heads of families would generally save themselves
the trouble of executing a Will, and allow the Law
to do as it pleased with their assets.   I think, however, if we look a little closely at the pre-Justinian-
ean scale of Intestate Succession, we shall discover
the key to the mystery.   The texture of the law
consists of two distinct parts.   One department of
rules comes from the Jus Civile, the Common Law
of Rome; the other from the Edict of the Prætor
The Civil Law, as I have already stated for another
purpose, calls to the inheritance only three orders
of successors in their turn; the unemancipated children, the nearest class of Agnatic kindred, and the
Gentiles.   Between these three orders, the Prætor
interpolates various classes of relatives, of whom
the Civil Law took no notice whatever.   Ultimately,
the combination of the Edict and of the Civil Law
forms a table of succession not materially different

from that which has descended to the generality of modern codes.

The point for recollection is, that there must anciently have been a time at which the rules of the Civil Law determined the scheme of Intestate Succession exclusively, and at which the arrangements of the Edict were non-existent, or not consistently carried out. We cannot doubt that, in its infancy, the Prætorian jurisprudence had to contend with formidable obstructions, and it is more than probable that, long after popular sentiment and legal opinion had acquiesced in it, the modifications which it periodically introduced were governed by no certain principles, and fluctuated with the varying bias of successive magistrates. The rules of Intestate Succession, which the Romans must at this period have practised, account, I think—and more than account—for that vehement distaste for an Intestacy to which Roman society during so many ages remained constant. The order of succession was this: on the death of a citizen, having no will or no valid will, his Unemancipated children became his Heirs. His *emancipated* sons had no share in the inheritance. If he left no direct descendants living at his death, the nearest grade of the Agnatic kindred succeeded, but no part of the inheritance was given to any relative united (however closely) with the dead man through female descents. All the other branches of the family were excluded, and the inheritance escheated to the *Gentiles*, or entire body of Roman

citizens bearing the same name with the deceased.
So that on failing to execute an operative Testament,
a Roman of the era under examination left his
emancipated children absolutely without provision,
while, on the assumption that he died childless, there
was imminent risk that his possessions would escape
from the family altogether, and devolve on a number of persons with whom he was merely connected
by the sacerdotal fiction that assumed all members
of the same *gens* to be descended from a common
ancestor. The prospect of such an issue is in itself
a nearly sufficient explanation of the popular sentiment; but, in point of fact, we shall only half understand it, if we forget that the state of things I
have been describing is likely to have existed at the
very moment when Roman society was in the first
stage of its transition from its primitive organisation
in detached families.   The empire of the father had
indeed received one of the earliest blows directed at
it through the recognition of Emancipation as a legitimate usage, but the law, still considering the
Patria Potestas to be the root of family connection,
persevered in looking on the emancipated children
as strangers to the rights of Kinship and aliens from
the blood.   We cannot, however, for a moment suppose that the limitations of the family imposed by
legal pedantry had their counterpart in the natural
affection of parents.   Family attachments must still
have retained that nearly inconceivable sanctity and
intensity which belonged to them under the Patri

archal system; and so little are they likely to have
been extinguished by the act of emancipation, that
the probabilities are altogether the other way. It
may be unhesitatingly taken for granted that enfran-
chisement from the father's power was a demonstration, rather than a severance, of affection—a mark
of grace and favour accorded to the best-beloved
and most esteemed of the children. If sons thus
honoured above the rest were absolutely deprived
of their heritage by an Intestacy, the reluctance to
incur it requires no farther explanation. We might
have assumed à *priori* that the passion for Testacy,
was generated by some moral injustice entailed by
the rules of Intestate succession; and here we find
them at variance with the very instinct by which
early society was cemented together. It is possible
to put all that has been urged in a very succinct form.
Every dominant sentiment of the primitive Romans
was entwined with the relations of the family. But
what was the Family? The Law defined it one way
—natural affection another. In the conflict between
the two, the feeling we would analyse grew up,
taking the form of an enthusiasm for the institution
by which the dictates of affection were permitted to
determine the fortunes of its objects.

I regard, therefore, the Roman horror of Intestacy as a monument of a very early conflict between
ancient law and slowly changing ancient sentiment
on the subject of the Family. Some passages in the
Roman Statute-Law, and one statute in particular

which limited the capacity for inheritance possessed
by women, must have contributed to keep alive the
feeling; and it is the general belief that the system
of creating Fidei-Commissa, or bequests in trust, was
devised to evade the disabilities imposed by those
statutes.　But the feeling itself, in its remarkable
intensity, seems to point back to some deeper antagonism between law and opinion; nor is it at all
wonderful that the improvements of jurisprudence
by the Praetor should not have extinguished it.
Everybody conversant with the philosophy of opinion is aware that a sentiment by no means dies out,
of necessity, with the passing away of the circumstances which produced it.　It may long survive
them; nay, it may afterwards attain to a pitch and
climax of intensity which it never attained during
their actual continuance.

The view of a Will which regards it as conferring the power of diverting property from the Family, or of distributing it in such uneven proportions
as the fancy or good sense of the Testator may dictate, is not older than that later portion of the Middle Ages in which Feudalism had completely consolidated itself.　When modern jurisprudence first
shows itself in the rough, Wills are rarely allowed
to dispose with absolute freedom of a dead man's
assets.　Wherever at this period the descent of
property was regulated by Will—and over the
greater part of Europe moveable or personal property was the subject of Testamentary disposition

—the exercise of the Testamentary power was seldom allowed to interfere with the right of the widow to a definite share, and of the children to certain fixed proportions, of the devolving inheritance. The shares of the children, as their amount shows, were determined by the authority of Roman law. The provision for the widow was attributable to the exertions of the Church, which never relaxed its solicitude for the interest of wives surviving their husbands—winning, perhaps one of the most arduous of its triumphs when, after exacting for two or three centuries an express promise from the husband at marriage to endow his wife, it at length succeeded in engrafting the principle of Dower on the Customary Law of all Western Europe. Curiously enough, the dower of lands proved a more stable institution than the analogous and more ancient reservation of certain shares of the personal property to the widow and children. A few local customs in France maintained the right down to the Revolution, and there are traces of similar usages in England; but on the whole the doctrine prevailed that moveables might be freely disposed of by Will, and, even when the claims of the widow continued to be respected, the privileges of the children were obliterated from jurisprudence. We need not hesitate to attribute the change to the influence of Primogeniture. As the Feudal law of land practically disinherited all the children in favour of one, the equal distribution even of those sorts of property which might have been equally divided ceased to be viewed as a duty. Testaments were the principal instruments employed in producing inequality, and in this condition of things originated the shade of difference which shows itself between the ancient and modern conception of a Will. But, though the liberty of bequest, enjoyed through Testaments, was thus an accidental fruit of Feudalism, there is no broader distinction than that which exists between a system of free Testamentary disposition and a system, like that of the Feudal land-law, under which property descends compulsorily in prescribed lines of devolution. This truth appears to have been lost sight of by the authors of the French Codes. In the social fabric which they determined to destroy, they saw Primogeniture resting chiefly on Family settlements, but they also perceived that Testaments were frequently employed to give the eldest son precisely the same preference which was reserved to him under the strictest of entails. In order, therefore, to make sure of their work, they not only rendered it impossible to prefer the eldest son to the rest in marriage-arrangements, but they almost expelled Testamentary succession from the law, lest it should be used to defeat their fundamental principle of an equal distribution of property among children at the parent's death. The result is that they have established a system of small perpetual entails, which is infinitely nearer akin to the system of feudal Europe than would be a perfect liberty of bequest.

The land-law of England, "the Herculaneum of Feudalism," is certainly much more closely allied to the land-law of the Middle Ages than that of any Continental country, and Wills with us are frequently used to aid or imitate that preference of the eldest son and his line which is a nearly universal feature in marriage settlements of real property. But nevertheless feeling and opinion in this country have been profoundly affected by the practice of free Testamentary disposition ; and it appears to me that the state of sentiment in a great part of French society, on the subject of the conservation of property in families, is much liker that which prevailed through Europe two or three centuries ago than are the current opinions of Englishmen.

The mention of Primogeniture introduces one of the most difficult problems of historical jurisprudence. Though I have not paused to explain my expressions, it may have been noticed that I have frequently spoken of a number of " co-heirs " as placed by the Roman Law of Succession on the same footing with a single Heir. In point of fact, we know of no period of Roman jurisprudence at which the place of the Heir, or Universal Successor, might not have been taken by a group of co-heirs. This group succeeded as a single unit, and the assets were afterwards divided among them in a separate legal proceeding. When the Succession was *ab intestato*, and the group consisted of the children of the deceased, they each took an equal share of the property; nor, though males had at one time some advantages over females, is there the faintest trace of Primogeniture. The mode of distribution is the same throughout archaic jurisprudence. It certainly seems that, when civil society begins and families cease to hold together through a series of generations, the idea which spontaneously suggests itself is to divide the domain equally among the members of each successive generation, and to reserve no privilege to the eldest son or stock. Some peculiarly significant hints as to the close relation of this phenomenon to primitive thought are furnished by systems yet more archaic than the Roman. Among the Hindoos, the instant a son is born, he acquires a vested right in his father's property, which cannot be sold without recognition of his joint-ownership. On the son's attaining full age, he can sometimes compel a partition of the estate even against the consent of the parent; and should the parent acquiesce, one son can always have a partition even against the will of the others On such partition taking place, the father has no advantage over his children, except that he has two of the shares instead of one. The ancient law of the German tribes was exceedingly similar. The *allod* or domain of the family was the joint-property of the father and his sons. It does not, however, appear to have been habitually divided even at the death of the parent, and in the same way the possessions of a Hindoo, however divisible theoretically, are so rarely dis

tributed in fact, that many generations constantly
succeed each other without a partition taking place,
and thus the Family in India has a perpetual tendency to expand into the Village Community, under
conditions which I shall hereafter attempt to eluci-
date.   All this points very clearly to the absolutely
equal division of assets among the male children at
death as the practice most usual with society at the
period when family-dependency is in the first stages
of disintegration.   Here then emerges the historical
difficulty of Primogeniture.   The more clearly we
perceive that, when the Feudal institutions were in
process of formation, there was no source in the
world whence they could derive their elements but
the Roman law of the provincials on the one hand
and the archaic customs of the barbarians on the
other, the more are we perplexed at first sight by
our knowledge that neither Roman nor barbarian
was accustomed to give any preference to the eldest
son or his line in the succession to property.

Primogeniture did not belong to the Customs
which the barbarians practised on their first establishment within the Roman Empire. It is known to
have had its origin in the *benefices* or beneficiary
gifts of the invading chieftains.   These benefices,
which were occasionally conferred by the earlier im
migrant kings, but were distributed on a great scale
by Charlemagne, were grants of Roman provincial
land to be holden by the beneficiary on condition
of military service. The *allodial* proprietors do not

seem to have followed their sovereign on distant or
difficult enterprises, and all the grander expeditions
of the Frankish chiefs and of Charlemagne were accomplished with forces composed of soldiers either
personally dependent on the royal house or com
pelled to serve it by the tenure of their land. The
benefices, however, were not at first in any sense
hereditary. They were held at the pleasure of the
grantor, or at most for the life of the grantee; but
still, from the very outset, no effort seems to have
been spared by the beneficiaries to enlarge their
tenure, and to continue their lands in their family af
ter death. Through the feebleness of Charlemagne's
successors these attempts were universally successful, and the Benefice gradually transformed itself
into the hereditary Fief. But, though the fiefs were
hereditary, they did not necessarily descend to the
eldest son. The rules of succession which they followed were entirely determined by the terms agreed
upon between the grantor and the beneficiary, or
imposed by one of them on the weakness of the
other. The original tenures were therefore extremely various; not indeed so capriciously various as is
sometimes asserted, for all which have hitherto been
described present some combination of the modes of
succession familiar to Romans and to barbarians, but
still exceedingly miscellaneous. In some of them,
the eldest son and his stock undoubtedly succeeded
to the fief before the others, but such successions,
so far from being universal, do not even appear to

have been general. Precisely the same phenomena recur during that more recent transmutation of European society which entirely substituted the feudal form of property for the domainial (or Roman) and the allodial (or German.) The allods were wholly absorbed by the fiefs. The greater allodial proprietors transformed themselves into feudal lords by conditional alienations of portions of their land to dependants ; the smaller sought an escape from the oppressions of that terrible time by surrendering their property to some powerful chieftain, and receiving it back at his hands on condition of service in his wars. Meantime, that vast mass of the population of Western Europe whose condition was servile or semi-servile—the Roman and German personal slaves, the Roman *coloni* and the German *lidi*—were concurrently absorbed by the feudal organisation, a few of them assuming a menial relation to the lords, but the greater part receiving land on terms which in those centuries were considered degrading. The tenures created during this era of universal infeudation were as various as the conditions which the tenants made with their new chiefs or were forced to accept from them. As in the case of benefices, the succession to some, but by no means to all, of the estates followed the rule of Primogeniture. No sooner, however, has the feudal system prevailed throughout the West, than it becomes evident that Primogeniture has some great advantage over every other mode of succession. It spread over Europe with re-

markable rapidity, the principal instrument of diffusion being Family Settlements, the Pactes de Fam
ille of France and Haus-Gesetze of Germany, which
universally stipulated that lands held by knightly
service should descend to the eldest son. Ultimately
the law resigned itself to follow inveterate practice,
and we find that in all the bodies of Customary Law,
which were gradually built up, the eldest son and
stock are preferred in the succession to estates of
which the tenure is free and military. As to lands
held by servile tenures (and originally all tenures
were servile which bound the tenant to pay money
or bestow manual labor), the system of succession
prescribed by custom differed greatly in different
countries and different provinces. The more general rule was that such lands were divided equally
at death among all the children, but still in some
instances the eldest son was preferred, in some the
youngest. But Primogeniture usually governed the
inheritance of that class of estates, in some respects
the most important of all, which were held by tenures that, like the English Socage, were of later origin than the rest, and were neither altogether free
nor altogether servile.

The diffusion of Primogeniture is usually accounted for by assigning what are called Feudal reasons for it. It is asserted that the feudal superior
had a better security for the military service he required when the fief descended to a single person,
instead of being distributed among a number on the

decease of the last holder. Without denying that
this consideration may partially explain the favour
gradually acquired by Primogeniture, I must point
out that Primogeniture became a custom of Europe
much more through its popularity with the tenants
than through any advantage it conferred on the
lords. For its origin, moreover, the reason given
does not account at all. Nothing in law springs entirely from a sense of convenience. There are always
certain ideas existing antecedently on which the
sense of convenience works, and of which it can do
no more than form some new combination; and to
find these ideas in the present case is exactly the
problem.

A valuable hint is furnished to us from a quarter
fruitful of such indications. Although in India the
possessions of a parent are divisible at his death, and
may be divisible during his life, among all his male
children in equal shares, and though this principle
of the equal distribution of *property* extends to every
part of the Hindoo institutions, yet wherever *public
office* or *political power* devolves at the decease of
the last Incumbent, the succession is nearly universally according to the rules of Primogeniture. Sov-
ereignties descend therefore to the eldest son, and
where the affairs of the Village Community, the
corporate unit of Hindoo society, are confided to a
single manager, it is generally the eldest son who
takes up the administration at his parent's death.
All offices, indeed, in India, tend to become heredi-

tary, and, when their nature permits it, to vest in
the eldest member of the oldest stock. Comparing
these Indian successions with some of the ruder social
organisations which have survived in Europe almost
to our own day, the conclusion suggests itself that,
when Patriarchal power is not only *domestic* but
political, it is not distributed among all the issue at
the parent's death, but is the birthright of the eldest
son. The chieftainship of a Highland clan, for example, followed the order of Primogeniture. There
seems, in truth, to be a form of family-dependency
still more archaic than any of those which we know
from the primitive records of organised civil societies.
The Agnatic Union of the kindred in ancient Roman
law, and a multitude of similar indications, point to
a period at which all the ramifying branches of the
family tree held together in one organic whole; and
it is no presumptuous conjecture, that, when the
corporation thus formed by the kindred was in itself
an independent society, it was governed by the eldest
male of the oldest line. It is true that we have no
actual knowledge of any such society. Even in the
most elementary communities, family-organisations,
as we know them, are at most *imperia in imperio*
But the position of some of them, of the Celtic clans
in particular, was sufficiently near independence
within historical times to force on us the conviction
that they were once separate *imperia*, and that Primogeniture regulated the succession to the chieftainship. It is, however, necessary to be on our guard

against modern associations with the term of law
We are speaking of a family-connection still closer
and more stringent than any with which we are
made acquainted by Hindoo society or ancient Roman law. If the Roman Paterfamilias was visibly
steward of the family possessions, if the Hindoo
father is only joint-sharer with his sons, still more
emphatically must the true patriarchal chieftain be
merely the administrator of a common fund.

The examples of succession by Primogeniture
which were found among the Benefices may, therefore, have been imitated from a system of family-
government known to the invading races, though
not in general use. Some rude tribes may have still
practised it, or, what is still more probable, society
may have been so slightly removed from its more
archaic condition that the minds of some men spontaneously recurred to it, when they were called upon
to settle the rules of inheritance for a new form of
property. But there is still the question, Why did
Primogeniture gradually supersede every other principle of succession? The answer, I think, is, that
European society decidedly retrograded during the
dissolution of the Carlovingian empire. It sank a
point or two back even from the miserably low degree which it had marked during the early barbarian
monarchies. The great characteristic of the period
was the feebleness, or rather the abeyance, of kingly
and therefore of civil authority; and hence it seems
as if, civil society no longer cohering, men univer-

sally flung themselves back on a social organisation older than the beginnings of civil communities. The lord with his vassals, during the ninth and tenth centuries, may be considered as a patriarchal household, recruited, not as in the primitive times by Adoption, but by Infeudation; and to such a confederacy, succession by Primogeniture was a source of strength and durability. So long as the land was kept together on which the entire organisation rested, it was powerful for defence and attack; to divide the land was to divide the little society, and voluntarily to invite aggression in an era of universal violence. We may be perfectly certain that into this preference for Primogeniture there entered no idea of disinheriting the bulk of the children in favour of one. Everybody would have suffered by the division of the fief. Everybody was a gainer by its consolidation. The Family grew stronger by the concentration of power in the same hands; nor is it likely that the lord who was invested with the inheritance had any advantage over his brethren and kinsfolk in occupations, interests, or indulgences. It would be a singular anachronism to estimate the privileges succeeded to by the heir of a fief, by the situation in which the eldest son is placed under an English strict settlement.

I have said that I regard the early feudal confederacies as descended from an archaic form of the Family, and as wearing a strong resemblance to it. But then in the ancient world, and in the societies

which have not passed through the crucible of feu
dalism, the Primogeniture which seems to have prevailed never transformed itself into the Primogeniture of the later feudal Europe.   When the group
of kinsmen ceased to be governed through a series
of generations by a hereditary chief, the domain
which had been managed for all appears to have
been equally divided among all.   Why did this not
occur in the feudal world ?   If during the confusions
of the first feudal period the eldest son held the
land for the behoof of the whole family, why was it
that when feudal Europe had consolidated itself, and
regular communities were again established, the
whole family did not resume that capacity for equal
inheritance which had belonged to Roman and German alike ?   The key which unlocks this difficulty
has rarely been seized by the writers who occupy
themselves in tracing the genealogy of Feudalism.
They perceive the materials of the feudal institutions, but they miss the cement.   The ideas and
social forms which contributed to the formation of
the system were unquestionably barbarian and archaic, but, as soon as Courts and lawyers were called
in to interpret and define it, the principles of interpretation which they applied to it were those of the
latest Roman jurisprudence, and were therefore excessively refined and matured.   In a patriarchally
governed society, the eldest son may succeed to the
government of the Agnatic group, and to the absolute disposal of its property.   But he is not there

fore a true proprietor. He has correlative duties not involved in the conception of proprietorship, but quite undefined and quite incapable of definition. The later Roman jurisprudence, however, like our own law, looked upon uncontrolled power over property as equivalent to ownership, and did not, and, in fact, could not, take notice of liabilities of such a kind, that the very conception of them belonged to a period anterior to regular law. The contact of the refined and the barbarous notion had inevitably for its effect the conversion of the eldest son into legal proprietor of the inheritance. The clerical and secular lawyers so defined his position from the first; but it was only by insensible degrees that the younger brother, from participating on equal terms in all the dangers and enjoyments of his kinsman, sank into the priest, the soldier of fortune, or the hanger-on of the mansion. The legal revolution was identical with that which occurred on a smaller scale, and in quite recent times, through the greater part of the Highlands of Scotland. When called in to determine the legal powers of the chieftain over the domains which gave sustenance to the clan, Scottish jurisprudence had long since passed the point at which it could take notice of the vague limitations on completeness of dominion imposed by the claims of the clansmen, and it was inevitable therefore, that it should convert the patrimony of many into the estate of one.

For the sake of simplicity, I have called the

mode of succession Primogeniture whenever a single
son or descendant succeeds to the authority over a
household or society. It is remarkable, however,
that in the few very ancient examples which remain
to us of this sort of succession, it is not always the
eldest son, in the sense familiar to us, who takes up
the representation. The form of Primogeniture
which has spread over Western Europe has also been
perpetuated among the Hindoos, and there is every
reason to believe that it is the normal form. Under
it, not only the eldest son, but the eldest line is
always preferred. If the eldest son fails, his eldest
son has precedence not only over brothers but over
uncles; and, if he too fails, the same rule is followed
in the next generation. But when the succession is
not merely to *civil* but to *political* power, a difficulty may present itself which will appear of
greater magnitude according as the cohesion of society is less perfect. The chieftain who last exercised authority may have outlived his eldest son,
and the grandson who is primarily entitled to succeed may be too young and immature to undertake
the actual guidance of the community, and the administration of its affairs. In such an event, the
expedient which suggests itself to the more settled
societies is to place the infant heir under guardianship till he reaches the age of fitness for government.
The guardianship is generally that of the male
Agnates; but it is remarkable that the contingency
supposed is one of the rare cases in which ancient

societies have consented to the exercise of power by women, doubtless out of respect to the overshadow-ing claims of the mother. In India, the widow of a Hindoo sovereign governs in the name of her in-fant son, and we cannot but remember that the cus-tom regulating succession to the throne of France —which, whatever be its origin, is doubtless of the highest antiquity—preferred the queen-mother to all other claimants for the Regency, at the same time that it rigorously excluded all females from the throne. There is, however, another mode of obvia-ting the inconvenience attending the devolution of sovereignty on an infant heir, and it is one which would doubtless occur spontaneously to rudely or-ganised communities. This is to set aside the infant heir altogether, and confer the chieftainship on the eldest surviving male of the first generation. The Celtic clan-associations, among the many phenomena which they have preserved of an age in which civil and political society were not yet even rudimentarily separated, have brought down this rule of succession to historical times. With them, it seems to have existed in the form of a positive canon, that, failing the eldest son, his next brother succeeds in priority to all grandsons, whatever be their age at the moment when the sovereignty devolves. Some writers have explained the principle by assuming that the Celtic customs took the last chieftain as a sort of root or stock, and then gave the succession to the descen-dant who should be least remote from him ; the uncle

thus being preferred to the grandson as being nearer
to the common root. No objection can be taken to
this statement if it be merely intended as a description of the system of succession ; but it would be a
serious error to conceive the men who first adopted
the rule as applying a course of reasoning which
evidently dates from the time when feudal schemes
of succession began to be debated among lawyers.
The true origin of the preference of the uncle to the
grandson is doubtless a simple calculation on the part
of rude men in a rude society that it is better to be
governed by a grown chieftain than by a child, and
that the younger son is more likely to have come to
maturity than any of the eldest son's descendants.
At the same time, we have some evidence that the
form of Primogeniture with which we are best acquainted is the primary form, in the tradition that
the assent of the clan was asked when an infant heir
was passed over in favour of his uncle. There is a
tolerably well authenticated instance of this ceremony in the annals of the Scottish Macdonalds;
and Irish Celtic antiquities, as interpreted by recent
inquirers, are said to disclose many traces of similar
practices. The substitution, by means of election,
of a " worthier " Agnatic relative for an elder is not
unknown, too, in the system of the Indian Village
Communities.

Under Mahometan law, which has probably preserved an ancient Arabian custom, inheritances of
property are divided equally among sons, the daugh-

ters taking a half share; but if any of the children
die before the division of the inheritance, leaving
issue behind, these grandchildren are entirely excluded by their uncles and aunts.　Consistently with
this principle, the succession, when political authority
devolves, is according to the form of Primogeniture
which appears to have obtained among the Celtic
societies.　In the two great Mahometan families of
the West, the rule is believed to be, that the uncle
succeeds to the throne in preference to the nephew,
though the latter be the son of an elder brother;
but though this rule has been followed quite recently
both in Egypt and in Turkey, I am informed that
there has always been some doubt as to its governing the devolution of the Turkish sovereignty.　The
policy of the Sultans has in fact generally prevented
cases for its application from occurring, and it is possible that their wholesale massacres of their younger
brothers may have been perpetrated quite as much
in the interest of their children as for the sake of
making away with dangerous competitors for the
throne.　It is evident, however, that in polygamous
societies the form of Primogeniture will always tend
to vary.　Many considerations may constitute a
claim on the succession, the rank of the mother, for
example, or her degree in the affections of the father.
Accordingly, some of the Indian Mahometan sovereigns, without pretending to any distinct testamentary power, claim the right of nominating the

son who is to succeed. The *blessing* mentioned in the Scriptural history of Isaac and his sons has sometimes been spoken of as a will, but it seems rather to have been a mode of naming an eldest son.

CHAPTER VIII.

THE EARLY HISTORY OF PROPERTY.

THE Roman Institutional Treatises, after giving their definition of the various forms and modifications of ownership, proceed to discuss the Natural Modes of Acquiring Property. Those who are unfamiliar with the history of jurisprudence are not likely to look upon these " natural modes " of acquisition as possessing, at first sight, either much speculative or much practical interest. The wild animal which is snared or killed by the hunter, the soil which is added to our field by the imperceptible deposits of a river, the tree which strikes its roots into our ground, are each said by the Roman lawyers to be ac· quired by us *naturally*. The older jurisconsults had doubtless observed that such acquisitions were universally sanctioned by the usages of the little societies around them, and thus the lawyers of a later age, finding them classed in the ancient Jus Gentium, and perceiving them to be of the simplest description, allotted them a place among the ordinances of

Nature. The dignity with which they were invested has gone on increasing in modern times till it is quite out of proportion to their original importance. Theory has made them its favourite food, and has enabled them to exercise the most serious influence on practice.

It will be necessary for us to attend to one only among these "natural modes of acquisition," Occupatio or Occupancy. Occupancy is the advisedly taking possession of that which at the moment is the property of no man, with the view (adds the technical definition) of acquiring property in it for yourself. The objects which the Roman lawyers called *res nullius*—things which have not or have never had an owner—can only be ascertained by enumerating them. Among things which *never had* an owner are wild animals, fishes, wild fowl, jewels disinterred for the first time, and land newly discovered or never before cultivated. Among things which *have not* an owner are moveables which have been abandoned, lands which have been deserted, and (an anomalous but most formidable item) the property of an enemy. In all these objects the full rights of dominion were acquired by the *Occupant*, who first took possession of them with the intention of keeping them as his own—an intention which, in certain cases, had to be manifested by specific acts It is not difficult, I think, to understand the universality which caused the practice of Occupancy to be placed by one generation of Roman lawyers in the

Law common to all Nations, and the simplicity which
occasioned its being attributed by another to the
Law of Nature.   But for its fortunes in modern legal history we are less prepared by *à priori* considerations.   The Roman principle of Occupancy, and
the rules into which the jurisconsults expanded it,
are the source of all modern International Law on
the subject of Capture in War and of the acquisition
of sovereign rights in newly discovered countries.
They have also supplied a theory of the Origin of
Property, which is at once the popular theory, and
the theory which, in one form or another, is acquiesced in by the great majority of speculative jurists.

I have said that the Roman principle of Occupancy has determined the tenor of that chapter of
International Law which is concerned with Capture
in War.   The Law of Warlike Capture derives its
rules from the assumption that communities are re-
mitted to a state of nature by the outbreak of hos-
tilities, and that, in the artificial natural condition
thus produced, the institution of private property
falls into abeyance so far as concerns the belligerents.
As the later writers on the Law of Nature have always been anxious to maintain that private property was in some sense sanctioned by the system
which they were expounding, the hypothesis that an
enemy's property is *res nullius* has seemed to them
perverse and shocking, and they were careful to
stigmatise it as a mere fiction of jurisprudence.   But,
as soon as the Law of Nature is traced to its source

in the Jus Gentium, we see at once how the goods
of an enemy came to be looked upon as nobody's
property, and therefore as capable of being acquired
by the first occupant. The idea would occur spontaneously to persons practising the ancient forms of
Warfare, when victory dissolved the organisation of
the conquering army and dismissed the soldiers to
indiscriminate plunder. It is probable, however, that
originally it was only moveable property which was
thus permitted to be acquired by the Captor. We
know on independent authority that a very different
rule prevailed in ancient Italy as to the acquisition
of ownership in the soil of a conquered country, and
we may therefore suspect that the application of the
principle of occupancy to land (always a matter of
difficulty) dates from the period when the Jus Gentium was becoming the Code of Nature, and that it
is the result of a generalisation effected by the jurisconsults of the golden age. Their dogmas on the
point are preserved in the Pandects of Justinian, and
amount to an unqualified assertion that enemy's property of every sort is *res nullius* to the other belligerent, and that Occupancy, by which the Captor
makes it his own, is an institution of Natural Law
The rules which International jurisprudence derives
from these positions have sometimes been stigma-
tised as needlessly indulgent to the ferocity and cu-
pidity of combatants, but the charge has been made,
I think, by persons who are unacquainted with the
history of wars, and who are consequently ignorant

how great an exploit it is to command obedience for a rule of any kind. The Roman principle of Occupancy, when it was admitted into the modern law of Capture in War, drew with it a number of subordinate canons, limiting and giving precision to its operation, and if the contests which have been waged since the treatise of Grotius became an authority, are compared with those of an earlier date, it will be seen that, as soon as the Roman maxims were received, Warfare instantly assumed a more tolerable complexion. If the Roman law of Occupancy is to be taxed with having had pernicious influence on any part of the modern Law of Nations, there is another chapter in it which may be said, with some reason, to have been injuriously affected. In applying to the discovery of new countries the same principles which the Romans had applied to the finding of a jewel, the Publicists forced into their service a doctrine altogether unequal to the task expected from it. Elevated into extreme importance by the discoveries of the great navigators of the 15th and 16th centuries, it raised more disputes than it solved. The greatest uncertainty was very shortly found to exist on the very two points on which certainty was most required, the extent of the territory which was acquired for his sovereign by the discoverer, and the nature of the acts which were necessary to complete the *apprehensio* or assumption of sovereign possession. Moreover, the principle itself, conferring as it did such enormous advantages as the consequence of

a piece of good luck, was instinctively mutinied
against by some of the most adventurous nations in
Europe, the Dutch, the English, and the Portuguese.
Our own countrymen, without expressly denying the
rule of International Law, never did, in practice, ad
mit the claim of the Spaniards to engross the whole
of America south of the Gulf of Mexico, or that of
the King of France to monopolise the valleys of the
Ohio and the Mississippi. From the accession of
Elizabeth to the accession of Charles the Second, it
cannot be said that there was at any time thorough
peace in the American waters, and the encroach-
ments of the New England Colonists on the territory of the French King continued for almost a century longer. Bentham was so struck with the confusion attending the application of the legal principle, that he went out of his way to eulogise the
famous Bull of Pope Alexander the Sixth, dividing
the undiscovered countries of the world between the
Spaniards and the Portuguese by a line drawn one
hundred leagues West of the Azores; and, grotesque
as his praises may appear at first sight, it may be
doubted whether the arrangement of Pope Alexan
der is absurder in principle than the rule of Public
law, which gave half a continent to the monarch
whose servants had fulfilled the conditions required
by Roman jurisprudence for the acquisition of property in a valuable object which could be covered by
the hand.

　　To all who pursue the inquiries which are the

subject of this volume, Occupancy is pre-eminently
interesting on the score of the service it has been
made to perform for speculative jurisprudence, in
furnishing a supposed explanation of the origin of
private property. It was once universally believed
that the proceeding implied in Occupancy was identical with the process by which the earth and its
fruits, which were at first in common, became the
allowed property of individuals. The course of
thought which led to this assumption is not difficult
to understand, if we seize the shade of difference
which separates the ancient from the modern conception of Natural Law. The Roman lawyers had
laid down that Occupancy was one of the Natural
modes of acquiring property, and they undoubtedly
believed that, were mankind living under the institutions of Nature, Occupancy would be one of their
practices. How far they persuaded themselves that
such a condition of the race had ever existed, is a
point, as I have already stated, which their language
leaves in much uncertainty; but they certainly do
seem to have made the conjecture, which has at all
times possessed much plausibility, that the institution
of property was not so old as the existence of mankind. Modern jurisprudence, accepting all their dogmas without reservation, went far beyond them in
the eager curiosity with which it dwelt on the supposed state of Nature. Since then it had received the
position that the earth and its fruits were once *res
nullius*, and since its peculiar view of Nature led it

to assume without hesitation that the human race had actually practised the Occupancy of *res nullius* long before the organisation of civil societies, the inference immediately suggested itself that Occupancy was the process by which the "no man's goods" of the primitive world became the private property of individuals in the world of history. It would be wearisome to enumerate the jurists who have subscribed to this theory in one shape or another, and it is the less necessary to attempt it because Blackstone, who is always a faithful index of the average opinions of his day, has summed them up in his 2d book and 1st chapter.

"The earth," he writes, "and all things therein were the general property of mankind from the immediate gift of the Creator. Not that the communion of goods seems ever to have been applicable, even in the earliest ages, to aught but the substance of the thing; nor could be extended to the use of it. For, by the law of nature and reason, he who first began to use it acquired therein a kind of transient property that lasted so long as he was using it, and no longer; or to speak with greater precision, the right of possession continued for the same time only that the act of possession lasted. Thus the ground was in common, and no part was the permanent property of any man in particular; yet whoever was in the occupation of any determined spot of it, for rest, for shade, or the like, acquired for the time a sort of ownership, from which it would have

been unjust and contrary to the law of nature to
have driven him by force, but the instant that he
quitted the use of occupation of it, another might
seize it without injustice." He then proceeds to
argue that " when mankind increased in number, it
became necessary to entertain conceptions of more
permanent dominion, and to appropriate to individuals not the immediate use only, but the very
substance of the thing to be used."

Some ambiguities of expression in this passage
lead to the suspicion that Blackstone did not quite
understand the meaning of the proposition which
he found in his authorities, that property in the
earth's surface was first acquired, under the law of
Nature, by the *occupant;* but the limitation which
designedly or through misapprehension he has imposed on the theory brings it into a form which it
has not infrequently assumed. Many writers more
famous than Blackstone for precision of language
have laid down that, in the beginning of things,
Occupancy first gave a right against the world to an
exclusive but temporary enjoyment, and that afterwards this right, while it remained exclusive, became
perpetual. Their object in so stating their theory
was to reconcile the doctrine that in the state of
Nature *res nullius* became property through Occupancy, with the inference which they drew from the
Scriptural history that the Patriarchs did not at first
permanently appropriate the soil which had been
grazed over by their flocks and herds.

The only criticism which could be directly applied to the theory of Blackstone would consist in
inquiring whether the circumstances which make up
his picture of a primitive society are more or less
probable than other incidents which could be imagined with equal readiness. Pursuing this method
of examination, we might fairly ask whether the
man who had *occupied* (Blackstone evidently uses
this word with its ordinary English meaning) a particular spot of ground for rest or shade would be
permitted to retain it without disturbance. The
chances surely are that his right to possession would
be exactly coextensive with his power to keep it,
and that he would be constantly liable to disturbance
by the first comer who coveted the spot and thought
himself strong enough to drive away the possessor.
But the truth is that all such cavil at these positions
is perfectly idle from the very baselessness of the
positions themselves. What mankind did in the
primitive state may not be a hopeless subject of inquiry, but of their motives for doing it it is impossible to know anything. These sketches of the
plight of human beings in the first ages of the world
are effected by first supposing mankind to be di-
vested of a great part of the circumstances by which
they are now surrounded, and by then assuming
that, in the condition thus imagined, they would preserve the same sentiments and prejudices by which
they are now actuated,—although, in fact, these
sentiments may have been created and engendered

by those very circumstances of which, by the hypothesis, they are to be stripped.

There is an aphorism of Savigny which has been sometimes thought to countenance a view of the origin of property somewhat similar to the theories epitomised by Blackstone. The great German jurist has laid down that all Property is founded on Adverse Possession ripened by Prescription. It is only with respect to Roman law that Savigny makes this statement, and before it can be fully appreciated much labour must be expended in explaining and defining the expressions employed. His meaning will, however, be indicated with sufficient accuracy if we consider him to assert that, how far soever we carry our inquiry into the ideas of property received among the Romans, however closely we approach in tracing them to the infancy of law, we can get no farther than a conception of ownership involving the three elements in the canon—Possession, Adverseness of Possession, that is, a holding not permissive or subordinate, but exclusive against the world, and Prescription, or a period of time during which the Adverse Possession has uninterruptedly continued. It is exceedingly probable that this maxim might be enunciated with more generality than was allowed to it by its author, and that no sound or safe conclusion can be looked for from investigations into any system of laws which are pushed farther back than the point at which these combined ideas constitute the notion of proprietary right. Meantime,

so far from bearing out the popular theory of the
origin of property, Savigny's canon is particularly
valuable as directing our attention to its weakest
point.   In the view of Blackstone and those whom
he follows, it was the mode of assuming the exclusive
enjoyment which mysteriously affected the minds of
the fathers of our race.   But the mystery does not
reside here.   It is not wonderful that property began
in adverse possession.   It is not surprising that the
first proprietor should have been the strong man
armed who kept his goods in peace.   But why it
was that lapse of time created a sentiment of respect
for his possession—which is the exact source of the
universal reverence of mankind for that which has
for a long period *de facto* existed—are questions
really deserving the profoundest examination, but
lying far beyond the boundary of our present inquiries.

Before pointing out the quarter in which we may
hope to glean some information, scanty and uncertain at best, concerning the early history of proprietary right, I venture to state my opinion that the
popular impression in reference to the part played
by Occupancy in the first stages of civilisation directly reverses the truth.   Occupancy is the advised
assumption of physical possession; and the notion
that an act of this description confers a title to " res
nullius," so far from being characteristic of very
early societies, is in all probability the growth of
a refined jurisprudence and of a settled condition of

the laws. It is only when the rights of property have gained a sanction from long practical inviolability, and when the vast majority of the objects of enjoyment have been subjected to private ownership, that mere possession is allowed to invest the first possessor with dominion over commodities in which no prior proprietorship has been asserted. The sentiment in which this doctrine originated is absolutely irreconcilable with that infrequency and uncertainty of proprietary rights which distinguish the beginnings of civilisation. Its true basis seems to be, not an instinctive bias towards the institution of Property, but a presumption, arising out of the long continuance of that institution, that *everything ought to have an owner*. When possession is taken of a " res nullius," that is, of an object which *is* not, or has *never* been, reduced to dominion, the possessor is permitted to become proprietor from a feeling that all valuable things are naturally the subjects of an exclusive enjoyment, and that in the given case there is no one to invest with the right of property except the Occupant. The Occupant, in short, becomes the owner, because all things are presumed to be somebody's property and because no one can be pointed out as having a better right than he to the proprietorship of this particular thing.

Even were there no other objection to the descriptions of mankind in their natural state which we have been discussing, there is one particular in which they are fatally at variance with the authentic

evidence possessed by us.   It will be observed, that
the acts and motives which these theories suppose
are the acts and motives of Individuals.   It is each
Individual who for himself subscribes the Social
Compact.   It is some shifting sandbank in which
the grains are Individual men, that according to the
theory of Hobbes is hardened into the social rock
by the wholesome discipline of force.   It is an Individual who, in the picture drawn by Blackstone, "is
in the occupation of a determined spot of ground
for rest, for shade, or the like."   The vice is one
which necessarily afflicts all the theories descended
from the Natural Law of the Romans, which differed
principally from their Civil Law in the account
which it took of Individuals, and which has rendered precisely its greatest service to civilisation in
enfranchising the individual from the authority of
archaic society.   But Ancient Law, it must again be
repeated, knows next to nothing of Individuals.   It
is concerned not with Individuals, but with Families,
not with single human beings, but groups.   Even
when the law of the State has succeeded in permea-
ting the small circles of kindred into which it had
originally no means of penetrating, the view it takes
of Individuals is curiously different from that taken
by jurisprudence in its maturest stage.   The life of
each citizen is not regarded as limited by birth and
death ; it is but a continuation of the existence of
his forefathers, and it will be prolonged in the ex
istence of his descendants.

The Roman distinction between the Law of Persons and the Law of Things, which though extremely
convenient is entirely artificial, has evidently done
much to divert inquiry on the subject before us from
the true direction.   The lessons learned in discussing
the Jus Personarum have been forgotten where the
Jus Rerum is reached, and Property, Contract, and
Delict, have been considered as if no hints concerning their original nature were to be gained from the
facts ascertained respecting the original condition
of Persons.   The futility of this method would be
manifest if a system of pure archaic law could be
brought before us, and if the experiment could be
tried of applying to it the Roman classifications.
It would soon be seen that the separation of the
Law of Persons from that of Things has no meaning
in the infancy of law, that the rules belonging to the
two departments are inextricably mingled together,
and that the distinctions of the later jurists are appropriate only to the later jurisprudence.   From
what has been said in the earlier portions of this
treatise, it will be gathered that there is a strong *à
priori* improbability of our obtaining any clue to
the early history of property, if we confine our notice to the proprietary rights of individuals.   It is
more than likely that joint-ownersh p, and not separate ownership, is the really archaic institution, and
that the forms of property which will afford us instruction will be those which are associated with
the rights of families and of groups of kindred.

The Roman jurisprudence will not here assist in enlightening us, for it is exactly the Roman jurispru dence which, transformed by the theory of Natural Law, has bequeathed to the moderns the impression that individual ownership is the normal state of proprietary right, and that ownership in common by groups of men is only the exception to a general rule. There is, however, one community which will always be carefully examined by the inquirer who is in quest of any lost institution of primeval society. How far soever any such institution may have under- gone change among the branch of the Indo-European family which has been settled for ages in India, it will seldom be found to have entirely cast aside the shell in which it was originally reared. It happens that, among the Hindoos, we do find a form of ownership which ought at once to rivet our atten- tion from its exactly fitting in with the ideas which our studies in the Law of Persons would lead us to entertain respecting the original condition of prop erty. The Village Community of India is at once an organised patriarchal society and an assemblage of co-proprietors. The personal relations to each other of the men who compose it are indistinguish- ably confounded with their proprietary rights, and to the attempts of English functionaries to separate the two may be assigned some of the most formi- dable miscarriages of Anglo-Indian administration. The Village Community is known to be of immense antiquity. In whatever direction research has been pushed into Indian history, general or local, it has always found the Community in existence at the farthest point of its progress. A great number of intelligent and observant writers, most of whom had no theory of any sort to support concerning its nature and origin, agree in considering it the least destructible institution of a society which never willingly surrenders any one of its usages to innovation. Conquests and revolutions seem to have swept over it without disturbing or displacing it, and the most beneficent systems of government in India have always been those which have recognised it as the basis of administration.

The mature Roman law, and modern jurisprudence following in its wake, look upon co-ownership as an exceptional and momentary condition of the rights of property. This view is clearly indicated in the maxim which obtains universally in Western Europe, *Nemo in communione potest invitus detineri* (" No one can be kept in co-proprietorship against his will "). But in India this order of ideas is reversed, and it may be said that separate proprietorship is always on its way to become proprietorship in common. The process has been adverted to already. As soon as a son is born, he acquires a vested interest in his father's substance, and on attaining years of discretion he is even, in certain contingencies, permitted by the letter of the law to call for a partition of the family estate. As a fact, however, a division rarely takes place even at the death of

the father, and the property constantly remains undivided for several generations, though every member of every generation has a legal right to an
undivided share in it. The domain thus held in
common is sometimes administered by an elected
manager, but more generally, and in some provinces
always, it is managed by the eldest agnate, by the
eldest representative of the eldest line of the stock.
Such an assemblage of joint proprietors, a body of
kindred holding a domain in common, is the simplest
form of an Indian Village Community, but the
Community is more than a brotherhood of relatives
and more than an association of partners. It is an
organised society, and besides providing for the
management of the common fund, it seldom fails to
provide, by a complete staff of functionaries, for internal government, for police, for the administration
of justice, and for the apportionment of taxes and
public duties.

The process which I have described as that under
which a Village Community is formed, may be regarded as typical. Yet it is not to be supposed that
every Village Community in India drew together
in so simple a manner. Although, in the North of
India, the archives, as I am informed, almost invariably show that the Community was founded by a
single assemblage of blood-relations, they also supply
information that men of alien extraction have always, from time to time, been engrafted on it, and
a mere purchaser of a share may generally, under

certain conditions, be admitted to the brotherhood.
In the South of the Peninsula there are often Communities which appear to have sprung not from one
but from two or more families; and there are some
whose composition is known to be entirely artificial,
indeed, the occasional aggregation of men of different castes in the same society is fatal to the hypothesis of a common descent. Yet in all these brotherhoods either the tradition is preserved, or the
assumption made, of an original common parentage.
Mountstuart Elphinstone, who writes more particularly of the Southern Village Communities, observes
of them (*History of India*, p. 71, 1905 edn.): "The
popular notion is that the Village landholders are all
descended from one or more individuals who settled
the Village; and that the only exceptions are
formed by persons who have derived their rights
by purchase or otherwise from members of the
original stock. The supposition is confirmed by the
fact that, to this day, there are only single families
of landholders in small villages and not many in
large ones; but each has branched out into so many
members that it is not uncommon for the whole
agricultural labour to be done by the landholders,
without the aid either of tenants or of labourers.
The rights of the landholders are theirs collectively,
and, though they almost always have a more or less
perfect partition of them, they never have an entire
separation. A landholder, for instance, can sell or
mortgage his rights; but he must first have the con-

sent of the Village, and the purchaser steps exactly into his place and takes up all his obligations. If a family becomes extinct, its share returns to the common stock."

Some considerations which have been offered in the fifth chapter of this volume will assist the reader, I trust, in appreciating the significance of Elphinstone's language. No institution of the primitive world is likely to have been preserved to our day, unless it has acquired an elasticity foreign to its original nature through some vivifying legal fiction. The Village Community then is not necessarily an assemblage of blood-relations, but it is *either* such an assemblage *or* a body of co-proprietors formed on the model of an association of kinsmen. The type with which it should be compared is evidently not the Roman Family, but the Roman Gens or House. The Gens was also a group on the model of the family; it was the family extended by a variety of fictions of which the exact nature was lost in antiquity. In historical times, its leading characteristics were the very two which Elphinstone remarks in the Village Community. There was always the assumption of a common origin, an assumption sometimes notoriously at variance with fact; and, to repeat the historian's words, "if a family became extinct, its share returned to the common stock." In old Roman law, unclaimed inheritances escheated to the Gentiles. It is further suspected by all who have examined their history that the Communities,

like the Gentes, have been very generally adulterated by the admission of strangers, but the exact mode
of absorption cannot now be ascertained. At present,
they are recruited, as Elphinstone tells us, by the
admission of purchasers, with the consent of the
brotherhood. The acquisition of the adopted mem
ber is, however, of the nature of a universal succession; together with the share he has bought, he
succeeds to the liabilities which the vendor had
incurred towards the aggregate group. He is an
Emptor Familiæ, and inherits the legal clothing of
the person whose place he begins to fill. The consent of the whole brotherhood required for his admission may remind us of the consent which the
Comitia Curiata, the Parliament of that larger brotherhood of self-styled kinsmen, the ancient Roman
commonwealth, so strenuously insisted on as essential
to the legalisation of an Adoption or the confirmation
of a Will.

The tokens of an extreme antiquity are discov
erable in almost every single feature of the Indian
Village Communities. We have so many independent reasons for suspecting that the infancy of law
is distinguished by the prevalence of co-ownership,
by the intermixture of personal with proprietary
rights, and by the confusion of public with private
duties, that we should be justified in deducing many
important conclusions from our observation of these
proprietary brotherhoods, even if no similarly compounded societies could be detected in any other

part of the world. It happens, however, that much
earnest curiosity has been very recently attracted to
a similar set of phenomena in those parts of Europe
which have been most slightly affected by the feudal
transformation of property, and which in many im
portant particulars have as close an affinity with the
Eastern as with the Western world. The researches
of M. de Haxthausen, M. Tengoborski, and others,
have shown us that the Russian villages are not fortuitous assemblages of men, nor are they unions
founded on contract; they are naturally organised
communities like those of India. It is true that these
villages are always in theory the patrimony of some
noble proprietor, and the peasants have within historical times been converted into the predial, and to
a great extent into the personal, serfs of the seignior.
But the pressure of this superior ownership has
never crushed the ancient organisation of the village,
and it is probable that the enactment of the Czar of
Russia, who is supposed to have introduced serfdom,
was really intended to prevent the peasants from
abandoning that co-operation without which the old
social order could not long be maintained. In the
assumption of an agnatic connection between the
villagers, in the blending of personal rights with
privileges of ownership, and in a variety of spontaneous provisions for internal administration, the
Russian village appears to be a nearly exact repeti-
tion of the Indian Community; but there is one
important difference which we note with the greatest

interest. The co-owners of an Indian village, though
their property is blended, have their rights distinct,
and this separation of rights is complete and continues indefinitely. The severance of rights is also
theoretically complete in a Russian village, but there
it is only temporary. After the expiration of a
given, but not in all cases of the same, period, separate ownerships are extinguished, the land of the
village is thrown into a mass, and then it is re-dis-
tributed among the families composing the community, according to their number. This repartition
having been effected, the rights of families and of
individuals are again allowed to branch out into
various lines, which they continue to follow till
another period of division comes round. An even
more curious variation from this type of ownership
occurs in some of those countries which long formed
a debateable land between the Turkish Empire and
the possessions of the House of Austria. In Servia,
in Croatia, and the Austrian Sclavonia, the villages
are also brotherhoods of persons who are at once co-
owners and kinsmen; but there the internal arrangements of the community differ from those adverted
to in the last two examples. The substance of the
common property is in this case neither divided in
practice nor considered in theory as divisible, but the
entire land is cultivated by the combined labour of
all the villagers, and the produce is annually distributed among the households, sometimes according to
their supposed wants, sometimes according to rules

which give to particular persons a fixed share of the
usufruct. All these practices are traced by the
jurists of the East of Europe to a principle which is
asserted to be found in the earliest Sclavonian laws,
the principle that the property of families cannot be
divided for a perpetuity.

The great interest of these phenomena in an inquiry like the present arises from the light they
throw on the development of distinct proprietary
rights *inside* the groups by which property seems to
have been originally held. We have the strongest
reason for thinking that property once belonged not
to individuals nor even to isolated families, but to
larger societies composed on the patriarchal model;
but the mode of transition from ancient to modern
ownerships, obscure at best, would have been infinitely obscurer if several distinguishable forms of
Village Communities had not been discovered and
examined. It is worth while to attend to the varieties of internal arrangement within the patriarchal
groups which are, or were till recently, observable
among races of Indo-European blood. The chiefs of
the ruder Highland clans used, it is said, to dole out
food to the heads of the households under their jurisdiction at the very shortest intervals, and sometimes day by day. A periodical distribution is also
made to the Sclavonian villagers of the Austrian and
Turkish provinces by the elders of their body, but
then it is a distribution once for all of the total produce of the year. In the Russian villages, however,

the substance of the property ceases to be looked upon as indivisible, and separate proprietary claims are allowed freely to grow up, but then the progress of separation is peremptorily arrested after it has continued a certain time.   In India, not only is there no indivisibility of the common fund, but separate proprietorship in parts of it may be indefinitely prolonged and may branch out into any number of derivative ownerships, the *de facto* partition of the stock being, however, checked by inveterate usage, and by the rule against the admission of strangers without the consent of the brotherhood.   It is not of course intended to insist that these different forms of the Village Community represent distinct stages in a process of transmutation which has been everywhere accomplished in the same manner.   But, though the evidence does not warrant our going so far as this, it renders less presumptuous the conjecture that private property, in the shape in which we know it, was chiefly formed by the gradual disentanglement of the separate rights of individuals from the blended rights of a community.   Our studies in the Law of Persons seemed to show us the Family expanding into the Agnatic group of kinsmen, then the Agnatic group dissolving into separate households; lastly, the household supplanted by the individual; and it is now suggested that each step in the change corresponds to an analogous alteration in the nature of Ownership.   If there be any truth in the suggestion, it is to be observed that it materially

affects the problem which theorists on the origin of
Property have generally proposed to themselves
The question—perhaps an insoluble one—which
they have mostly agitated is, what were the motives
which first induced men to respect each other's possessions? It may still be put, without much hope
of finding an answer to it, in the form of an inquiry
into the reasons which led one composite group to
keep aloof from the domain of another. But, if it
be true that far the most important passage in the
history of Private Property is its gradual separation
from the co-ownership of kinsmen, then the great
point of inquiry is identical with that which lies on
the threshold of all historical law—what were the
motives which originally prompted men to hold together in the family union? To such a question,
Jurisprudence, unassisted by other sciences, is not
competent to give a reply. The fact can only be
noted.

The undivided state of property in ancient societies is consistent with a peculiar sharpness of division, which shows itself as soon as any single share
is completely separated from the patrimony of the
group. This phenomenon springs, doubtless, from the
circumstance that the property is supposed to become
the domain of a new group, so that any dealing with
it, in its divided state, is a transaction between two
highly complex bodies. I have already compared
Ancient Law to Modern International Law, in respect of the size of the corporate associations, whose

rights and duties it settles. As the contracts and
conveyances known to ancient law are contracts and
conveyances to which not single individuals, but or·
ganised companies of men, are parties, they are in
the highest degree ceremonious ; they require a variety of symbolical acts and words intended to impress the business on the memory of all who take
part in it ; and they demand the presence of an inordinate number of witnesses. From these peculiarities, and others allied to them, springs the universally unmalleable character of the ancient forms of
property. Sometimes the patrimony of the family
is absolutely inalienable, as was the case with the
Sclavonians, and still oftener, though alienations may
not be entirely illegitimate, they are virtually im·
practicable, as among most of the Germanic tribes,
from the necessity of having the consent of a large
number of persons to the transfer. Where these impediments do not exist, or can be surmounted, the act
of conveyance itself is generally burdened with a perfect load of ceremony, in which not one iota can be
safely neglected. Ancient law uniformly refuses to
dispense with a single gesture, however grotesque ;
with a single syllable, however its meaning may have
been forgotten ; with a single witness, however super·
fluous may be his testimony. The entire solemnities must be scrupulously completed by persons le-
gally entitled to take part in it, or else the convey·
ance is null, and the seller is re-established in the

rights of which he had vainly attempted to divest himself.

These various obstacles to the free circulation of the objects of use and enjoyment, begin of course to make themselves felt as soon as society has acquired even a slight degree of activity, and the expedients by which advancing communities endeavour to over-come them form the staple of the history of Property. Of such expedients there is one which takes prece-dence of the rest from its antiquity and universality. The idea seems to have spontaneously suggested it-self to a great number of early societies, to classify property into kinds. One kind or sort of property is placed on a lower footing of dignity than the others, but at the same time is relieved from the fetters which antiquity has imposed on them. Sub-sequently, the superior convenience of the rules gov-erning the transfer and descent of the lower order of property becomes generally recognised, and by a gradual course of innovation the plasticity of the less dignified class of valuable objects is communicated to the classes which stand conventionally higher. The history of Roman Property Law is the history of the assimilation of Res Mancipi to Res Nec Mancipi. The history of Property on the European Continent is the history of the subversion of the feudalised law of land by the Romanised law of moveables; and though the history of ownership in England is not nearly completed, it is visibly the law of personalty which threatens to absorb and annihilate the law of realty.

The only *natural* classification of the objects of enjoyment, the only classification which corresponds with an essential difference in the subject matter, is that which divides them into Moveables and Immoveables. Familiar as is this classification to jurisprudence, it was very slowly developed by Roman law, from which we inherit it, and was only finally adopted by it in its latest stage. The classifications of Ancient Law have sometimes a superficial resemblance to this. They occasionally divide property into categories, and place immoveables in one of them; but then it is found that they either class along with immoveables a number of objects which have no sort of relation with them, or else divorce them from various rights to which they have a close affinity. Thus, the Res Mancipi of Roman Law included not only land but slaves, horses, and oxen. Scottish law ranks with land a certain class of securities, and Hindoo law associates it with slaves. English law, on the other hand, parts leases of land for years from other interests in the soil, and joins them to personalty under the name of chattels real. Moreover, the classifications of Ancient Law are classifications implying superiority and inferiority; while the distinction between moveables and immoveables, so long at least as it was confined to Roman jurisprudence, carried with it no suggestion whatever of a difference in dignity. The Res Mancipi, however,

did certainly at first enjoy a precedence over the Res
Nec Mancipi, as did heritable property in Scotland,
and realty in England, over the personalty to which
they were opposed. The lawyers of all systems have
spared no pains in striving to refer these classifications to some intelligible principle ; but the reasons
of the severance must ever be vainly sought for in
the philosophy of law ; they belong not to its philosophy, but to its history. The explanation which appears to cover the greatest number of instances is
that the objects of enjoyment honoured above the
rest were forms of property known first and earliest
to each particular community, and dignified therefore emphatically with the designation of *Property.*
On the other hand, the articles not enumerated
among the favoured objects seem to have been placed
on a lower standing, because the knowledge of their
value was posterior to the epoch at which the cata-
logue of superior property was settled. They were
at first unknown, rare, limited in their uses, or else
regarded as mere appendages to the privileged objects. Thus, though the Roman Res Mancipi included a number of moveable articles of great value,
still the most costly jewels were never allowed to
take rank as Res Mancipi, because they were unknown to the early Romans. In the same way chattels real in England are said to have been degraded
to the footing of personalty, from the infrequency
and valuelessness of such estates under the feudal
land-law. But the grand point of interest is, the con-

tinued degradation of these commodities when their importance had increased and their number had multiplied. Why were they not successively included among the favoured objects of enjoyment? One reason is found in the stubbornness with which Ancient Law adheres to its classifications. It is a characteristic both of uneducated minds and of early societies, that they are little able to conceive a general rule apart from the particular applications of it with which they are practically familiar. They cannot dissociate a general term or maxim from the special examples which meet them in daily experience; and in this way the designation covering the best-known forms of property is denied to articles which exactly resemble them in being objects of enjoyment and subjects of right. But to these influences, which exert peculiar force in a subject-matter so stable as that of law, are afterwards added others more consistent with progress in enlightenment and in the conceptions of general expediency. Courts and lawyers become at last alive to the inconvenience of the embarrassing formalities required for the transfer, recovery, or devolution of the favoured commodities, and grow unwilling to fetter the newer descriptions of property with the technical trammels which characterised the infancy of law Hence arises a disposition to keep these last on a lower grade in the arrangements of Jurisprudence, and to permit their transfer by simpler processes than those which, in archaic conveyances, serve as stumbling-blocks to

good faith and stepping-stones to fraud. We are
perhaps in some danger of underrating the inconveniences of the ancient modes of transfer. Our instruments of conveyance are written, so that their language, well pondered by the professional drafts-
man, is rarely defective in accuracy. But an ancient
conveyance was not written, but *acted*. Gestures and
words took the place of written technical phraseology, and any formula mispronounced, or symbolical
act omitted, would have vitiated the proceeding as fatally as a material mistake in stating the uses or setting out the remainders would, two hundred years
ago, have vitiated an English deed.   Indeed, the mischiefs of the archaic ceremonial are even thus only
half stated.   So long as elaborate conveyances, written or acted, are required for the alienation of *land*
alone, the chances of mistake are not considerable in
the transfer of a description of property which is
seldom got rid of with much precipitation.   But the
higher class of property in the ancient world comprised not only land but several of the commonest
and several of the most valuable moveables.   When
once the wheels of society had begun to move quick-
ly, there must have been immense inconvenience in
demanding a highly intricate form of transfer for a
horse or an ox, or for the most costly chattel of the
old world—the Slave. Such commodities must have
been constantly and even ordinarily conveyed with
incomplete forms, and held, therefore, under imperfect titles.

The Res Mancipi of old Roman law were, land,
—in historical times, land on Italian soil,—slaves
and beasts of burden, such as horses and oxen. It
is impossible to doubt that the objects which make
up the class are the instruments of agricultural labour, the commodities of first consequence to a
primitive people. Such commodities were at first,
I imagine, called emphatically Things or Property,
and the mode of conveyance by which they were
transferred was called a Mancipium or Mancipation;
but it was not probably till much later that they received the distinctive appellation of Res Mancipi,
" Things which require a Mancipation." By their
side there may have existed or grown up a class of
objects, for which it was not worth while to insist
upon the full ceremony of Mancipation. It would
be enough if, in transferring these last from owner
to owner, a part only of the ordinary formalities
were proceeded with, namely, that actual delivery,
physical transfer, or *tradition*, which is the most obvious index of a change of proprietorship. Such
commodities were the Res Nec Mancipi of the ancient jurisprudence, " things which did not require
a Mancipation," little prized probably at first, and
not often passed from one group of proprietors to
another. While, however, the list of the Res Mancipi was irrevocably closed, that of the Res Nec
Mancipi admitted of indefinite expansion; and hence
every fresh conquest of man over material nature
added an item to the Res Nec Mancipi, or effected

an improvement in those already recognised. In
sensibly, therefore, they mounted to an equality
with the Res Mancipi, and the impression of an
intrinsic inferiority being thus dissipated, men began
to observe the manifold advantages of the simple
formality which accompanied their transfer over the
more intricate and more venerable ceremonial. Two
of the agents of legal amelioration, Fictions and
Equity, were assiduously employed by the Roman
lawyers to give the practical effects of a Mancipation to a Tradition; and, though Roman legislators
long shrank from enacting that the right of property
in a Res Mancipi should be immediately transferred
by bare delivery of the article, yet even this step
was at last ventured upon by Justinian, in whose
jurisprudence the difference between Res Mancipi
and Res Nec Mancipi disappears, and Tradition or
Delivery becomes the one great conveyance known
to the law. The marked preference which the Roman lawyers very early gave to Tradition caused
them to assign it a place in their theory which has
helped to blind their modern disciples to its true
history. It was classed among the " natural " modes
of acquisition, both because it was generally practised among the Italian tribes, and because it was a
process which attained its object by the simplest
mechanism. If the expressions of the jurisconsults
be pressed, they undoubtedly imply that Tradition,
which belongs to the Law Natural, is more ancient
than Mancipation, which is an institution of Civil

Society; and this, I need not say, is the exact reverse of the truth.

The distinction between Res Mancipi and Res Nec Mancipi is the type of a class of distinctions to which civilisation is much indebted, distinctions which run through the whole mass of commodities, placing a few of them in a class by themselves, and relegating the others to a lower category. The inferior kinds of property are first, from disdain and disregard, released from the perplexed ceremonies in which primitive law delights, and then afterwards, in another state of intellectual progress, the simple methods of transfer and recovery which have been allowed to come into use serve as a model which condemns by its convenience and simplicity the cumbrous solemnities inherited from ancient days. But, in some societies, the trammels in which Property is tied up are much too complicated and stringent to be relaxed in so easy a manner. Whenever male children have been born to a Hindoo, the law of India, as I have stated, gives them all an interest in his property, and makes their consent a necessary condition of its alienation. In the same spirit, the general usage of the old Germanic peoples—it is remarkable that the Anglo-Saxon customs seem to have been an exception—forbade alienations without the consent of the male children; and the primitive law of the Sclavonians even prohibited them altogether. It is evident that such impediments as these cannot be overcome by a distinction between kinds

of property, inasmuch as the difficulty extends to
commodities of all sorts; and accordingly, Ancient
Law, when once launched on a course of improvement, encounters them with a distinction of another
character, a distinction classifying property, not according to its nature but according to its origin. In
India, where there are traces of both systems of
classification, the one which we are considering is
exemplified in the difference which Hindoo law
establishes between Inheritances and Acquisitions.
The inherited property of the father is shared by
the children as soon as they are born; but according
to the custom of most provinces, the acquisitions
made by him during his lifetime are wholly his own,
and can be transferred by him at pleasure. A similar distinction was not unknown to Roman law, in
which the earliest innovation on the Parental Powers
took the form of a permission given to the son to
keep for himself whatever he might have acquired
in military service. But the most extensive use
ever made of this mode of classification appears to
have been among the Germans. I have repeatedly
stated that the *allod*, though not inalienable, was
commonly transferable with the greatest difficulty;
and moreover, it descended exclusively to the agnatic
kindred. Hence an extraordinary variety of distinctions came to be recognised, all intended to diminish the inconveniences inseparable from allodial
property. The *wehrgeld*, for example, or composi
tion for the homicide of a relative, which occupies

so large a space in German jurisprudence, formed no
part of the family domain, and descended according
to rules of succession altogether different. Similarly, the *reipus*, or fine leviable on the re-marriage
of a widow, did not enter into the *allod* of the per
son to whom it was paid, and followed a line of
devolution in which the privileges of the agnates
were neglected. The law, too, as among the Hindoos, distinguished the Acquisitions of the chief of
the household from his Inherited property, and permitted him to deal with them under much more
liberal conditions. Classifications of the other sort
were also admitted, and the familiar distinction
drawn between land and moveables; but moveable
property was divided into several subordinate categories, to each of which different rules applied. This
exuberance of classification, which may strike us as
strange in so rude a people as the German conquerors of the Empire, is doubtless to be explained by
the presence in their systems of a considerable element of Roman law, absorbed by them during their
long sojourn on the confines of the Roman dominion.
It is not difficult to trace a great number of the rules
governing the transfer and devolution of the commodities which lay outside the *allod*, to their source
in Roman jurisprudence, from which they were probably borrowed at widely distant epochs, and in fragmentary importations. How far the obstacles to
the free circulation of property were surmounted by
such contrivances, we have not the means even of

conjecturing, for the distinctions adverted to have
no modern history. As I before explained, the allodial form of property was entirely lost in the feudal,
and when the consolidation of feudalism was once
completed, there was practically but one distinction
left standing of all those which had been known to
the western world—the distinction between land
and goods, immoveables and moveables. Externally
this distinction was the same with that which Roman
law had finally accepted, but the law of the middle
ages differed from that of Rome in distinctly considering immoveable property to be more dignified
than moveable. Yet this one sample is enough to
show the importance of the class of expedients to
which it belongs. In all the countries governed by
systems based on the French codes, that is, through
much the greatest part of the Continent of Europe,
the law of moveables, which was always Roman law,
has superseded and annulled the feudal law of land.
England is the only country of importance in which
this transmutation, though it has gone some way, is
not nearly accomplished. Our own, too, it may be
added, is the only considerable European country in
which the separation of moveables from immoveables has been somewhat disturbed by the same in
fluences which caused the ancient classifications to
depart from the only one which is countenanced by
nature. In the main, the English distinction has
been between land and goods; but a certain class of
goods have gone as heir-looms with the land, and a

certain description of interests in land have from historical causes been ranked with personalty. This is not the only instance in which English jurisprudence, standing apart from the main current of legal modification, has reproduced phenomena of archaic law.

I proceed to notice one or two more contrivances by which the ancient trammels of proprietary right were more or less successfully relaxed, premising that the scheme of this treatise only permits me to mention those which are of great antiquity. On one of them in particular it is necessary to dwell for a moment or two, because persons unacquainted with the early history of law will not be easily persuaded that a principle, of which modern jurisprudence has very slowly and with the greatest difficulty obtained the recognition, was really familiar to the very infancy of legal science. There is no principle in all law which the moderns, in spite of its beneficial character, have been so loath to adopt and to carry to its legitimate consequences as that which was known to the Romans as Usucapion, and which has descended to modern jurisprudence under the name of Prescription. It was a positive rule of the oldest Roman law, a rule older than the Twelve Tables, that commodities which had been uninterruptedly possessed for a certain period became the property of the possessor. The period of possession was exceedingly short—one or two years, according to the nature of the commodities—and in historical times

Usucapion was only allowed to operate when possession had commenced in a particular way; but I
think it likely that at a less advanced epoch possession was converted into ownership under conditions
even less severe than we read of in our authorities.
As I have said before, I am far from asserting that
the respect of men for *de facto* possession is a phenomenon which jurisprudence can account for by
itself, but it is very necessary to remark that primitive societies, in adopting the principle of Usucapion, were not beset with any of the speculative
doubts and hesitations which have impeded its reception among the moderns.   Prescriptions were
viewed by the modern lawyers, first with repug-
nance, afterwards with reluctant approval.   In several countries, including our own, legislation long
declined to advance beyond the rude device of
barring all actions based on a wrong which had
been suffered earlier than a fixed point of time in
the past, generally the first year of some preceding
reign; nor was it till the middle ages had finally
closed, and James the First had ascended the throne
of England, that we obtained a true statute of limitation of a very imperfect kind.   This tardiness in
copying one of the most famous chapters of Roman
law, which was no doubt constantly read by the
majority of European lawyers, the modern world
owes to the influence of the Canon Law.   The
ecclesiastical customs out of which the Canon Law
grew, concerned as they were with sacred or quasi

sacred interests, very naturally regarded the privileges which they conferred as incapable of being lost through disuse however prolonged; and in accordance with this view, the spiritual jurisprudence, when afterwards consolidated, was distinguished by a marked leaning against Prescriptions. It was the fate of the Canon Law, when held up by the clerical lawyers as a pattern to secular legislation, to have a peculiar influence on first principles. It gave to the bodies of custom which were formed throughout Europe far fewer express rules than did the Roman law, but then it seems to have communicated a bias to professional opinion on a surprising number of fundamental points, and the tendencies thus produced progressively gained strength as each system was developed. One of the dispositions it produced was a disrelish for Prescriptions; but I do not know that this prejudice would have operated as powerfully as it has done, if it had not fallen in with the doctrine of the scholastic jurists of the realist sect, who taught that, whatever turn actual legislation might take, a *right*, how long soever neglected, was in point of fact indestructible. The remains of this state of feeling still exist. Wherever the philosophy of law is earnestly discussed, questions respecting the speculative basis of Prescription are always hotly disputed; and it is still a point of the greatest interest in France and Germany, whether a person who has been out of possession for a series of years is deprived of his ownership as a penalty for his

neglect, or loses it through the summary interposition of the law in its desire to have a *finis litium*.
But no such scruples troubled the mind of early
Roman society.   Their ancient usages directly took
away the ownership of everybody who had been
out of possession, under certain circumstances, during
one or two years.   What was the exact tenor of the
rule of Usucapion in its earliest shape, it is not easy
to say; but, taken with the limitations which we
find attending it in the books, it was a most useful
security against the mischiefs of a too cumbrous
system of conveyance.   In order to have the benefit
of Usucapion, it was necessary that the adverse possession should have begun in good faith, that is,
with belief on the part of the possessor that he was
lawfully acquiring the property, and it was further
required that the commodity should have been
transferred to him by some mode of alienation
which, however unequal to conferring a complete
title in the particular case, was at least recognised
by the law.   In the case therefore of a Mancipation,
however slovenly the performance might have been,
yet if it had been carried so far as to involve a Tradition or Delivery, the vice of the title would be
cured by Usucapion in two years at most.   I know
nothing in the practice of the Romans which testifies
so strongly to their legal genius as the use which
they made of the Usucapion.   The difficulties which
beset them were nearly the same with those which
embarrassed and still embarrass the lawyers of

England. Owing to the complexity of their system, which as yet they had neither the courage nor the power to reconstruct, actual right was constantly getting divorced from technical right, the equitable ownership from the legal. But Usucapion, as manipulated by the jurisconsults, supplied a self-acting machinery, by which the defects of titles to property were always in course of being cured, and by which the ownerships that were temporarily separated were again rapidly cemented together with the briefest possible delay. Usucapion did not lose its advantages till the reforms of Justinian. But as soon as law and equity had been completely fused, and when Mancipation ceased to be the Roman conveyance, there was no further necessity for the ancient contrivance, and Usucapion, with its periods of time considerably lengthened, became the Prescription which has at length been adopted by nearly all systems of modern law.

I pass by with brief mention another expedient having the same object with the last, which, though it did not immediately make its appearance in English legal history, was of immemorial antiquity in Roman law; such indeed is its apparent age that some German civilians, not sufficiently aware of the light thrown on the subject by the analogies of English law, have thought it even older than the Mancipation. I speak of the Cessio in Jure, a collusive recovery, in a Court of Law, of property sought to be conveyed. The plaintiff claimed the

subject of this proceeding with the ordinary forms
of a litigation; the defendant made default; and
the commodity was of course adjudged to the plaintiff. I need scarcely remind the English lawyer that
this expedient suggested itself to our forefathers,
and produced those famous Fines and Recoveries
which did so much to undo the harshest trammels
of the feudal land-law. The Roman and English
contrivances have very much in common, and illustrate each other most instructively, but there is this
difference between them, that the object of the
English lawyers was to remove complications already
introduced into the title, while the Roman jurisconsults sought to prevent them by substituting a mode
of transfer necessarily unimpeachable for one which
too often miscarried. The device is in fact one
which suggests itself as soon as Courts of Law are
in steady operation, but are nevertheless still under
the empire of primitive notions. In an advanced
state of legal opinion, tribunals regard collusive
litigation as an abuse of their procedure; but there
has always been a time when, if their forms were
scrupulously complied with, they never dreamed of
looking further.

The influence of Courts of Law and of their
procedure upon property has been most extensive,
but the subject is too large for the dimensions of
this treatise, and would carry us further down the
course of legal history than is consistent with its
scheme. It is desirable, however, to mention, that

to this influence we must attribute the importance
of the distinction between Property and Possession
—not, indeed, the distinction itself, which (in the
language of an eminent English civilian) is the same
thing as the distinction between the legal right to
act upon a thing and the physical power to do so—
but the extraordinary importance which the distinc
tion has obtained in the philosophy of the law. Few
educated persons are so little versed in legal literature as not to have heard that the language of the
Roman jurisconsults on the subject of Possession
long occasioned the greatest possible perplexity, and
that the genius of Savigny is supposed to have
chiefly proved itself by the solution which he discovered for the enigma. Possession, in fact, when
employed by the Roman lawyers, appears to have
contracted a shade of meaning not easily accounted
for. The word, as appears from its etymology, must
have originally denoted physical contact or physical
contact resumeable at pleasure ; but as actually used,
without any qualifying epithet, it signifies not simply
physical detention, but physical detention coupled
with the intention to hold the thing detained as
one's own. Savigny, following Niebuhr, perceived
that for this anomaly there could only be a historical origin. He pointed out that the Patrician
burghers of Rome, who had become tenants of the
greatest part of the public domain at nominal rents,
were, in the view of the old Roman law, mere possessors, but then they were possessors intending to

keep their land against all comers. They, in truth, put forward a claim almost identical with that which has recently been advanced in England by the les· sees of Church lands. Admitting that in theory they were the tenants-at-will of the state, they contended that time and undisturbed enjoyment had ripened their holding into a species of ownership, and that it would be unjust to eject them for the purpose of redistributing the domain. The association of this claim with the Patrician tenancies, permanently influenced the sense of "possession." Meanwhile the only legal remedies of which the tenants could avail themselves, if ejected or threat· ened with disturbance, were the Possessory Inter· dicts, summary processes of Roman law which were either expressly devised by the Prætor for their protection, or else, according to another theory, had in older times been employed for the provisional maintenance of possessions pending the settlement of questions of legal right. It came, therefore, to be understood that everybody who possessed property *as his own* had the power of demanding the Interdicts, and, by a system of highly artificial pleading, the Interdictal process was moulded into a shape fitted for the trial of conflicting claims to a disputed possession. Then commenced a movement which, as Mr. John Austin pointed out, exactly reproduced itself in English law. Proprietors, *domini*, began to prefer the simpler forms or speedier course of the Interdict to the lagging and intricate formal ities of the Real Action, and for the purpose of availing themselves of the possessory remedy fell back upon the possession which was supposed to be involved in their proprietorship. The liberty con ceded to persons who were not true Possessors, but Owners, to vindicate their rights by possessory remedies, though it may have been at first a boon, had ultimately the effect of seriously deteriorating both English and Roman jurisprudence. The Roman law owes to it those subtleties on the subject of Possession which have done so much to discredit it, while English law, after the actions which it appropriated to the recovery of real property had fallen into the most hopeless confusion, got rid at last of the whole tangled mass by a heroic remedy No one can doubt that the virtual abolition of the English real actions which took place nearly thirty years since was a public benefit, but still persons sensitive to the harmonies of jurisprudence will lament that, instead of cleansing, improving, and simplifying the true proprietary actions, we sacrificed them all to the possessory action of ejectment, thus basing our whole system of land recovery upon a legal fiction.

Legal tribunals have also powerfully assisted to shape and modify conceptions of proprietary right by means of the distinction between Law and Equity, which always makes its first appearance as a distinction between jurisdictions. Equitable property in England is simply property held under the

jurisdiction of the Court of Chancery. At Rome
the Prætor's Edict introduced its novel principles in
the guise of a promise that under certain circum
stances a particular action or a particular plea would
be granted ; and, accordingly, the property *in bonis,*
or Equitable Property, of Roman law was property
exclusively protected by remedies which had their
source in the Edict. The mechanism by which equitable rights were saved from being overridden by
the claims of the legal owner was somewhat different
in the two systems. With us their independence is
secured by the Injunction of the Court of Chancery.
Since however Law and Equity, while not as yet
consolidated, were administered under the Roman
system by the same Court, nothing like the Injunction was required, and the Magistrate took the simpler course of refusing to grant to the Civil Law
Owner those actions and pleas by which alone he
could obtain the property that belonged in equity
to another. But the practical operation of both
systems was nearly the same. Both, by means of a
distinction in procedure, were able to preserve new
forms of property in a sort of provisional existence,
until the time should come when they were recognised by the whole law. In this way, the Roman
Prætor gave an immediate right of property to the
person who had acquired a Res Mancipi by mere
delivery, without waiting for the ripening of Usucapion. Similarly he in time recognised an ownership
in the Mortgagee, who had at first been a mere

"bailee" or depositary, and in the Emphyteuta, or
tenant of land which was subject to a fixed perpetual rent. Following a parallel line of progress,
the English Court of Chancery created a special
proprietorship for the Mortgagor, for the Cestui
que Trust, for the Married Woman who had the
advantage of a particular kind of settlement, and
for the Purchaser who had not yet acquired a complete legal ownership. All these are examples in
which forms of proprietary right, distinctly new,
were recognised and preserved. But indirectly
Property has been affected in a thousand ways by
equity, both in England and at Rome. Into whatever corner of jurisprudence its authors pushed the
powerful instrument in their command, they were
sure to meet, and touch, and more or less materially
modify the law of property. When in the preceding
pages I have spoken of certain ancient legal distinctions and expedients as having powerfully affected
the history of ownership, I must be understood to
mean that the greatest part of their influence has
arisen from the hints and suggestions of improvement infused by them into the mental atmosphere
which was breathed by the fabricators of equitable
systems.

But to describe the influence of Equity on Ownership would be to write its history down to our
own days. I have alluded to it principally because
several esteemed contemporary writers have thought
that in the Roman severance of Equitable from Le-

gal property we have the clue to that difference in the conception of Ownership, which apparently distinguishes the law of the middle ages from the law of the Roman Empire. The leading characteristic of the feudal conception is its recognition of a double proprietorship, the superior ownership of the lord of the fief coexisting with the inferior property or estate of the tenant. Now, this duplication of proprietary right looks, it is urged, extremely like a generalised form of the Roman distribution of rights over property into *Quiritarian* or legal, and (to use a word of late origin) *Bonitarian* or equitable. Gaius himself observes upon the splitting of *dominion* into two parts as a singularity of Roman law, and expressly contrasts it with the entire or allodial ownership to which other nations were accustomed. Justinian, it is true, reconsolidated dominion into one, but then it was the partially reformed system of the Western Empire, and not Justinian's jurisprudence, with which the barbarians were in contact during so many centuries. While they remained poised on the edge of the Empire, it may well be that they learned this distinction, which afterwards bore remarkable fruit. In favour of this theory, it must at all events be admitted that the element of Roman law in the various bodies of barbarian custom has been very imperfectly examined. The erroneous or insufficient theories which have served to explain Feudalism resemble each other in their tendency to draw off attention from this particular in

gredient in its texture. The older investigators,
who have been mostly followed in this country,
attached an exclusive importance to the circum
stances of the turbulent period during which the
Feudal system grew to maturity ; and in later times
a new source of error has been added to those already
existing, in that pride of nationality which has led
German writers to exaggerate the completeness of
the social fabric which their forefathers had built up
before their appearance in the Roman world.   One
or two English inquirers who looked in the right
quarter for the foundations of the feudal system,
failed nevertheless to conduct their investigations to
any satisfactory result, either from searching too exclusively for analogies in the compilations of Justinian, or from confining their attention to the compendia of Roman law which are found appended to
some of the extant barbarian codes.   But, if Roman
jurisprudence had any influence on the barbarous
societies, it had probably produced the greatest part
of its effects before the legislation of Justinian, and
before the preparation of these compendia.   It was
not the reformed and purified jurisprudence of Justinian, but the undigested system which prevailed in
the Western Empire, and which the Eastern *Corpus
Juris* never succeeded in displacing, that I conceive
to have clothed with flesh and muscle the scanty
skeleton of barbarous usage.   The change must be
supposed to have taken place before the Germanic
tribes had distinctly appropriated, as conquerors,

any portion of the Roman dominions, and therefore long before Germanic monarchs had ordered breviaries of Roman law to be drawn up for the use of their Roman subjects. The necessity for some such hypothesis will be felt by everybody who can appreciate the difference between archaic and developed law. Rude as are the *Leges Barbarorum* which remain to us, they are not rude enough to satisfy the theory of their purely barbarous origin; nor have we any reason for believing that we have received, in written records, more than a fraction of the fixed rules which were practised among themselves by the members of the conquering tribes. If we can once persuade ourselves that a considerable element of debased Roman law already existed in the barbarian systems, we shall have done something to remove a grave difficulty. The German law of the conquerors and the Roman law of their subjects would not have combined if they had not possessed more affinity for each other than refined jurisprudence has usually for the customs of savages. It is extremely likely that the codes of the barbarians, archaic as they seem, are only a compound of true primitive usage with half-understood Roman rules, and that it was the foreign ingredient which enabled them to coalesce with a Roman jurisprudence that had already receded somewhat from the comparative finish which it had acquired under the Western Emperors.

But, though all this must be allowed, there are several considerations which render it unlikely that

the feudal form of ownership was directly suggested
by the Roman duplication of domainial rights. The
distinction between legal and equitable property
strikes one as a subtlety little likely to be appreciated
by barbarians; and, moreover, it can scarcely be understood unless Courts of Law are contemplated in
regular operation. But the strongest reason against
this theory is the existence in Roman law of a form
of property—a creation of Equity, it is true—which
supplies a much simpler explanation of the transition from one set of ideas to the other. This is the
Emphyteusis, upon which the Fief of the middle
ages has often been fathered, though without much
knowledge of the exact share which it had in bringing feudal ownership into the world. The truth is
that the Emphyteusis, not probably as yet known
by its Greek designation, marks one stage in a current of ideas which led ultimately to feudalism. The
first mention in Roman history of estates larger than
could be farmed by a Paterfamilias, with his household of sons and slaves, occurs when we come to the
holdings of the Roman patricians. These great proprietors appear to have had no idea of any system
of farming by free tenants. Their *latifundia* seem
to have been universally cultivated by slave-gangs,
under bailiffs who were themselves slaves or freed
men; and the only organisation attempted appears
to have consisted in dividing the inferior slaves into
small bodies, and making them the *peculium* of the
better and trustier sort, who thus acquired a kind

of interest in the efficiency of their labour. This system was, however, especially disadvantageous to one class of estated proprietors, the Municipalities. Functionaries in Italy were changed with the rapidity which often surprises us in the administration of Rome herself; so that the superintendence of a large landed domain by an Italian corporation must have been excessively imperfect. Accordingly, we are told that with the municipalities began the practice of letting out *agri vectigules*, that is, of leasing land for a perpetuity to a free tenant, at a fixed rent, and under certain conditions. The plan was afterwards extensively imitated by individual proprietors, and the tenant, whose relation to the owner had originally been determined by his contract, was subsequently recognised by the Prætor as having himself a qualified proprietorship, which in time became known as an Emphyteusis. From this point the history of tenure parts into two branches. In the course of that long period during which our records of the Roman Empire are most incomplete, the slave-gangs of the great Roman families became transformed into the *coloni*, whose origin and situation constitute one of the obscurest questions in all history. We may suspect that they were formed partly by the elevation of the slaves, and partly by the degradation of the free farmers; and that they prove the richer classes of the Roman Empire to have become aware of the increased value which landed property obtains when the cultivator has an

interest in the produce of the land.　We know that
their servitude was predial; that it wanted many
of the characteristics of absolute slavery, and that
they acquitted their service to the landlord in rendering to him a fixed portion of the annual crop.
We know further that they survived all the muta-
tions of society in the ancient and modern worlds.
Though included in the lower courses of the feudal
structure, they continued in many countries to render to the landlord precisely the same dues which
they had paid to the Roman *dominus*, and from a
particular class among them, the *coloni medietarii*,
who reserved half the produce for the owner, are
descended the *metayer* tenantry, who still conduct
the cultivation of the soil in almost all the South of
Europe.　On the other hand, the Emphyteusis, if
we may so interpret the allusions to it in the *Corpus
Juris*, became a favorite and beneficial modification
of property; and it may be conjectured that wherever free farmers existed, it was this tenure which
regulated their interest in the land.　The Prætor,
as has been said, treated the Emphyteuta as a true
proprietor.　When ejected, he was allowed to rein-
state himself by a Real Action, the distinctive badge
of proprietary right, and he was protected from disturbance by the author of his lease so long as the
canon, or quit-rent, was punctually paid.　But at
the same time it must not be supposed that the
ownership of the author of the lease was either ex
tinct or dormant.　It was kept alive by a power of

re-entry on non-payment of the rent, a right of pre-
emption in case of sale, and a certain control over
the mode of cultivation.　We have, therefore, in the
Emphyteusis a striking example of the double ownership which characterised feudal property, and one,
moreover, which is much simpler and much more
easily imitated than the juxtaposition of legal and
equitable rights.　The history of the Roman tenure
does not end, however, at this point.　We have
clear evidence that between the great fortresses
which, disposed along the line of the Rhine and
Danube, long secured the frontier of the Empire
against its barbarian neighbours, there extended a
succession of strips of land, the *agri limitrophi*,
which were occupied by veteran soldiers of the Roman army on the terms of an Emphyteusis.　There
was a double ownership.　The Roman State was
landlord of the soil, but the soldiers cultivated it
without disturbance so long as they held themselves
ready to be called out for military service whenever
the state of the border should require it.　In fact, a
sort of garrison-duty, under a system closely resembling that of the military colonies on the Austro-
Turkish border, had taken the place of the quit-rent
which was the service of the ordinary Emphyteuta.
It seems impossible to doubt that this was the precedent copied by the barbarian monarchs who
founded feudalism.　It had been within their view
for some hundred years, and many of the veterans
who guarded the border were, it is to be remem-

bered, themselves of barbarian extraction, who
probably spoke the Germanic tongues. Not only
does the proximity of so easily followed a model explain whence the Frankish and Lombard Sovereigns
got the idea of securing the military service of their
followers by granting away portions of their public
domain; but it perhaps explains the tendency which
immediately showed itself in the Benefices to become
hereditary, for an Emphyteusis, though capable of
being moulded to the terms of the original contract,
nevertheless descended as a general rule to the
heirs of the grantee. It is true that the holder of
a benefice, and more recently the lord of one of
those fiefs into which the benefices were transformed,
appears to have owed certain services which were
not likely to have been rendered by the military
colonist, and were certainly not rendered by the
Emphyteuta. The duty of respect and gratitude to
the feudal superior, the obligation to assist in endowing his daughter and equipping his son, the liability to his guardianship in minority, and many
other similar incidents of tenure, must have been
literally borrowed from the relations of Patron and
Freedman under Roman law, that is, of quondam
master and quondam-slave. But then it is known
that the earliest beneficiaries were the personal companions of the sovereign, and it is indisputable that
this position, brilliant as it seems, was at first attended by some shade of servile debasement. The

person who ministered to the Sovereign in his Court
had given up something of that absolute personal
freedom which was the proudest privilege of the
allodial proprietor.

CHAPTER IX.

THE EARLY HISTORY OF CONTRACT.

THERE are few general propositions concerning the age to which we belong which seem at first sight likely to be received with readier concurrence than the assertion that the society of our day is mainly distinguished from that of preceding generations by the largeness of the sphere which is occupied in it by Contract. Some of the phenomena on which this proposition rests are among those most frequently singled out for notice, for comment, and for eulogy. Not many of us are so unobservant as not to perceive that in innumerable cases where old law fixed a man's social position irreversibly at his birth, modern law allows him to create it for himself by convention; and indeed several of the few exceptions which remain to this rule are constantly denounced with passionate indignation. The point, for instance, which is really debated in the vigorous controversy still carried on upon the subject of negro servitude, is whether the status of the slave does not

belong to by-gone institutions, and whether the only
relation between employer and labourer which com
mends itself to modern morality be not a relation determined exclusively by contract.   The recognition
of this difference between past ages and the present
enters into the very essence of the most famous contemporary speculations. It is certain that the science
of Political Economy, the only department of moral
inquiry which has made any considerable progress in
our day, would fail to correspond with the facts of
life if it were not true that Imperative Law had
abandoned the largest part of the field which it once
occupied, and had left men to settle rules of conduct
for themselves with a liberty never allowed to them
till recently. The bias indeed of most persons trained
in political economy is to consider the general truth
on which their science reposes as entitled to become
universal, and, when they apply it as an art, their efforts are ordinarily directed to enlarging the province
of Contract and to curtailing that of Imperative Law,
except so far as law is necessary to enforce the performance of Contracts. The impulse given by thinkers who are under the influence of these ideas is beginning to be very strongly felt in the Western
world. Legislation has nearly confessed its inability
to keep pace with the activity of man in discovery,
in invention, and in the manipulation of accumulated
wealth ; and the law even of the least advanced
communities tends more and more to become a mere
surface-stratum, having under it an ever-changing as-

semblage of contractual rules with which it rarely interferes except to compel compliance with a few fundamental principles, or unless it be called in to punish the violation of good faith.

Social inquiries, so far as they depend on the consideration of legal phenomena, are in so backward a condition that we need not be surprised at not finding these truths recognised in the commonplaces which pass current concerning the progress of society. These commonplaces answer much more to our prejudices than to our convictions. The strong disinclination of most men to regard morality as advancing seems to be especially powerful when the virtues on which Contract depends are in question, and many of us have an almost instinctive reluctance to admitting that good faith and trust in our fellows are more widely diffused than of old, or that there is anything in contemporary manners which parallels the loyalty of the antique world. From time to time, these prepossessions are greatly strengthened by the spectacle of frauds, unheard of before the period at which they were observed, and astonishing from their complication as well shocking from criminality. But the very character of these frauds shows clearly that, before they became possible, the moral obligations of which they are the breach must have been more than proportionately developed. It is the confidence reposed and deserved by the many which affords facilities for the bad faith of the few, so that, if colossal examples of dishonesty occur, there is no surer conclusion than that scrupulous honesty is displayed in the average of the transactions which, in the particular case, have supplied the delinquent with his opportunity.   If we insist on reading the history of morality as reflected in jurisprudence, by turning our eyes not on the law of Contract but on the law of Crime, we must be careful that we read it aright. The only form of dishonesty treated of in the most ancient Roman law is Theft.   At the moment at which I write, the newest chapter in the English criminal law is one which attempts to prescribe punishment for the frauds of Trustees.   The proper inference from this contrast is not that the primitive Romans practised a higher morality than ourselves. We should rather say that, in the interval between their day and ours, morality had advanced from a very rude to a highly refined conception—from viewing the rights of property as exclusively sacred, to looking upon the rights growing out of the mere unilateral reposal of confidence as entitled to the protection of the penal law.

The definite theories of jurists are scarcely nearer the truth in this point than the opinions of the multitude. To begin with the views of the Roman lawyers, we find them inconsistent with the true history of moral and legal progress. One class of contracts, in which the plighted faith of the contracting parties was the only material ingredient, they specifically denominated Contracts *juris gentium*, and though these contracts were undoubtedly the latest born

into the Roman system, the expression employed
implies, if a definite meaning be extracted from
it, that they were more ancient than certain other
forms of engagement treated of in Roman law, in
which the neglect of a mere technical formality was
as fatal to the obligation as misunderstanding or
deceit. But then the antiquity to which they were
referred was vague, shadowy, and only capable of
being understood through the Present; nor was it
until the language of the Roman lawyers became the
language of an age which had lost the key to their
mode of thought that a " Contract of the Law of Nations" came to be distinctly looked upon as a Contract
known to man in a state of Nature. Rousseau adopted
both the judicial and the popular error. In the Dis-
sertation on the effects of Art and Science upon
Morals, the first of his works which attracted attention and the one in which he states most unreservedly the opinions which made him the founder of a sect,
the veracity and good faith attributed to the ancient
Persians are repeatedly pointed out as traits of primitive innocence which have been gradually obliterated by civilisation; and at a later period he found a
basis for all his speculations in the doctrine of an
original Social Contract. The Social Contract or
Compact is the most systematic form which has ever
been assumed by the error we are discussing. It is
a theory which, though nursed into importance by
political passions, derived all its sap from the speculations of lawyers. True it certainly is that the fa-

mous Englishmen, for whom it had first had attraction, valued it chiefly for its political serviceableness, but, as I shall presently attempt to explain, they would never have arrived at it, if politicians had not long conducted their controversies in legal phraseology.   Nor were the English authors of the theory blind to that speculative amplitude which recommended it so strongly to the Frenchmen who inherited it from them.   Their writings show they perceived that it could be made to account for all social, quite as well as for all political phenomena. They had observed the fact, already striking in their day, that of the positive rules obeyed by men, the greater part were created by Contract, the lesser by imperative Law.   But they were ignorant or careless of the historical relation of these two constituents of jurisprudence.   It was for the purpose, therefore, of gratifying their speculative tastes by attributing all jurisprudence to a uniform source, as much as with the view of eluding the doctrines which claimed a divine parentage for Imperative Law, that they devised the theory that all Law had its origin in Contract.   In another stage of thought, they would have been satisfied to leave their theory in the condition of an ingenious hypothesis or a convenient verbal formula.   But that age was under the dominion of legal superstitions.   The State of Nature had been talked about till it had ceased to be regarded as paradoxical, and hence it seemed easy to give a fallacious reality and definiteness to the contractual origin of Law by insisting on the Social Compact as a historical fact.

Our own generation has got rid of these erroneous juridical theories, partly by outgrowing the intellectual state to which they belong, and partly by almost ceasing to theorise on such subjects altogether. The favorite occupation of active minds at the present moment, and the one which answers to the speculations of our forefathers on the origin of the social state, is the analysis of society as it exists and moves before our eyes; but, through omitting to call in the assistance of history, this analysis too often degenerates into an idle exercise of curiosity, and is especially apt to incapacitate the inquirer for comprehending states of society which differ considerably from that to which he is accustomed. The mistake of judging the men of other periods by the morality of our own day has its parallel in the mistake of supposing that every wheel or bolt in the modern social machine had its counterpart in more rudimentary societies. Such impressions ramify very widely, and masque themselves very subtly, in historical works written in the modern fashion ; but I find the trace of their presence in the domain of jurisprudence in the praise which is frequently bestowed on the little apologue of Montesquieu concerning the Troglodytes, inserted in the *Lettres Persanes.* The Troglodytes were a people who systematically violated their Contracts, and so perished utterly. If the story bears the moral which its author intended, and is employ-

ed to expose an anti-social heresy by which this century and the last have been threatened, it is most un-
exceptionable; but if the inference be obtained from
it that society could not possibly hold together without attaching a sacredness to promises and agreements which should be on something like a par with
the respect that is paid to them by a mature civilisation, it involves an error so grave as to be fatal to
all sound understanding of legal history. The fact is
that the Troglodytes have flourished and founded
powerful states with very small attention to the obligations of Contract. The point which before all
others has to be apprehended in the constitution of
primitive societies is that the individual creates for
himself few or no rights, and few or no duties. The
rules which he obeys are derived first from the station into which he is born, and next from the imperative commands addressed to him by the chief of
the household of which he forms a part. Such a system leaves the very smallest room for Contract. The
members of the same family (for so we may interpret
the evidence) are wholly incapable of contracting
with each other, and the family is entitled to disregard the engagements by which any one of its subordinate members has attempted to bind it. Family,
it is true, may contract with family, and chieftain with
chieftain, but the transaction is one of the same nature, and encumbered by as many formalities, as the
alienation of property, and the disregard of one iota
of the performance is fatal to the obligation. The

positive duty resulting from one man's reliance on
the word of another is among the slowest conquests
of advancing civilisation.

Neither Ancient Law nor any other source of
evidence discloses to us society entirely destitute of
the conception of Contract. But the conception
when it first shows itself, is obviously rudimentary.
No trustworthy primitive record can be read without perceiving that the habit of mind which induces
us to make good a promise is as yet imperfectly developed, and that acts of flagrant perfidy are often
mentioned without blame and sometimes described
with approbation. In the Homeric literature, for
instance, the deceitful cunning of Ulysses appears
as a virtue of the same rank with the prudence of
Nestor, the constancy of Hector, and the gallantry
of Achilles. Ancient law is still more suggestive
of the distance which separates the crude form of
Contract from its maturity. At first, nothing is
seen like the interposition of law to compel the performance of a promise. That which the law arms
with its sanctions is not a promise, but a promise
accompanied with a solemn ceremonial. Not only
are the formalities of equal importance with the
promise itself, but they are, if anything, of greater
importance; for that delicate analysis which mature
jurisprudence applies to the conditions of mind under
which a particular verbal assent is given appears, in
ancient law, to be transferred to the words and gestures of the accompanying performance. No pledge

is enforced if a single form be omitted or misplaced, but, on the other hand, if the forms can be shown to have been accurately proceeded with, it is of no avail to plead that the promise was made under duress or deception. The transmutation of this ancient view into the familiar notion of a Contract is plainly seen in the history of jurisprudence. First one or two steps in the ceremonial are dispensed with; then the others are simplified or permitted to be neglected on certain conditions; lastly, a few specific contracts are separated from the rest and allowed to be entered into without form, the selected contracts being those on which the activity and energy of social intercourse depend. Slowly, but most distinctly, the mental engagement isolates itself amid the technicalities, and gradually becomes the sole ingredient on which the interest of the jurisconsult is concentrated. Such a mental engage-ment, signified through external acts, the Romans called a Pact or Convention; and when the Conven-tion has once been conceived as the nucleus of a Contract, it soon becomes the tendency of advancing jurisprudence to break away the external shell of form and ceremony. Forms are thenceforward only retained so far as they are guarantees of authenticity, and securities for caution and deliberation. The idea of a Contract is fully developed, or, to employ the Roman phrase, Contracts are absorbed in Pacts.

The history of this course of change in Roman law is exceedingly instructive. At the earliest dawn

of the jurisprudence, the term in use for a Contract
was one which is very familiar to the students of
historical Latinity. It was *nexum*, and the parties
to the contract were said to be *nexi*, expressions
which must be carefully attended to on account of
the singular durableness of the metaphor on which
they are founded. The notion that persons under
a contractual engagement are connected together by
a strong *bond* or *chain*, continued till the last to
influence the Roman jurisprudence of Contract; and
flowing thence it has mixed itself with modern ideas.
What then was involved in this nexum or bond?
A definition which has descended to us from one of
the Latin antiquarians describes *nexum* as *omne quod
geritur per æs et libram*, " every transaction with
the copper and the balance," and these words have
occasioned a good deal of perplexity. The copper
and the balance are the well-known accompaniments
of the Mancipation, the ancient solemnity described
in a former chapter, by which the right of owner
ship in the highest form of Roman Property was
transferred from one person to another. Mancipation was a *conveyance*, and hence has arisen the
difficulty, for the definition thus cited appears to
confound Contracts and Conveyances, which in the
philosophy of jurisprudence are not simply kept
apart, but are actually opposed to each other. The
jus in re, right *in rem*, right " availing against all
the world," or Proprietary Right, is sharply distinguished by the analyst of mature jurisprudence from

the *jus ad rem*, right *in personam*, right " availing against a single individual or group," or Obligation. Now Conveyances transfer Proprietary Rights, Contracts create Obligations—how then can the two be included under the same name or same general conception? This, like many similar embarrassments, has been occasioned by the error of ascribing to the mental condition of an unformed society a faculty which pre-eminently belongs to an advanced stage of intellectual development, the faculty of distinguishing in speculation ideas which are blended in practice. We have indications not to be mistaken of a state of social affairs in which Conveyances and Contracts were practically confounded; nor did the discrepance of the conceptions become perceptible till men had begun to adopt a distinct practice in contracting and conveying.

It may here be observed that we know enough of ancient Roman law to give some idea of the mode of transformation followed by legal conceptions and by legal phraseology in the infancy of Jurisprudence. The change which they undergo appears to be a change from general to special; or, as we might otherwise express it, the ancient conceptions and the ancient terms are subjected to a process of gradual specialisation. An ancient legal conception corresponds not to one but to several modern conceptions. An ancient technical expression serves to indicate a variety of things which in modern law have separate names allotted to them. If, however, we take up the history of Jurisprudence at the next stage, we find that the subordinate conceptions have gradually disengaged themselves, and that the old general names are giving way to special appellations. The old general conception is not obliterated, but it has ceased to cover more than one or a few of the notions which it first included. So too the old technical name remains, but it discharges only one of the functions which it once performed. We may exemplify this phenomenon in various ways. Patriarchal Power of all sorts appears, for instance, to have been once conceived as identical in character, and it was doubtless distinguished by one name. The Power exercised by the ancestor was the same whether it was exercised over the family or the material property—over flocks, herds, slaves, children, or wife. We cannot be absolutely certain of its old Roman name, but there is very strong reason for believing, from the number of expressions indicating shades of the notion of *power* into which the word *manus* enters, that the ancient general term was *manus*. But, when Roman law has advanced a little, both the name and the idea have become specialised. Power is discriminated, both in word and in conception, according to the object over which it is exerted. Exercised over material commodities or slaves, it has become *dominium*—over children it is *Potestas* —over free persons whose services have been made away to another by their own ancestor, it is *mancipium*—over a wife, it is still *manus*. The old

word, it will be perceived, has not altogether fallen
into desuetude, but is confined to one very special
exercise of the authority it had formerly denoted.
This example will enable us to comprehend the
nature of the historical alliance between Contracts
and Conveyances. There seems to have been one
solemn ceremonial at first for all solemn transactions,
and its name at Rome appears to have been *nexum.*
Precisely the same forms which were in use when
a conveyance of property was effected seem to have
been employed in the making of a contract. But
we have not very far to move onwards before we
come to a period at which the notion of a Contract
has disengaged itself from the notion of a Conveyance. A double change has thus taken place. The
transaction " with the copper and the balance," when
intended to have for its office the transfer of property, is known by the new and special name of
Mancipation. The ancient Nexum still designates
the same ceremony, but only when it is employed
for the special purpose of solemnising a contract.

When two or three legal conceptions are spoken
of as anciently blended in one, it is not intended to
imply that some one of the included notions may
not be older than the others, or, when those others
have been formed, may not greatly predominate over
and take precedence over them. The reason why
one legal conception continues so long to cover sev
eral conceptions, and one technical phrase to do
instead of several, is doubtless that practical changes

are accomplished in the law of primitive societies long before men see occasion to notice or name them. Though I have said that Patriarchal Power was not at first distinguished according to the objects over which it was exercised, I feel sure that Power over Children was the root of the old conception of Power; and I cannot doubt that the earliest use of the Nexum, and the one primarily regarded by those who resorted to it, was to give proper solemnity to the alienation of property. It is likely that a very slight perversion of the Nexum from its original functions first gave rise to its employment in Contracts, and that the very slightness of the change long prevented its being appreciated or noticed. The old name remained because men had not become conscious that they wanted a new one; the old notion clung to the mind because nobody had seen reason to be at the pains of examining it. We have had the process clearly exemplified in the history of Testaments. A Will was at first a simple conveyance of Property. It was only the enormous practical difference that gradually showed itself between this particular conveyance and all others which caused it to be regarded separately, and even as it was, centuries elapsed before the ameliorators of law cleared away the useless encumbrance of the nominal mancipation, and consented to care for nothing in the Will but the expressed intentions of the Testator. It is unfortunate that we cannot track the early history of Contracts with

the same absolute confidence as the early history of
Wills, but we are not quite without hints that contracts first showed themselves through the *nexum*
being put to a new use and afterwards obtained
recognition as distinct transactions through the im
portant practical consequences of the experiment.
There is some, but not very violent, conjecture in
the following delineation of the process. Let us
conceive a sale for ready money as the normal type
of the Nexum. The seller brought the property of
which he intended to dispose—a slave, for example
—the purchaser attended with the rough ingots of
copper which served for money—and an indispensable assistant, the *libripens*, presented himself with a
pair of scales. The slave with certain fixed formalities was handed over to the vendee—the copper
was weighed by the *libripens* and passed to the vendor. So long as the business lasted it was a *nexum*,
and the parties were *nexi;* but the moment it was
completed, the *nexum* ended, and the vendor and
purchaser ceased to bear the name derived from
their momentary relation. But now, let us move a
step onward in commercial history. Suppose the
slave transferred, but the money not paid. In *that*
case the *nexum* is finished, so far as the seller is concerned, and when he has once handed over his property, he is no longer *nexus;* but, in regard to the
purchaser, the *nexum* continues. The transaction,
as to his part of it, is incomplete, and he is still considered to be *nexus*. It follows, therefore, that the

same term described the conveyance by which the right of property was transmitted, and the personal obligation of the debtor for the unpaid purchase-money. We may still go forward, and picture to ourselves a proceeding wholly formal, in which *nothing* is handed over and *nothing* paid ; we are brought at once to a transaction indicative of much higher commercial activity, an *executory Contract of Sale.*

If it be true that, both in the popular and in the professional view, a *Contract* was long regarded as an *incomplete Conveyance*, the truth has importance for many reasons. The speculations of the last century concerning mankind in a state of nature, are not unfairly summed up in the doctrine that "in the primitive society property was nothing, and obligation everything;" and it will now be seen that, if the proposition were reversed, it would be nearer the reality. On the other hand, considered historically, the primitive association of Conveyances and Contracts explains something which often strikes the scholar and jurist as singularly enigmatical, I mean the extraordinary and uniform severity of very ancient systems of law to *debtors*, and the extravagant powers which they lodge with *creditors*. When once we understand that the *nexum* was artificially prolonged to give time to the debtor, we can better comprehend his position in the eye of the public and of the law. His indebtedness was doubtless regarded as an anomaly, and suspense of payment in general as an artifice and a distortion of strict rule. The person who had duly consummated his part in the transaction must, on the contrary, have stood in peculiar favour; and nothing would seem more natural than to arm him with stringent facilities for enforcing the completion of a proceeding which, of strict right, ought never to have been extended or deferred.

Nexum, therefore, which originally signified a Conveyance of property, came insensibly to denote a Contract also, and ultimately so constant became the association between this word and the notion of a Contract, that a special term, Mancipium or Mancipatio, had to be used for the purpose of designating the true nexum or transaction in which the property was really transferred. Contracts are therefore now severed from Conveyances, and the first stage in their history is accomplished, but still they are far enough from that epoch of their development when the promise of the contractor has a higher sacredness than the formalities with which it is coupled. In attempting to indicate the character of the changes passed through in this interval, it is necessary to tres-pass a little on a subject which lies properly beyond the range of these pages, the analysis of Agreement effected by the Roman jurisconsults. Of this analy-sis, the most beautiful monument of their sagacity, I need not say more than that it is based on the theoretical separation of the Obligation from the Convention or Pact. Bentham and Mr. Austin have laid down that the "two main essentials of a contract are these : first, a signification by the promis-ing party of his *intention* to do the acts or to observe the forbearances which he promises to do or to ob-serve. Secondly, a signification by the promisee that he *expects* the promising party will fulfil the prof ferred promise." This is virtually identical with the doctrine of the Roman lawyers, but then, in their view, the result of these "significations" was not a Contract, but a Convention or Pact. A Pact was the utmost product of the engagements of indi-viduals agreeing among themselves, and it distinctly fell short of a Contract. Whether it ultimately be-came a Contract depended on the question whether the law annexed an Obligation to it. A Contract was a Pact (or Convention) *plus* an Obligation. So long as the Pact remained unclothed with the Obli-gation, it was called *nude* or *naked*.

What was an Obligation ? It is defined by the Roman lawyers as "Juris vinculum, quo necessitate adstringimur alicujus solvendæ rei." This definition connects the Obligation with the Nexum through the common metaphor on which they are founded, and shows us with much clearness the pedigree of a peculiar conception. The obligation is the "bond" or "chain," with which the law joins together per-sons or groups of persons, in consequence of certain voluntary acts. The acts which have the effect of attracting an Obligation are chiefly those classed under the heads of Contract and Delict, of Agree-

ment and Wrong; but a variety of other acts have
a similar consequence which are not capable of being comprised in an exact classification. It is to be
remarked, however, that the Pact does not draw to
itself the Obligation in consequence of any moral
necessity; it is the law which annexes it in the pleni-
tude of its power, a point the more necessary to be
noted, because a different doctrine has sometimes
been propounded by modern interpreters of the
Civil Law who had moral or metaphysical theories
of their own to support. The image of a *vinculum
juris* colours and pervades every part of the Roman
law of Contract and Delict. The law bound the
parties together, and the *chain* could only be un-
done by the process called *solutio*, an expression still
figurative, to which our word "payment" is only
occasionally and incidentally equivalent. The consistency with which the figurative image was allowed
to present itself, explains an otherwise puzzling peculiarity of Roman legal phraseology, the fact that
"Obligation" signifies rights as well as duties, the
right, for example, to have a debt paid as well as
the duty of paying it. The Romans kept, in fact,
the entire picture of the "legal chain" before their
eyes, and regarded one end of it no more and no
less than the other.

In the developed Roman law, the Convention, as
soon as it was completed, was, in almost all cases, at
once crowned with the Obligation, and so became a
Contract; and this was the result to which contract-

law was surely tending. But for the purpose of this inquiry, we must attend particularly to the inter-mediate stage—that in which something more than a perfect agreement was required to attract the Ob-ligation. This epoch is synchronous with the period at which the famous Roman classification of Con-tracts into four sorts—the Verbal, the Literal, the Real, and the Consensual—had come into use, and during which these four orders of Contract consti-tuted the only descriptions of engagement which the law would enforce. The meaning of the fourfold dis-tribution is readily understood as soon as we appre-hend the theory which severed the Obligation from the Convention. Each class of contracts was in fact named from certain formalities which were required over and above the mere agreement of the contract-ing parties. In the Verbal Contract, as soon as the Convention was effected, a form of words had to be gone through before the vinculum juris was attached to it. In the Literal Contract, an entry in a ledger or table-book had the effect of clothing the Convention with the Obligation, and the same result followed, in the case of the Real Contract, from the delivery of the Res or Thing which was the subject of the preliminary engagement. The Contracting parties came, in short, to an understanding in each case; but, if they went no further, they were not *obliged* to one another, and could not compel performance or ask redress for a breach of faith. But let them comply with certain prescribed formalities, and the

Contract was immediately complete, taking its name
from the particular form which it had suited them
to adopt. The exceptions to this practice will be
noticed presently.

I have enumerated the four Contracts in their
historical order, which order, however, the Roman
Institutional writers did not invariably follow. There
can be no doubt that the Verbal Contract was the
most ancient of the four, and that it is the eldest
known descendant of the primitive Nexum. Several
species of Verbal Contract were anciently in use, but
the most important of all, and the only one treated
of by our authorities, was effected by means of a
stipulation, that is, a Question and Answer; a question addressed by the person who exacted the promise,
and an answer given by the person who made it.
This question and answer constituted the additional
ingredient which, as I have just explained, was demanded by the primitive notion over and above th
mere agreement of the persons interested. They
formed the agency by which the Obligation was annexed. The old Nexum has now bequeathed to
maturer jurisprudence first of all the conception
of a chain uniting the contracting parties, and this
has become the Obligation. It has further transmitted the notion of a ceremonial accompanying and
consecrating the engagement, and this ceremonial
has been transmuted into the Stipulation. The conversion of the solemn conveyance, which was the
prominent feature of the original Nexum, into a

mere question and answer, would be more of a mystery than it is if we had not the analogous history
of Roman Testaments to enlighten us. Looking at
that history, we can understand how the formal conveyance was first separated from the part of the
proceeding which had immediate reference to the
business in hand, and how afterwards it was omitted altogether. As then the question and answer of
the Stipulation were unquestionably the Nexum in
a simplified shape, we are prepared to find that they
long partook of the nature of a technical term. It
would be a mistake to consider them exclusively re-
commending themselves to the older Roman lawyers
through their usefulness in furnishing persons meditating an agreement with an opportunity for consideration and reflection. It is not to be disputed that
they had a value of this kind, which was gradually recognised; but there is proof that their function
in respect to Contracts was at first formal and ceremonial in the statement of authorities, that not every
question and answer was of old sufficient to constitute a Stipulation, but only a question and answer
couched in technical phraseology specially appropriated to the particular occasion.

But although it is essential for the proper appreciation of the history of contract-law that the Stipulation should be understood to have been looked
upon as a solemn form before it was recognised as a
useful security, it would be wrong on the other hand
to shut our eyes to its real usefulness. The Verbal

Contract, though it had lost much of its ancient im
portance, survived to the latest period of Roman
jurisprudence; and we may take it for granted that
no institution of Roman law had so extended a lon-
gevity unless it served some practical advantage
I observe in an English writer some expressions of
surprise that the Romans even of the earliest times
were content with so meagre a protection against
haste and irreflection.   But on examining the Stipu
lation closely, and remembering that we have to do
with a state of society in which written evidence
was not easily procurable, I think we must admit
that this Question and Answer, had it been expressly
devised to answer the purpose which it served, would
have been justly designated a highly ingenious expedient.   It was the *promisee* who, in the character
of stipulator, put all the terms of the contract into
the form of a question, and the answer was given by
the *promisor*.   " Do you promise that you will de-
liver me such and such a slave, at such and such a
place, on such and such a day ? "   " I do promise."
Now, if we reflect for a moment, we shall see that
this obligation to put the promise interrogatively
inverts the natural position of the parties, and, by
effectually breaking the tenor of the conversation,
prevents the attention from gliding over a dangerous
pledge.   With us, a verbal promise is, generally
speaking, to be gathered exclusively from the words
of the promisor.   In old Roman law, another step
was absolutely required; it was necessary for the

promisee, after the agreement had been made, to
sum up all its terms in a solemn interrogation ; and
it was of this interrogation, of course, and of the
assent to it, that proof had to be given at the trial
—*not* of the promise, which was not in itself bind
ing. How great a difference this seemingly insignificant peculiarity may make in the phraseology of
contract-law is speedily realised by the beginner in
Roman jurisprudence, one of whose first stumbling
blocks is almost universally created by it. When
we in English have occasion, in mentioning a contract, to connect it for convenience' sake with one
of the parties,—for example, if we wished to speak
generally of a contractor,—it is always the promis*or*
at whom our words are pointing. But the general
language of Roman law takes a different turn ; it
always regards the contract, if we may so speak,
from the point of view of the promis*ee* ; in speaking
of a party to a contract, it is always the Stipulator,
the person who asks the question, who is primarily
alluded to. But the serviceableness of the stipulation is most vividly illustrated by referring to the
actual examples in the pages of the Latin comic
dramatists. If the entire scenes are read down in
which these passages occur (ex. gra. Plautus, *Pseu-
dolus*, Act I. sc. 1 ; Act IV. sc. 6 ; *Trinummus*, Act
V. sc. 2), it will be perceived how effectually the attention of the person meditating the promise must
have been arrested by the question, and how ample

was the opportunity for withdrawal from an improvident undertaking.

In the Literal or Written Contract, the formal
act by which an Obligation was superinduced on
the Convention, was an entry of the sum due, where
it could be specifically ascertained, on the debit side
of a ledger. The explanation of this contract turns
on a point of Roman domestic manners, the systematic character and exceeding regularity of book-
keeping in ancient times. There are several minor
difficulties of old Roman law, as, for example, the
nature of the Slave's Peculium, which are only
cleared up when we recollect that a Roman household consisted of a number of persons strictly ac-
countable to its head, and that every single item of
domestic receipt and expenditure, after being entered
in waste books, was transferred at stated periods to
a general household ledger. There are some obscu-
rities, however, in the descriptions we have received
of the Literal Contract, the fact being that the habit
of keeping books ceased to be universal in later
times, and the expression " Literal Contract," came
to signify a form of engagement entirely different
from that originally understood. We are not, therefore, in a position to say, with respect to the primitive Literal Contract, whether the obligation was
created by a simple entry on the part of the creditor
or whether the consent of the debtor or a correspond
ent entry in his own books was necessary to give it
legal effect. The essential point is however estab-

lished, that, in the case of this Contract, all formalities were dispensed with on a condition being com
plied with. This is another step downwards in the
history of contract-law.

The Contract which stands next in historical
succession, the Real Contract, shows a great advance
in ethical conceptions. Whenever any agreement
had for its object the delivery of a specific thing—
and this is the case with the large majority of simple
engagements—the Obligation was drawn down as
soon as the delivery had actually taken place. Such
a result must have involved a serious innovation on
the oldest ideas of Contract; for doubtless, in the
primitive times, when a contracting party had neglected to clothe his agreement in a stipulation, nothing done in pursuance of the agreement would be
recognised by the law. A person who had paid
over money on loan would be unable to sue for its
repayment unless he had formally *stipulated* for it.
But, in the Real Contract, performance on one side
is allowed to impose a legal duty on the other—
evidently on ethical grounds. For the first time
then moral considerations appear as an ingredient
in Contract-law, and the Real Contract differs from
its two predecessors in being founded on these, rather
than on respect for technical forms or on deference
to Roman domestic habits.

We now reach the fourth class, or Consensual
Contracts, the most interesting and important of all.
Four specified Contracts were distinguished by this

name : Mandatum, *i. e.* Commission or Agency; Societas or Partnership ; Emtio Venditio or Sale ; and Locatio Conductio or Letting and Hiring. A few pages back, after stating that a Contract consisted of a Pact or Convention to which an Obligation had been superadded, I spoke of certain acts or formalities by which the law permitted the Obligation to be attracted to the Pact. I used this language on account of the advantage of a general expression, but it is not strictly correct unless it be understood to include the negative as well as the positive. For, in truth, the peculiarity of these Consensual Contracts is that *no* formalities are required to create them out of the Pact. Much that is indefensible, and much more that is obscure, has been written about the Consensual Contracts, and it has even been asserted that in them the *consent* of the Parties is more emphatically given than in any other species of agreement. But the term Consensual merely indicates that the Obligation is here annexed at once to the *Consensus.* The Consensus, or mutual assent of the parties, is the final and crowning ingredient in the Convention, and it is the special characteristic of agreements falling under one of the four heads of Sale, Partnership, Agency, and Hiring, that, as soon as the assent of the parties has supplied this ingredient, there is *at once* a Contract. The Consensus draws with it the Obligation, performing, in transactions of the sort specified, the exact functions which are discharged, in the other contracts, by the

Res or Thing, by the *Verba* stipulationis, and by the *Literæ* or written entry in a ledger. Consensual is therefore a term which does not involve the slightest anomaly, but is exactly analogous to Real, Verbal, and Literal.

In the intercourse of life the commonest and most important of all the contracts are unquestiona bly the four styled Consensual. The larger part of the collective existence of every community is consumed in transactions of buying and selling, of letting and hiring, of alliances between men for purposes of business, of delegation of business from one man to another; and this is no doubt the consideration which led the Romans, as it has led most societies, to relieve these transactions from technical incumbrance, to abstain as much as possible from clogging the most efficient springs of social movement. Such motives were not of course confined to Rome, and the commerce of the Romans with their neighbours must have given them abundant opportunities for observing that the contracts before us tended everywhere to become *Consensual*, obligatory on the mere signification of mutual assent. Hence, following their usual practice, they distinguished these contracts as contracts *Juris Gentium.* Yet I do not think that they were so named at a very early period. The first notions of a Jus Gentium may have been deposited in the minds of the Roman lawyers long before the appointment of a Prætor Peregrinus, but it would only be through

extensive and regular trade that they would be
familiarised with the contractual system of other
Italian communities, and such a trade would scarcely
attain considerable proportions before Italy had
been thoroughly pacified, and the supremacy of
Rome conclusively assured. Although, however,
there is strong probability that the Consensual Contracts were the latest-born into the Roman system,
and though it is likely that the qualification, *Juris
Gentium*, stamps the recency of their origin, yet
this very expression, which attributes them to the
" Law of Nations," has in modern times produced
the notion of their extreme antiquity. For, when
the " Law of Nations " had been converted into the
" Law of Nature," it seemed to be implied that the
Consensual Contracts were the type of the agreements most congenial to the natural state ; and hence
arose the singular belief that the younger the civilisation, the simpler must be its forms of contract.

The Consensual Contracts, it will be observed,
were extremely limited in number. But it cannot
be doubted that they constituted the stage in the
history of Contract-law from which all modern conceptions of contract took their start. The motion
of the will which constitutes agreement was now
completely insulated, and became the subject of separate contemplation ; forms were entirely elimina-
ted from the notion of contract, and external acts
were only regarded as symbols of the internal act
of volition. The Consensual Contracts had, more-

over, been classed in the Jus Gentium, and it was
long before this classification drew with it the inference that they were the species of agreement which
represented the engagements approved of by Nature
and included in her code.   This point once reached,
we are prepared for several celebrated doctrines and
distinctions of the Roman lawyers.   One of them is
the distinction between Natural and Civil Obligations.   When a person of full intellectual maturity
had deliberately bound himself by an engagement,
he was said to be under a *natural obligation*, even
though he had omitted some necessary formality, and
even though through some technical impediment he
was devoid of the formal capacity for making a valid
contract.   The law (and this is what the distinction implies) would not enforce the obligation, but
it did not absolutely refuse to recognise it; and *natural obligations* differed in many respects from obligations which were merely null and void, more particularly in the circumstance that they could be
civilly confirmed, if the capacity for contract were
subsequently acquired.   Another very peculiar doctrine of the jurisconsults could not have had its origin earlier than the period at which the Convention
was severed from the technical ingredients of Contract.   They taught that though nothing but a Contract could be the foundation of an *action*, a mere
Pact or Convention could be the basis of a *plea*.   It
followed from this, that though nobody could sue
upon an agreement which he had not taken the pre

caution to mature into a Contract by complying with the proper forms, nevertheless a claim arising out of a valid contract could be rebutted by proving a counter-agreement which had never got beyond the state of a simple convention. An action for the recovery of a debt could be met by showing a mere informal agreement to waive or postpone the payment.

The doctrine just stated indicates the hesitation of the Prætors in making their advances towards the greatest of their innovations. Their theory of Natural law must have led them to look with especial favour on the Consensual Contracts and on those Pacts or Conventions of which the Consensual Contracts were only particular instances; but they did not at once venture on extending to all Conventions the liberty of the Consensual Contracts. They took advantage of that special superintendence over procedure which had been confided to them since the first beginnings of Roman law, and, while they still declined to permit a suit to be launched which was not based on a formal contract, they gave full play to their new theory of agreement in directing the ulterior stages of the proceeding. But when they had proceeded thus far, it was inevitable that they should proceed farther. The revolution of the ancient law of Contract was consummated when the Prætor of some one year announced in his Edict that he would grant equitable actions upon Pacts which had never been matured at all into Contracts, provided only that the Pacts in question had been founded on a

consideration (*causa*). Pacts of this sort are always
enforced under the advanced Roman jurisprudence
The principle is merely the principle of the Consensual Contract carried to its proper consequence;
and, in fact, if the technical language of the Romans
had been as plastic as their legal theories, these
Pacts enforced by the Prætor would have been
styled new Contracts, new Consensual Contracts.
Legal phraseology is, however, the part of the law
which is the last to alter, and the Pacts equitably
enforced continued to be designated simply Prætorian Pacts. It will be remarked that unless there
were consideration for the Pact, it would continue
nude so far as the new jurisprudence was concerned;
in order to give it effect, it would be necessary to
convert it by a stipulation into a Verbal Contract.

The extreme importance of this history of Contract, as a safeguard against almost innumerable
delusions, must be my justification for discussing it
at so considerable a length. It gives a complete
account of the march of ideas from one great land-
mark of jurisprudence to another. We begin with
the Nexum, in which a Contract and a Conveyance
are blended, and in which the formalities which ac
company the agreement are even more important
than the agreement itself. From the Nexum we
pass to the Stipulation, which is a simplified form of
the older ceremonial. The Literal Contract comes
next and here all formalities are waived, if proof
of the agreement can be supplied from the rigid

observances of a Roman household. In the Real
Contract a moral duty is for the first time recognised,
and persons who have joined or acquiesced in the
partial performance of an engagement are forbidden
to repudiate it on account of defects in form. Lastly,
the Consensual Contracts emerge, in which the mental attitude of the contractors is solely regarded,
and external circumstances have no title to notice
except as evidence of the inward undertaking. It is
of course uncertain how far this progress of Roman
ideas from a gross to a refined conception exemplifies
the necessary progress of human thought on the subject of Contract. The Contract-law of all other
ancient societies but the Roman is either too scanty
to furnish information, or else is entirely lost; and
modern jurisprudence is so thoroughly leavened with
the Roman notions that it furnishes us with no contrasts or parallels from which instruction can be
gleaned. From the absence, however, of everything
violent, marvellous, or unintelligible in the changes
I have described, it may be reasonably believed that
the history of Ancient Roman Contracts is, up to a
certain point, typical of the history of this class of
legal conceptions in other ancient societies. But it
is only up to a certain point that the progress of
Roman law can be taken to represent the progress
of other systems of jurisprudence. The theory of
Natural law is exclusively Roman. The notion of
the *vinculum juris*, so far as my knowledge extends,
is exclusively Roman. The many peculiarities of

the mature Roman law of Contract and Delict which
are traceable to these two ideas, whether singly or
in combination, are therefore among the exclusive
products of one particular society. These later legal
conceptions are important, not because they typify
the necessary results of advancing thought under all
conditions, but because they have exercised perfectly
enormous influence on the intellectual diathesis of
the modern world.

I know nothing more wonderful than the variety
of sciences to which Roman law, Roman Contract-
law more particularly, has contributed modes of
thought, courses of reasoning, and a technical language. Of the subjects which have whetted the
intellectual appetite of the moderns, there is scarcely
one, except Physics, which has not been filtered
through Roman jurisprudence. The science of pure
Metaphysics had, indeed, rather a Greek than a
Roman parentage, but Politics, Moral Philosophy,
and even Theology, found in Roman law not only a
vehicle of expression, but a nidus in which some of
their profoundest inquiries were nourished into maturity. For the purpose of accounting for this phenomenon, it is not absolutely necessary to discuss the
mysterious relation between words and ideas, or to
explain how it is that the human mind has never
grappled with any subject of thought, unless it has
been provided beforehand with a proper store of
language and with an apparatus of appropriate
logical methods. It is enough to remark, that,

when the philosophical interests of the Eastern and
Western worlds were separated, the founders of
Western thought belonged to a society which spoke
Latin and reflected in Latin. But in the Western
provinces the only language which retained sufficient
precision for philosophical purposes was the language of Roman law, which by a singular fortune
had preserved nearly all the purity of the Augustan
age, while vernacular Latin was degenerating into
a dialect of portentous barbarism. And if Roman
jurisprudence supplied the only means of exactness
in speech, still more emphatically did it furnish
the only means of exactness, subtlety, or depth in
thought. For at least three centuries, philosophy
and science were without a home in the West; and
though metaphysics and metaphysical theology were
engrossing the mental energies of multitudes of
Roman subjects, the phraseology employed in these
ardent inquiries was exclusively Greek, and their
theatre was the Eastern half of the Empire. Sometimes, indeed, the conclusions of the Eastern disputants became so important that every man's assent
to them, or dissent from them, had to be recorded,
and then the West was introduced to the results of
Eastern controversy, which it generally acquiesced
in without interest and without resistance. Meanwhile, one department of inquiry, difficult enough
for the most laborious, deep enough for the most
subtle, delicate enough for the most refined, had
never lost its attractions for the educated classes of

the Western provinces.   To the cultivated citizen of
Africa, of Spain, of Gaul, and of Northern Italy
it was jurisprudence, and jurisprudence only, which
stood in the place of poetry and history, of philosophy and science.   So far then from there being anything mysterious in the palpably legal complexion
of the earliest efforts of Western thought, it would
rather be astonishing if it had assumed any other
hue.   I can only express my surprise at the scantiness of the attention which has been given to the
difference between Western ideas and Eastern, between Western theology and Eastern, caused by the
presence of a new ingredient.   It is precisely because the influence of jurisprudence begins to be
powerful that the foundation of Constantinople and
the subsequent separation of the Western empire
from the Eastern, are epochs in philosophical history.
But continental thinkers are doubtless less capable
of appreciating the importance of this crisis by the
very intimacy with which notions derived from Roman law are mingled up with their every-day ideas.
Englishmen, on the other hand, are blind to it
through the monstrous ignorance to which they con-
demn themselves of the most plentiful source of the
stream of modern knowledge, of the one intellectual
result of the Roman civilisation.   At the same time,
an Englishman, who will be at the pains to familiar-
ise himself with the classical Roman law, is perhaps,
from the very slightness of the interest which his
countrymen have hitherto taken in the subject, a

better judge than a Frenchman or German of the
value of the assertions I have ventured to make
Anybody who knows what Roman jurisprudence is
as actually practised by the Romans, and who will
observe in what characteristics the earliest Western
theology and philosophy differ from the phases of
thought which preceded them, may be safely left to
pronounce what was the new element which had begun to pervade and govern speculation.

The part of Roman law which has had most extensive influence on foreign subjects of inquiry has
been the law of Obligation, or, what comes nearly
to the same thing, of Contract and Delict. The
Romans themselves were not unaware of the offices
which the copious and malleable terminology belonging to this part of their system might be made to
discharge, and this is proved by their employment
of the peculiar adjunct *quasi* in such expressions as
Quasi-Contract and Quasi-Delict. " Quasi," so used,
is exclusively a term of classification. It has been
usual with English critics to identify the quasi-contracts with *implied* contracts, but this is an error, for
implied contracts are true contracts, which quasi-
contracts are not. In implied contracts, acts and
circumstances are the symbols of the same ingredients which are symbolised, in express contracts,
by words; and whether a man employs one set of
symbols or the other must be a matter of indifference so far as concerns the theory of agreement.
But a Quasi-Contract is not a contract at all. The

commonest sample of the class is the relation sub-
sisting between two persons, one of whom has paid
money to the other through mistake. The law,
consulting the interests of morality, imposes an obligation on the receiver to refund, but the very nature of the transaction indicates that it is not a
contract, inasmuch as the Convention, the most
essential ingredient of Contract, is wanting. This
word "quasi," prefixed to a term of Roman law, implies that the conception to which it serves as an
index is connected with the conception with which
the comparison is instituted by a strong superficial
analogy or resemblance. It does not denote that
the two conceptions are the same, or that they belong to the same genus. On the contrary, it nega-
tives the notion of an identity between them; but
it points out that they are sufficiently similar for one
to be classed as the sequel to the other, and that the
phraseology taken from one department of law may
be transferred to the other, and employed without
violent straining in the statement of rules which
would otherwise be imperfectly expressed.

It has been shrewdly remarked, that the confusion between Implied Contracts, which are true
contracts, and Quasi-Contracts, which are not contracts at all, has much in common with the famous
error which attributed political rights and duties to
an Original Compact between the governed and the
governor. Long before this theory had clothed
itself in definite shape, the phraseology of Roman

contract-law had been largely drawn upon to describe that reciprocity of rights and duties which men had always conceived as existing between sovereigns and subjects. While the world was full of maxims setting forth with the utmost positiveness the claims of kings to implicit obedience—maxims which pre tended to have had their origin in the New Testament, but which were really derived from indelible recollections of the Cæsarian despotism—the consciousness of correlative rights possessed by the governed would have been entirely without the means of expression if the Roman law of Obligation had not supplied a language capable of shadowing forth an idea which was as yet imperfectly developed. The antagonism between the privileges of kings and their duties to their subjects was never, I believe, lost sight of since Western history began, but it had interest for few except speculative writers so long as feudalism continued in vigour, for feudalism effectually controlled by express customs the exorbitant theoretical pretensions of most European sovereigns. It is notorious, however, that as soon as the decay of the Feudal System had thrown the mediæval constitutions out of working order, and when the Reformation had discredited the authority of the Pope, the doctrine of the divine right of Kings rose immediately into an importance which had never before attended it. The vogue which it obtained entailed still more constant resort to the phraseology of Roman law, and a controversy which

had originally worn a theological aspect assumed
more and more the air of a legal disputation. A
phenomenon then appeared which has repeatedly
shown itself in the history of opinion. Just when
the argument for monarchical authority rounded
itself into the definite doctrine of Filmer, the phraseology, borrowed from the Law of Contract, which
had been used in defence of the rights of subjects,
crystallised into the theory of an actual original
compact between king and people, a theory which,
first in English and afterwards, and more particularly, in French hands, expanded into a comprehensive explanation of all the phenomena of society and
law. But the only real connection between political
and legal science had consisted in the last giving to
the first the benefit of its peculiarly plastic terminology. The Roman jurisprudence of Contract had
performed for the relation of sovereign and subject
precisely the same service which, in a humbler
sphere, it rendered to the relation of persons bound
together by an obligation of " quasi-contract." It
had furnished a body of words and phrases which
approximated with sufficient accuracy to the ideas
which then were from time to time forming on the
subject of political obligation. The doctrine of an
Original Compact can never be put higher than it is
placed by Dr. Whewell, when he suggests that,
though unsound, "it may be a *convenient* form for
the expression of moral truths."

The extensive employment of legal language on

political subjects previously to the invention of the
Original Compact, and the powerful influence which
that assumption has exercised subsequently, amply
account for the plentifulness in political science of
words and conceptions, which were the exclusive
creation of Roman jurisprudence. Of their plentifulness in Moral Philosophy a rather different explanation must be given, inasmuch as ethical writings
have laid Roman law under contribution much more
directly than political speculations, and their authors
have been much more conscious of the extent of
their obligation. In speaking of moral philosophy
as extraordinarily indebted to Roman jurisprudence,
I must be understood to intend moral philosophy
as understood previously to the break in its history
effected by Kant, that is, as the science of the rules
governing human conduct, of their proper interpretation and of the limitations to which they are subject. Since the rise of the Critical Philosophy, moral
science has almost wholly lost its older meaning,
and, except where it is preserved under a debased
form in the casuistry still cultivated by Roman
Catholic theologians, it seems to be regarded nearly
universally as a branch of ontological inquiry. I do
not know that there is a single contemporary English writer, with the exception of Dr. Whewell, who
understands moral philosophy as it was understood
before it was absorbed by metaphysics and before
the groundwork of its rules came to be a more important consideration than the rules themselves. So

long, however, as ethical science had to do with the
practical regimen of conduct, it was more or less
saturated with Roman law.   Like all the great sub·
jects of modern thought, it was originally incorporated with theology.   The science of Moral Theology
as it was at first called, and as it is still designated
by the Roman Catholic divines, was undoubtedly
constructed, to the full knowledge of its authors, by
taking principles of conduct from the system of the
Church, and by using the language and methods of
jurisprudence for their expression and expansion.
While this process went on, it was inevitable that
jurisprudence, though merely intended to be the
vehicle of thought, should communicate its colour to
the thought itself.   The tinge received through con·
tact with legal conceptions is perfectly perceptible
in the earliest ethical literature of the modern world,
and it is evident, I think, that the Law of Contract,
based as it is on the complete reciprocity and indis
soluble connection of rights and duties, has acted as
a wholesome corrective to the predispositions of
writers who, if left to themselves, might have ex·
clusively viewed a moral obligation as the public
duty of a citizen in the Civitas Dei.   But the amount
of Roman Law in moral theology becomes sensibly
smaller at the time of its cultivation by the great
Spanish moralists.   Moral theology, developed by
the juridical method of doctor commenting on doctor,
provided itself with a phraseology of its own, and
Aristotelian peculiarities of reasoning and expres-

sion, imbibed doubtless in great part from the Disputations on Morals in the academical schools, take the place of that special turn of thought and speech which can never be mistaken by any person conversant with the Roman law. If the credit of the Spanish school of moral theologians had continued, the juridical ingredient in ethical science would have been insignificant, but the use made of their conclusions by the next generation of Roman Catholic writers on these subjects almost entirely destroyed their influence. Moral Theology, degraded into Casuistry, lost all interest for the leaders of European speculation; and the new science of Moral Philosophy, which was entirely in the hands of the Protestants, swerved greatly aside from the path which the moral theologians had followed. The effect was vastly to increase the influence of Roman law on ethical inquiry.

"Shortly * after the Reformation, we find two great schools of thought dividing this class of subjects between them. The most influential of the two was at first the sect or school known to us as the Casuists, all of them in spiritual communion with the Roman Catholic Church, and nearly all of them affiliated to one or other of her religious orders. On the other side were a body of writers connected with each other by a common intellectual descent from the great author of the treatise *De Jure Belli et*

* The passage quoted is transcribed, with slight alterations, from a paper contributed by the author to the *Cambridge Essays* for 1856.

Pacis, Hugo Grotius.   Almost all of the latter were
adherents of the Reformation ; and though it cannot
be said that they were formally and avowedly at
conflict with the Casuists, the origin and object of
their system were nevertheless essentially different
from those of Casuistry.   It is necessary to call attention to this difference, because it involves the
question of the influence of Roman law on that department of thought with which both systems are
concerned.   The book of Grotius, though it touches
questions of pure Ethics in every page, and though
it is the parent immediate or remote of innumerable volumes of formal morality, is not, as is well
known, a professed treatise on Moral Philosophy ; it
is an attempt to determine the Law of Nature, or
Natural Law.   Now, without entering upon the
question, whether the conception of a Law Natural
be not exclusively a creation of the Roman jurisconsults, we may lay down that, even on the admission
of Grotius himself, the dicta of the Roman jurisprudence as to what parts of known positive law must
be taken to be parts of the Law of Nature, are, if
not infallible, to be received at all events with the
profoundest respect.   Hence the system of Grotius
is implicated with Roman law at its very foundation,
and this connection rendered inevitable—what the
legal training of the writer would perhaps have entailed without it—the free employment in every
paragraph of technical phraseology, and of modes
of reasoning, defining, and illustrating, which must

sometimes conceal the sense, and almost always the force and cogency, of the argument from the reader who is unfamiliar with the sources whence they have been derived. On the other hand, Casuistry borrows little from Roman law, and the views of mo rality contended for have nothing whatever in com mon with the undertaking of Grotius. All that philosophy of right and wrong which has become famous, or infamous, under the name of Casuistry, had its origin in the distinction between Mortal and Venial sin. A natural anxiety to escape the awful consequences of determining a particular act to be mortally sinful, and a desire, equally intelligible, to assist the Roman Catholic Church in its conflict with Protestantism by disburthening it of an inconvenient theory, were the motives which impelled the authors of the Casuistical philosophy to the invention of an elaborate system of criteria, intended to remove immoral actions, in as many cases as possible, out of the category of mortal offences, and to stamp them as venial sins. The fate of this experiment is matter of ordinary history. We know that the distinctions of Casuistry, by enabling the priesthood to adjust spiritual control to all the varieties of human character, did really confer on it an influence with princes, statesmen, and generals, unheard of in the ages before the Reformation, and did really contribute largely to that great reaction which checked and narrowed the first successes of Protestantism. But beginning in the attempt, not to establish, but

to evade—not to discover a principle, but to escape
a postulate—not to settle the nature of right and
wrong, but to determine what was not wrong of a
particular nature,—Casuistry went on with its dex-
terous refinements till it ended in so attenuating the
moral features of actions, and so belying the moral
instincts of our being, that at length the conscience
of mankind rose suddenly in revolt against it, and
consigned to one common ruin the system and its
doctors. The blow, long pending, was finally struck
in the *Provincial Letters* of Pascal, and since the
appearance of those memorable Papers, no moralist
of the smallest influence or credit has ever avowedly
conducted his speculations in the footsteps of the
Casuists. The whole field of ethical science was
thus left at the exclusive command of the writers
who followed Grotius; and it still exhibits in an extraordinary degree the traces of that entanglement
with Roman law which is sometimes imputed as a
fault, and sometimes the highest of its recommendations, to the Grotian theory. Many inquirers since
Grotius's day have modified his principles, and many,
of course, since the rise of the critical philosophy,
have quite deserted them; but even those who have
departed most widely from his fundamental assumptions have inherited much of his method of statement, of his train of thought, and of his mode of
illustration; and these have little meaning and no
point to the person ignorant of Roman jur'spru
dence."

I have already said that, with the exception of the physical sciences, there is no walk of knowledge which has been so slightly affected by Roman law as Metaphysics. The reason is that discussion on metaphysical subjects has always been conducted in Greek, first in pure Greek, and afterwards in a dia lect of Latin expressly constructed to give expression to Greek conceptions. The modern languages have only been fitted to metaphysical inquiries by adopting this Latin dialect, or by imitating the process which was originally followed in its formation. The source of the phraseology which has been always employed for metaphysical discussion in modern times was the Latin translations of Aristotle, in which, whether derived or not from Arabic versions, the plan of the translator was not to seek for analogous expressions in any part of Latin literature, but to construct anew from Latin roots a set of phrases equal to the expression of Greek philosophical ideas. Over such a process the terminology of Roman law can have exercised little influence; at most, a few Latin law terms in a transmuted shape have made their way into metaphysical language. At the same time it is worthy of remark that whenever the problems of metaphysics are those which have been most strongly agitated in Western Europe, the thought, if not the language, betrays a legal parentage. Few things in the history of speculation are more im pressive than the fact that no Greek-speaking people has ever felt itself seriously perplexed by the great

question of Free-will and Necessity. I do not pretend to offer any summary explanation of this, but
it does not seem an irrelevant suggestion that neither
the Greeks, nor any society speaking and thinking
in their language, ever showed the smallest capacity
for producing a philosophy of law. Legal science
is a Roman creation, and the problem of Free-will
arises when we contemplate a metaphysical conception under a legal aspect. How came it to be a
question whether invariable sequence was identical
with necessary connection? I can only say that the
tendency of Roman law, which became stronger as
it advanced, was to look upon legal consequences as
united to legal causes by an inexorable necessity, a
tendency most markedly exemplified in the definition of Obligation which I have repeatedly cited,
" Juris vinculum quo necessitate adstringimur alicujus solvendæ rei."

But the problem of Free-will was theological before it became philosophical, and, if its terms have
been affected by jurisprudence, it will be because
Jurisprudence has made itself felt in Theology. The
great point of inquiry which is here suggested has
never been satisfactorily elucidated. What has to be
determined, is whether jurisprudence has ever served
as the medium through which theological principles
have been viewed; whether, by supplying a peculiar
language, a peculiar mode of reasoning and a peculiar solution of many of the problems of life, it has
ever opened new channels in which theological spec-

ulation could flow out and expand itself. For the purpose of giving an answer it is necessary to recol·lect what is already agreed upon by the best writers as to the intellectual food which theology first assimilated. It is conceded on all sides that the earliest language of the Christian Church was Greek, and that the problems to which it first addressed itself were those for which Greek philosophy in its later forms had prepared the way. Greek metaphysical literature contained the sole stock of words and ideas out of which the human mind could provide itself with the means of engaging in the profound controversies as to the Divine Persons, the Divine Substance, and the Divine Natures. The Latin language and the meagre Latin philosophy were quite unequal to the undertaking, and accordingly the Western or Latin speaking provinces of the Empire adopted the conclusions of the East without disputing or reviewing them. "Latin Christianity," says Dean Milman, "accepted the creed which its narrow and barren vocabulary could hardly express in adequate terms. Yet, throughout, the adhesion of Rome and the West was a passive acquiescence in the dogmatic system which had been wrought out by the profounder theology of the Eastern divines, rather than a vigorous and original examination on her part of those mysteries. The Latin Church was the scholar as well as the loyal partizan of Athanasius." But when the separation of East and West became wider, and the Latin-speaking Western Empire began to

live with an intellectual life of its own, its deference
to the East was all at once exchanged for the agita-
tion of a number of questions entirely foreign to
Eastern speculation. " While Greek theology (Milman, *Latin Christianity*, Preface, 5) went on defining with still more exquisite subtlety the Godhead
and the nature of Christ "—" while the interminable
controversy still lengthened out and cast forth sect
after sect from the enfeebled community "—the
Western Church threw itself with passionate ardour
into a new order of disputes, the same which from
those days to this have never lost their interest for
any family of mankind at any time included in the
Latin communion. The nature of Sin and its transmission by inheritance—the debt owed by man and its
vicarious satisfaction—the necessity and sufficiency
of the Atonement—above all the apparent antagonism between Free-will and the Divine Providence—
these were points which the West began to debate
as ardently as ever the East had discussed the articles of its more special creed.   Why is it then that
on the two sides of the line which divides the Greek-
speaking from the Latin-speaking provinces there lie
two classes of theological problems so strikingly different from one another?   The historians of the
Church have come close upon the solution when they
remark that the new problems were more " practical," less absolutely speculative, than those which
had torn Eastern Christianity asunder, but none of
them, so far as I am aware, has quite reached it.   I

affirm without hesitation that the difference between the two theological systems is accounted for by the fact that, in passing from the East to the West, theological peculation had passed from a climate of Greek metaphysics to a climate of Roman law. For some centuries before these controversies rose into overwhelming importance, all the intellectual activity of the Western Romans had been expended on jurisprudence exclusively. They had been occupied in applying a peculiar set of principles to all combinations in which the circumstances of life are capable of being arranged. No foreign pursuit or taste called off their attention from this engrossing occupation, and for carrying it on they possessed a vocabulary as accurate as it was copious, a strict method of reasoning, a stock of general propositions on conduct more or less verified by experience, and a rigid moral philosophy. It was impossible that they should not select from the questions indicated by the Christian records those which had some affinity with the order of speculations to which they were accustomed, and that their manner of dealing with them should borrow something from their forensic habits. Almost everybody who has knowledge enough of Roman law to appreciate the Roman penal system, the Roman theory of the obligations established by Contract or Delict, the Roman view of Debts and of the modes of incurring, extinguishing, and transmitting them, the Roman notion of the continuance of individual existence by Universal Succession, may be

trusted to say whence arose the frame of mind to
which the problems of Western theology proved so
congenial, whence came the phraseology in which
these problems were stated, and whence the description of reasoning. employed in their solution. It
must only be recollected that the Roman law which
had worked itself into Western thought was neither
the archaic system of the ancient city, nor the prun-
ed and curtailed jurisprudence of the Byzantine Emperors; still less, of course, was it the mass of rules,
nearly buried in a parasitical overgrowth of modern
speculative doctrine, which passes by the name of
Modern Civil Law. I only speak of that philosophy
of jurisprudence, wrought out by the great juridical
thinkers of the Antonine age, which may still be
partially reproduced from the Pandects of Justinian,
a system to which few faults can be attributed except perhaps that it aimed at a higher degree of elegance, certainty, and precision than human affairs
will permit to the limits within which human laws
seek to confine them.

It is a singular result of that ignorance of Roman
law which Englishmen readily confess, and of which
they are sometimes not ashamed to boast, that many
English writers of note and credit have been led by
it to put forward the most untenable of paradoxes
concerning the condition of human intellect during
the Roman empire. It has been constantly asserted,
as unhesitatingly as if there were no temerity in advancing the proposition, that from the close of the

Augustan era to the general awakening of interest on the points of the Christian faith, the mental energies of the civilised world were smitten with a paralysis. Now there are two subjects of thought—the only two perhaps with the exception of physical science—which are able to give employment to all the powers and capacities which the mind possesses. One of them is Metaphysical inquiry, which knows no limits so long as the mind is satisfied to work on itself; the other is Law, which is as extensive as the concerns of mankind. It happens that, during the very period indicated, the Greek-speaking provinces were devoted to one, the Latin-speaking provinces to the other, of these studies. I say nothing of the fruits of speculation in Alexandria and the East, but I confidently affirm that Rome and the West had an occupation in hand fully capable of compensating them for the absence of every other mental exercise, and I add that the results achieved, so far as we know them, were not unworthy of the continuous and exclusive labor bestowed on producing them. Nobody except a professional lawyer is perhaps in a position completely to understand how much of the intellectual strength of individuals Law is capable of absorbing, but a layman has no difficulty in comprehending why it was that an unusual share of the collective intellect of Rome was engrossed by juris prudence. " The proficiency * of a given communi ty in jurisprudence depends in the long run on the same conditions as its progress in any other line of inquiry; and the chief of these are the proportion of the national intellect devoted to it, and the length of time during which it is so devoted. Now, a combination of all the causes, direct and indirect, which contribute to the advancing and perfecting of a science continued to operate on the jurisprudence of Rome through the entire space between the Twelve Tables and the severance of the two Empires,—and that not irregularly or at intervals, but in steadily increasing force and constantly augmenting number. We should reflect that the earliest intellectual exercise to which a young nation devotes itself is the study of its laws. As soon as the mind makes its first conscious efforts towards generalisation, the concerns of every-day life are the first to press for inclusion within general rules and comprehensive formulas. The popularity of the pursuit on which all the energies of the young commonwealth are bent is at the outset unbounded; but it ceases in time. The monopoly of mind by law is broken down. The crowd at the morning audience of the great Roman jurisconsult lessens. The students are counted by hundreds instead of thousands in the English Inns of Court. Art, Literature, Science, and Politics, claim their share of the national intellect; and the practice of jurisprudence is confined within the circle of a profession, never indeed limited or insignificant, but attracted as much by the rewards as by the intrinsic recommendations of their science. This succession of changes exhibited itself evenmore strikingly in Rome than in England. To the close of the Republic the law was the sole field for all ability except the special talent of a capacity for generalship. But a new stage of intellectual progress began with the Augustan age, as it did with our own Elizabethan era. We all know what were its achievements in poetry and prose ; but there are some indications, it should be remarked, that, besides its efflorescence in ornamental literature, it was on the eve of throwing out new aptitudes for conquest in physical science. Here, however, is the point at which the history of mind in the Roman States ceases to be parallel to the routes which mental progress has since then pursued. The brief span of Roman literature, strictly so called, was suddenly closed under a variety of influences, which though they may partially be traced, it would be im proper in this place to analyse. Ancient intellect was forcibly thrust back into its old courses, and law again became no less exclusively the proper sphere for talent than it had been in the days when the Ro mans despised philosophy and poetry as the toys of a childish race. Of what nature were the external in ducements which, during the Imperial period, tended to draw a man of inherent capacity to the pursuits of the jurisconsult may best be understood by considering the option which was practically before him in the choice of a profession. He might become a teacher of rhetoric, a commander of frontier-posts, or a professional writer of panegyrics. The only other walk of active life which was open to him was the practice of the law. Through *that* lay the approach to wealth, to fame, to office, to the council-chamber of the monarch—it may be to the very throne itself.

The premium on the study of jurisprudence was so enormous that there were schools of law in every part of the Empire, even in the very domain of Metaphysics. But, though the transfer of the seat of empire to Byzantium gave a perceptible impetus to its cultivation in the East, jurisprudence never dethroned the pursuits which there competed with it. Its language was Latin, an exotic dialect in the Eastern half of the Empire. It is only of the West that we can lay down that law was not only the mental food of the ambitious and aspiring, but the sole aliment of all intellectual activity. Greek philosophy had never been more than a transient fashionable taste with the educated class of Rome itself, and when the new Eastern capital had been created, and the Empire subsequently divided into two, the divorce of the Western provinces from Greek speculation, and their exclusive devotion to jurisprudence, became more decided than ever. As soon then as they ceased to sit at the feet of the Greeks and began to ponder out a theology of their own, the theology proved to be permeated with forensic ideas and couched in a forensic phraseology. It is certain that this substratum of law in Western theology lies exceedingly deep. A new set of Greek theories, the Aristotelian philosophy, made their way afterwards into the West, and almost entirely buried its indigenous doctrines. But when at the Reformation it partially shook itself free from their influence, it instantly supplied their place with Law. It is difficult to say whether the religious system of Calvin or the religious system of the Arminians has the more markedly legal character.

The vast influence of this specific jurisprudence of Contract produced by the Romans upon the corresponding department of modern Law belongs rather to the history of mature jurisprudence than to a treatise like the present. It did not make itself felt till the school of Bologna founded the legal science of modern Europe. But the fact that the Romans, before their Empire fell, had so fully developed the conception of Contract becomes of importance at a much earlier period than this. Feudalism, I have repeatedly asserted, was a compound of archaic barbarian usage with Roman law; no other explanation of it is tenable, or even intelligible. The earliest social forms of the feudal period differ in little from the ordinary associations in which the men of primitive civilisations are everywhere seen united. A Fief was an organically complete brotherhood of associates whose proprietary and personal rights were inextricably blended together. It had much in common with an Indian Village Community and much in common with a Highland clan. But still it presents some phenomena which we never find in the associations which are spontaneously formed by beginners in civilisation. True archaic communities are held together not by express rules, but by sentiment, or, we should perhaps say, by instinct; and new comers into the brotherhood are brought within the range of this instinct by falsely pretending to share in the blood-relationship from which it naturally springs. But the earliest feudal communities were neither bound together by mere sentiment nor recruited by a fiction. The tie which united them was Contract, and they obtained new associates by contracting with them. The relation of the lord to the vassals had originally been settled by express engagement, and a person wishing to engraft himself on the brotherhood by *commendation* or *infeudation* came to a distinct understanding as to the conditions on which he was to be admitted. It is therefore the sphere occupied in them by Contract which principally distinguishes the feudal institutions from the unadulterated usages of primitive races. The lord had many of the characteristics of a patriarchal chieftain, but his prerogative was limited by a variety of settled customs traceable to the express conditions which had been agreed upon when the infeudation took place. Hence flow the chief differences which forbid us to class the feudal societies with true archaic communities. They were much more durable and much more various; more durable, because express rules are less destructible than instinctive habits, and more various, because the contracts on which they were founded were adjusted to the minutest circumstances and wishes of the persons who surrendered or granted away their lands.   This last consideration may serve to indicate how greatly the vulgar opinions current among us as to the origin of modern society stand in need of revision.   It is often said that the irregular and various contour of modern civilisation is due to the exuberant and erratic genius of the Germanic races, and it is often contrasted with the dull routine of the Roman Empire.   The truth is that the Empire bequeathed to modern society the legal conception to which all this irregularity is attributable; if the customs and institutions of barbarians have one characteristic more striking than another, it is their extreme uniformity.

CHAPTER X.

THE Teutonic Codes, including those of our Anglo-Saxon ancestors, are the only bodies of archaic secular law which have come down to us in such a state that we can form an exact notion of their original dimensions. Although the extant fragments of Roman and Hellenic codes suffice to prove to us their general character, there does not remain enough of them for us to be quite sure of their precise magnitude or of the proportion of their parts to each other. But still on the whole all the known collections of ancient law are characterised by a feature which broadly distinguishes them from systems of mature jurisprudence. The proportion of criminal to civil law is exceedingly different. In the German codes, the civil part of the law has trifling dimensions as compared with the criminal. The traditions which speak of the sanguinary penalties inflicted by the code of Draco seem to indicate that it had the same characteristic. In the Twelve Tables alone

produced by a society of greater legal genius and at
first of gentler manners, the civil law has something
like its modern precedence ; but the relative amount
of space given to the modes of redressing wrong,
though not enormous, appears to have been large.
It may be laid down, I think, that the more archaic
the code, the fuller and the minuter is its penal legislation.   The phenomenon has often been observed
and has been explained, no doubt to a great extent
correctly, by the violence habitual to the communities which for the first time reduced their laws to
writing.   The legislator, it is said, proportioned the
divisions of his work to the frequency of a certain
class of incidents in barbarian life.   I imagine, however, that this account is not quite complete.   It
should be recollected that the comparative barren-
ness of civil law in archaic collections is consistent
with those other characteristics of ancient jurisprudence which have been discussed in this treatise.
Nine-tenths of the civil part of the law practised by
civilised societies are made up of the Law of Persons,
of the Law of Property and of Inheritance, and of
the Law of Contract.   But it is plain that all these
provinces of jurisprudence must shrink within nar-
rower boundaries, the nearer we make our approaches
to the infancy of social brotherhood.   The Law of
Persons, which is nothing else than the Law of
Status, will be restricted to the scantiest limits as
long as all forms of status are merged in common
subjection to Paternal Power, as long as the Wife

has no rights against her Husband, the Son none against his Father, and the infant Ward none against the Agnates who are his Guardians. Similarly, the rules relating to Property and Succession can never be plentiful, so long as land and goods devolve within the family, and, if distributed at all, are distributed inside its circle. But the greatest gap in ancient civil law will always be caused by the absence of Contract, which some archaic codes do not mention at all, while others significantly attest the immaturity of the moral notions on which Contract depends by supplying its place with an elaborate jurisprudence of Oaths. There are no corresponding reasons for the poverty of penal law, and accordingly, even if it be hazardous to pronounce that the childhood of nations is always a period of ungoverned violence, we shall still be able to understand why the modern relation of criminal law to civil should be inverted in ancient codes.

I have spoken of primitive jurisprudence as giving to *criminal* law a priority unknown in a later age. The expression has been used for convenience' sake, but in fact the inspection of ancient codes shows that the law which they exhibit in unusual quantities is not true criminal law. All civilised systems agree in drawing a distinction between offences against the State or Community and offences against the Individual, and the two classes of injuries, thus kept apart, I may here, without pretending that the terms have always been employed consistently in jurispru-

dence, call Crimes and Wrongs, *crimina* and *delicta.*
Now the penal Law of ancient communities is not
the law of Crimes; it is the law of Wrongs, or, to
use the English technical word, of Torts.   The person injured proceeds against the wrong-doer by an
ordinary civil action, and recovers compensation in
the shape of money-damages if he succeeds.   If the
Commentaries of Gaius be opened at the place where
the writer treats of the penal jurisprudence founded
on the Twelve Tables, it will be seen that at the
head of the civil wrongs recognised by the Roman
law stood *Furtum* or *Theft.*   Offences which we are
accustomed to regard exclusively as *crimes* are exclusively treated as *torts*, and not theft only, but
assault and violent robbery, are associated by the
jurisconsult with trespass, libel and slander.   All
alike gave rise to an Obligation or *vinculum juris*,
and were all requited by a payment of money.   This
peculiarity, however, is most strongly brought out
in the consolidated Laws of the Germanic tribes.
Without an exception they describe an immense
system of money compensations for homicide, and
with few exceptions, as large a scheme of compensation for minor injuries.   "Under Anglo-Saxon law,'
writes Mr. Kemble (*Anglo-Saxons*, i. 177), "a sum
was placed on the life of every free man, according
to his rank, and a corresponding sum on every wound
that could be inflicted on his person, for nearly every
injury that could be done to his civil rights, honour
or peace; the sum being aggravated according to

adventitious circumstances." These compositions
are evidently regarded as a valuable source of income; highly complex rules regulate the title to
them and the responsibility for them; and, as I have
already had occasion to state, they often follow a
very peculiar line of devolution, if they have not
been acquitted at the decease of the person to whom
they belong. If therefore the criterion of a *delict*,
wrong, or *tort* be that the person who suffers it, and
not the State, is conceived to be wronged, it may be
asserted that in the infancy of jurisprudence the
citizen depends for protection against violence or
fraud not on the Law of Crime but on the Law of
Tort.

Torts then are copiously enlarged upon in primitive jurisprudence. It must be added that Sins are
known to it also. Of the Teutonic codes it is almost
unnecessary to make this assertion, because those
codes, in the form in which we have received them,
were compiled or recast by Christian legislators.
But it is also true that the non-Christian bodies of archaic law entail penal consequences on certain classes
of acts and on certain classes of omissions, as being violations of divine prescriptions and commands.
The law administered at Athens by the Senate of
Areopagus was probably a special religious code, and
at Rome, apparently from a very early period, the
Pontifical jurisprudence punished adultery, sacrilege,
and perhaps murder. There were therefore in the
Athenian and in the Roman States laws punishing

sins. There were also laws punishing *torts.* The conception of offence against God produced the first class of ordinances; the conception of offence against one's neighbour produced the second; but the idea of offence against the State or aggregate community did not at first produce a true criminal jurisprudence.

Yet it is not to be supposed that a conception so simple and elementary as that of wrong done to the State was wanting in any primitive society. It seems rather that the very distinctness with which this conception is realised is the true cause which at first prevents the growth of a criminal law. At all events, when the Roman community conceived itself to be injured, the analogy of a personal wrong received was carried out to its consequences with absolute literalness, and the State avenged itself by a single act on the individual wrong-doer. The result was that, in the infancy of the commonwealth, every offence vitally touching its security or its interests was punished by a separate enactment of the legislature. And this is the earliest conception of a *crimen* or Crime—an act involving such high issues that the State, instead of leaving its cognisance to the civil tribunal or the religious court, directed a special law or *privilegium* against the perpetrator. Every indictment therefore took the form of a bill of pains and penalties, and the trial of a *criminal* was a proceeding wholly extraordinary, wholly irregular, wholly independent of settled rules and fixed conditions. Consequently, both for the reason that the tribunal dispensing justice was the sovereign State itself, and also for the reason that no classification of the acts prescribed or forbidden was possible, there was not at this epoch any *Law* of crimes, any criminal jurisprudence.   The procedure was identical with the forms of passing an ordinary statute; it was set in motion by the same persons and conducted with precisely the same solemnities. And it is to be observed that, when a regular criminal law with an apparatus of Courts and officers for its administration had afterwards come into being, the old procedure, as might be supposed from its conformity with theory, still in strictness remained practicable; and, much as resort to such an expedient was discredited, the people of Rome always retained the power of punishing by a special law offences against its majesty.   The classical scholar does not require to be reminded that in exactly the same manner the Athenian Bill of Pains and Penalties, or *εἰσαγγελία,* survived the establishment of regular tribunals.   It is known too that when the freemen of the Teutonic races assembled for legislation, they also claimed authority to punish offences of peculiar blackness or perpetrated by criminals of exalted station.   Of this nature was the criminal jurisdiction of the Anglo-Saxon Witenagemot.

It may be thought that the difference which I have asserted to exist between the ancient and modern view of penal law has only a verbal existence. The community, it may be said, besides interposing

to punish crimes legislatively, has from the earliest
times interfered by its tribunals to compel the wrong-
doer to compound for his wrong, and if it does this,
it must always have supposed that in some way it
was injured through his offence. But, however rigorous this inference may seem to us now a-days, it is
very doubtful whether it was actually drawn by the
men of primitive antiquity. How little the notion of
injury to the community had to do with the earliest
interferences of the State *through its tribunals*, is
shown by the curious circumstance that in the original administration of justice, the proceedings were
a close imitation of the series of acts which were
likely to be gone through in private life by persons
who were disputing, but who afterwards suffered
their quarrel to be appeased. The magistrate carefully simulated the demeanour of a private arbitrator
casually called in.

In order to show that this statement is not a
mere fanciful conceit, I will produce the evidence on
which it rests. Very far the most ancient judicial
proceeding known to us is the Legis Actio Sacramenti of the Romans, out of which all the later Roman law of Actions may be proved to have grown.
Gaius carefully describes its ceremonial. Unmeaning
and grotesque as it appears at first sight, a little at
tention enables us to decipher and interpret it.

The subject of litigation is supposed to be in
Court. If it is moveable, it is actually there. If it
be immoveable, a fragment or sample of it is brought

in its place.; land, for instance, is represented by a
clod, a house by a single brick. In the example
selected by Gaius, the suit is for a slave. The proceeding begins by the plaintiff's advancing with a
rod, which as Gaius expressly tells, symbolised a
spear. He lays hold of the slave and asserts a right
to him with the words, " *Hunc ego hominem ex Jure
Quiritium meum esse dico secundum suam causam
sicut dixi ;* " and then saying, " *Ecce tibi Vindictam
imposui,* " he touches him with the spear. The defendant goes through the same series of acts and
gestures. On this the Prætor intervenes, and bids
the litigants relax their hold, " *Mittite ambo hominem.* " They obey, and the plaintiff demands from
the defendant the reason of his interference, " *Pos-
tulo anne dicas quâ ex causâ vindicaveris,*" a question which is replied to by a fresh assertion of right,
" *Jus peregi sicut vindictam imposui.*" On this, the
first claimant offers to stake a sum of money, called
a Sacramentum, on the justice of his own case,
" *Quando tu injuriâ provocasti, D æris Sacramento
te provoco,* " and the defendant, in the phrase, " *Sim-
iliter ego te,* " accepts the wager. The subsequent
proceedings were no longer of a formal kind, but it is
to be observed that the Prætor took security for the
Sacramentum, which always went into the coffers of
the State.

Such was the necessary preface of every ancient
Roman suit. It is impossible, I think, to refuse assent to the suggestion of those who see in it a dra-

matization of the origin of Justice. Two armed men
are wrangling about some disputed property. The
Prætor, *vir pietate gravis*, happens to be going by
and interposes to stop the contest. The disputants
state their case to him, and agree that he shall arbi
trate between them, it being arranged that the loser
besides resigning the subject of the quarrel, shall pay
a sum of money to the umpire as a remuneration
for his trouble and loss of time. This interpretation
would be less plausible than it is, were it not that,
by a surprising coincidence, the ceremony described
by Gaius as the imperative course of proceeding in a
Legis Actio is substantially the same with one of
the two subjects which the God Hephæstus is described by Homer as moulding into the First Com-
partment of the Shield of Achilles. In the Homeric
trial-scene, the dispute, as if expressly intended to
bring out the characteristics of primitive society, is
not about property but about the composition for a
homicide. One person asserts that he has paid it,
the other that he has never received it. The point
of detail, however, which stamps the picture as the
counterpart of the archaic Roman practice is the reward designed for the judges. Two talents of gold
lie in the middle, to be given to him who shall explain the grounds of the decision most to the satisfaction of the audience. The magnitude of this sum
as compared with the trifling amount of the Sacramentum seems to me indicative of the difference bo-
tween fluctuating usage ard usage consolidated into

law. The scene introduced by the poet as a striking
and characteristic, but still only occasional, feature
of city-life in the heroic age has stiffened, at the
opening of the history of civil process, into the reg
ular, ordinary formalities of a lawsuit. It is natural
therefore that in the Legis Actio the remuneration
of the Judge should be reduced to a reasonable sum,
and that, instead of being adjudged to one of a number of arbitrators by popular acclamation, it should
be paid as a matter of course to the State which the
Prætor represents. But that the incidents described
so vividly by Homer, and by Gaius with even more
than the usual crudity of technical language, have
substantially the same meaning, I cannot doubt; and,
in confirmation of this view it may be added that
many observers of the earliest judicial usages of modern Europe have remarked that the fines inflicted by
Courts on offenders were originally *sacramenta*. The
State did not take from the defendant a composition
for any wrong supposed to be done to itself, but
claimed a share in the compensation awarded to the
plaintiff simply as the fair price of its time and
trouble.   Mr. Kemble expressly assigns this character to the Anglo-Saxon *bannum* or *fredum*.

Ancient law furnishes other proofs that the earliest administrators of justice simulated the probable
acts of persons engaged in a private quarrel. In
settling the damages to be awarded, they took as
their guide the measure of vengeance likely to be
exacted by an aggrieved person under the circum-

stances of the case. This is the true explanation of
the very different penalties imposed by ancient law
on offenders caught in the act or soon after it and on
offenders detected after considerable delay. Some
strange exemplifications of this peculiarity are supplied by the old Roman law of Theft. The Laws
of the Twelve Tables seem to have divided Thefts
into Manifest and Non-Manifest, and to have allotted
extraordinarily different penalties to the offence according as it fell under one head or the other. The
Manifest Thief was he who was caught within the
house in which he had been pilfering, or who was
taken while making off to a place of safety with the
stolen goods; the Twelve Tables condemned him to
be put to death if he were already a slave, and, if
he was a freeman, they made him the bondsman of
the owner of the property. The Non-Manifest
Thief was he who was detected under any other circumstances than those described; and the old code
simply directed that an offender of this sort should
refund double the value of what he had stolen. In
Gaius's day the excessive severity of the Twelve Tables to the Manifest Thief had naturally been much
mitigated, but the law still maintained the old princi
ple by mulcting him in fourfold the value of the stolen
goods, while the Non-Manifest Thief still continued
to pay merely the double. The ancient lawgiver
doubtless considered that the injured proprietor, if
left to himself, would inflict a very different punishment when his blood was hot from that with which

he would be satisfied when the Thief was detected
after a considerable interval ; and to this calculation
the legal scale of penalties was adjusted.   The principle is precisely the same as that followed in the
Anglo-Saxon and other Germanic codes, when they
suffer a thief chased down and caught with the
booty to be hanged or decapitated on the spot,
while they exact the full penalties of homicide from
anybody who kills him after the pursuit has been
intermitted.   These archaic distinctions bring home
to us very forcibly the distance of a refined from a
rude jurisprudence.   The modern administrator of
justice has confessedly one of his hardest tasks before
him when he undertakes to discriminate between
the degrees of criminality which belong to offences
falling within the same technical description.   It is
always easy to say that a man is guilty of man-
slaughter, larceny, or bigamy, but it is often most
difficult to pronounce what extent of moral guilt he
has incurred, and consequently what measure of
punishment he has deserved.   There is hardly any
perplexity in casuistry, or in the analysis of motive,
which we may not be called upon to confront, if
we attempt to settle such a point with precision;
and accordingly the law of our day shows an increasing tendency to abstain as much as possible
from laying down positive rules on the subject.   In
France the jury is left to decide whether the offence
which it finds committed has been attended by ex-
tenuating circumstances ; in England, a nearly un-

bounded latitude in the selection of punishments is now allowed to the judge; while all States have in reserve an ultimate remedy for the miscarriages of law in the Prerogative of Pardon, universally lodged with the Chief Magistrate. It is curious to observe how little the men of primitive times were troubled with these scruples, how completely they were persuaded that the impulses of the injured person were the proper measure of the vengeance he was entitled to exact, and how literally they imitated the probable rise and fall of his passions in fixing their scale of punishment. I wish it could be said that their method of legislation is quite extinct. There are, however, several modern systems of law which, in cases of graver wrong, admit the fact of the wrongdoer having been taken in the act to be pleaded in justification of inordinate punishment inflicted on him by the sufferer—an indulgence which, though superficially regarded it may seem intelligible, is based, as it seems to me, on a very low morality.

Nothing, I have said, can be simpler than the considerations which ultimately led ancient societies to the formation of a true criminal jurisprudence. The State conceived itself to be wronged, and the Popular Assembly struck straight at the offender with the same movement which accompanied its legislative action. It is further true of the ancient world—though not precisely of the modern, as I shall have occasion to point out—that the earliest criminal tribunals were merely subdivisions, or committees, of the legislature. This, at all events, is the conclusion pointed at by the legal history of the two great states of antiquity. with tolerable clearness in one case, and with absolute distinctness in the other. The primitive penal law of Athens entrusted the castigation of offences partly to the Archons, who seem to have punished them as *torts*, and partly to the Senate of Areopagus, which punished them as *sins*. Both jurisdictions were substantially transferred in the end to the Heliæa, the High Court of Popular Justice, and the functions of the Archons and the Areopagus became either merely ministerial or quite insignificant. But " Heliæa " is only an old word for Assembly ; the Heliæa of classical times was simply the Popular Assembly convened for judicial purposes, and the famous Dikasteries of Athens were only its subdivisions or panels. The corresponding changes which occurred at Rome are still more easily interpreted, because the Romans confined their experiments to the penal law, and did not, like the Athenians, construct popular courts with a civil as well as a criminal jurisdiction. The history of Roman criminal jurisprudence begins with the Old Judicia Populi, at which the Kings are said to have presided. These were simply solemn trials of great offenders under legislative forms. It seems, however, that from an early period the Comitia had occasionally delegated its criminal jurisdiction to a Quæstio or Commission, which bore much the same relation to the Assembly

which a Committee of the House of Commons bears
to the House itself, except that the Roman Commis-
sioners or Quæstores did not merely *report* to the
Comitia, but exercised all powers which that body
was itself in the habit of exercising, even to the
passing sentence on the Accused. A Quæstio of
this sort was only appointed to try a particular
offender, but there was nothing to prevent two or
three Quæstiones sitting at the same time ; and it is
probable that several of them were appointed simultaneously, when several grave cases of wrong to the
community had occurred together. There are also
indications that now and then these Quæstiones approached the character of our *Standing* Committees,
in that they were appointed periodically, and without waiting for occasion to arise in the commission
of some serious crime. The old Quæstores Parricidii, who are mentioned in connection with transactions of very ancient date, as being deputed to try
(or, as some take it, to search out and try) all cases
of parricide and murder, seem to have been appointed
regularly every year ; and the Duumviri Perduellionis, or Commission of Two for trial of violent
injury to the Commonwealth, are also believed by
most writers to have been named periodically. The
delegations of power to these latter functionaries
bring us some way forwards. Instead of being appointed *when and as* state-offences were committed
they had a general, though a temporary jurisdiction
over such as *might* be perpetrated. Our proximity

to a regular criminal jurisprudence is also indicated
by the general terms "Parricidium" and "Perduel-
lio," which mark the approach to something like a
classification of crimes.

The true criminal law did not however come
into existence till the year B.C. 149, when L. Cal-
purnius Piso carried the statute known as the Lex
Calpurnia de Repetundis. The law applied to cases
Repetundarum Pecuniarum, that is, claims by Provincials to recover monies improperly received by
a Governor-General, but the great and permanent
importance of this statute arose from its establish-
ing the first Quæstio Perpetua. A Quæstio Perpetua
was a *Permanent* Commission as opposed to those
which were occasional and to those which were temporary. It was a regular criminal tribunal, whose
existence dated from the passing of the statute creating it and continued till another statute should
pass abolishing it. Its members were not specially
nominated, as were the members of the older Quæstiones, but provision was made in the law constituting it for selecting from particular classes the
judges who were to officiate, and for renewing them
in conformity with definite rules. The offences of
which it took cognisance were also expressly named
and defined in this statute, and the new Quæstio
had authority to try and sentence all persons in
future whose acts should fall under the definitions
of crime supplied by the law It was therefore a

regular criminal judicature, administering a true criminal jurisprudence.

The primitive history of criminal law divides itself therefore into four stages.   Understanding that the conception of *Crime*, as distinguished from that of *Wrong* or *Tort* and from that of *Sin*, involves the idea of injury to the State or collective community, we first find that the commonwealth, in literal conformity with the conception, itself inter-posed directly, and by isolated acts, to avenge itself on the author of the evil which it had suffered This is the point from which we start; each indict-ment is now a bill of pains and penalties, a special law naming the criminal and prescribing his punish-ment.   A *second* step is accomplished when the mul-tiplicity of crimes compels the legislature to delegate its powers to particular Quæstiones or Commissions, each of which is deputed to investigate a particular accusation, and if it be proved, to punish the par-ticular offender.   Yet *another* movement is made when the legislature, instead of waiting for the al-leged commission of a crime as the occasion of ap-pointing a Quæstio, periodically nominates Com-missioners like the Quæstores Parricidii and the Duumviri Perduellionis, on the chance of certain classes of crimes being committed, and in the expec-tation that they *will* be perpetrated.   The *last* stage is reached when the Quæstiones from being periodical or occasional become permanent Benches or Chambers—when the judges, instead of being named in the particular law nominating the Commission, are directed to be chosen through all future time in a particular way and from a particular class —and when certain acts are described in general language and declared to be crimes, to be visited, in the event of their perpetration, with specified penalties appropriated to each description.

If the Quæstiones Perpetuæ had had a longer history, they would doubtless have come to be regarded as a distinct institution, and their relation to the Comitia would have seemed no closer than the connection of our own Courts of Law with the Sovereign, who is theoretically the fountain of justice. But the Imperial despotism destroyed them before their origin had been completely forgotten, and so long as they lasted, these Permanent Commissions were looked upon by the Romans as the mere depositaries of a delegated power. The cognisance of crimes was considered a natural attribute of the legislature, and the mind of the citizen never ceased to be carried back from the Quæstiones to the Comitia which had deputed them to put into exercise some of its own inalienable functions. The view which regarded the Quæstiones, even when they became permanent, as mere Committees of the Popular Assembly—as bodies which only ministered to a higher authority--had some important legal consequences which left their mark on the criminal law to the very latest period. One immediate result was that the Comitia continued to exercise criminal jurisdiction by way of bill of pains and penalties, long after the Quæstiones had been established. Though the legislature had consented to delegate its powers for the sake of convenience to bodies external to itself, it did not follow that it surrendered them. The Comitia and the Quæstiones went on trying and punishing offenders side by side; and any unusual outburst of popular indignation was sure, until the extinction of the Republic, to call down upon its object an indictment before the Assembly of the Tribes.

One of the most remarkable peculiarities of the institutions of the Republic is also traceable to this dependance of the Quæstiones on the Comitia. The disappearance of the punishment of Death from the penal system of Republican Rome used to be a very favorite topic with the writers of the last century, who were perpetually using it to point some theory of the Roman character or of modern social economy. The reason which can be confidently assigned for it stamps it as purely fortuitous. Of the three forms which the Roman legislature successively assumed, one, it is well known—the Comitia Centuriata—was exclusively taken to represent the State as embodied for military operations. The Assembly of the Centuries, therefore, had all powers which may be supposed to be properly lodged with a General commanding an army, and, among them, it had authority to subject all offenders to the same correction to

which a soldier rendered himself liable by breaches
of discipline. The Comitia Centuriata could therefore inflict capital punishment. Not so, however,
the Comitia Curiata or Comitia Tributa. They were
fettered on this point by the sacredness with which
the person of a Roman citizen, inside the walls of the
city, was invested by religion and law; and, with
respect to the last of them, the Comitia Tributa, we
know for certain that it became a fixed principle that
the Assembly of the Tribes could at most impose a
fine. So long as criminal jurisdiction was confined
to the legislature, and so long as the assemblies of
the Centuries and of the Tribes continued to exercise
co-ordinate powers, it was easy to prefer indictments
for graver crimes before the legislative body which
dispensed the heavier penalties; but then it happened that the more democratic assembly, that of the
Tribes, almost entirely superseded the others, and
became the ordinary legislature of the later Republic. Now the decline of the Republic was exactly
the period during which the Quæstiones Perpetuæ
were established, so that the statutes creating them
were all passed by a legislative assembly which itself
could not, at its ordinary sittings, punish a criminal
with death. It followed that the Permanent Judicial
Commissions, holding a delegated authority, were cir-
cumscribed in their attributes and capacities by the
limits of the powers residing with the body which
deputed them. They could do nothing which the
Assembly of the tribes could not have done; and, as

the Assembly could not sentence to death, the Quæstiones were equally incompetent to award capital
punishment. The anomaly thus resulting was not
viewed in ancient times with anything like the favour
which it has attracted among the moderns, and in
deed, while it is questionable whether the Roman
character was at all the better for it, it is certain that
the Roman Constitution was a great deal the worse.
Like every other institution which has accompanied
the human race down the current of its history, the
punishment of death is a necessity of society in certain stages of the civilising process. There is a time
when the attempt to dispense with it baulks both of
the two great instincts which lie at the root of all penal law. Without it, the community neither feels that
it is sufficiently revenged on the criminal, nor thinks
that the example of his punishment is adequate to
deter others from imitating him. The incompetence
of the Roman Tribunals to pass sentence of death led
distinctly and directly to those frightful Revolutionary intervals, known as the Proscriptions, during
which all law was formally suspended simply because
party violence could find no other avenue to the vengeance for which it was thirsting. No cause contrib
uted so powerfully to the decay of political capacity
in the Roman people as this periodical abeyance of
the laws; and, when it had once been resorted to, we
need not hesitate to assert that the ruin of Roman
liberty became merely a question of time. If the
practice of the Tribunals had afforded an adequate

vent for popular passion, the forms of judicial procedure would no doubt have been as flagrantly perverted as with us in the reigns of the later Stuarts,
but national character would not have suffered as
deeply as it did, nor would the stability of Roman
institutions have been as seriously enfeebled.

I will mention two more singularities of the Roman Criminal System which were produced by the
same theory of judicial authority. They are, the extreme multiplicity of the Roman criminal tribunals,
and the capricious and anomalous classification of
crimes which characterised Roman penal jurisprudence throughout its entire history. Every *Quæstio*,
it has been said, whether Perpetual or otherwise,
had its origin in a distinct statute. From the law
which created it, it derived its authority; it rigorously observed the limits which its charter prescribed to it, and touched no form of criminality
which that charter did not expressly define. As then
the statutes which constituted the various Quæstiones
were all called forth by particular emergencies, each
of them being in fact passed to punish a class of acts
which the circumstances of the time rendered particularly odious or particularly dangerous, these enactments made not the slightest reference to each
other, and were connected by no common principle.
Twenty or thirty different criminal laws were in ex
istence together, with exactly the same number of
Quæstiones to administer them; nor was any attempt
made during the Republic to fuse these distinct ju

dicial bodies into one, or to give symmetry to the pro·
visions of the statutes which appointed them and
defined their duties. The state of the Roman criminal jurisdiction at this period, exhibited some resemblance to the administration of civil remedies in
England at the time when the English Courts of
Common Law had not as yet introduced those ficti·
tious averments into their writs which enabled them
to trespass on each other's peculiar province. Like
the Quæstiones, the Courts of Queen's Bench, Common Pleas, and Exchequer, were all theoretical
emanations from a higher authority, and each entertained a special class of cases supposed to be committed to it by the fountain of its jurisdiction ; but
then the Roman Quæstiones were many more than
three in number, and it was infinitely less easy to
discriminate the acts which fell under the cognisance
of each Quæstio, than to distinguish between the provinces of the three Courts in Westmnister Hall.
The difficulty of drawing exact lines between the
spheres of the different Quæstiones made the multi·
plicity of Roman tribunals something more than a
mere inconvenience ; for we read with astonishment
that when it was not immediately clear under what
general description a man's alleged offence ranged
themselves, he might be indicted at once, or suc·
cessively before several different Commissions, on
the chance of some of them declaring itself compe·
tent to convict him ; and, although conviction by one
Quæstio ousted the jurisdiction of the rest, acquittal

by one of them could not be pleaded to an accusation before another. This was directly contrary to
the rule of the Roman civil law ; and we may be sure
that a people so sensitive as the Romans to anomalies
(or, as their significant phrase was, to *inelegancies*)
in jurisprudence, would not long have tolerated it,
had not the melancholy history of the Quæstiones
caused them to be regarded much more as temporary
weapons in the hands of factions than as permanent
institutions for the correction of crime. The Empe
rors soon abolished this multiplicity and conflict of
jurisdiction; but it is remarkable that they did not
remove another singularity of the criminal law which
stands in close connection with the number of the
Courts. The classifications of crimes which are contained even in the Corpus Juris of Justinian are remarkably capricious. Each Quæstio had, in fact,
confined itself to the crimes committed to its cognisance by its charter. These crimes, however, were
only classed together in the original statute because
they happened to call simultaneously for castigation
at the moment of passing it. They had not therefore
anything necessarily in common ; but the fact of
their constituting the particular subject-matter of
trials before a particular Quæstio impressed itself naturally on the public attention, and so inveterate did
the association become between the offences mentioned in the same statute that, even when formal
attempts were made by Sylla and by the Emperor
Augustus to consolidate the Roman criminal law, the

legislator preserved the old grouping. The Statutes
of Sylla and Augustus were the foundation of the
penal jurisprudence of the Empire, and nothing can
be more extraordinary than some of the classifications
which they bequeathed to it. I need only give a
single example in the fact that *perjury* was always
classed with *cutting and wounding* and with *poison-
ing*, no doubt because a law of Sylla, the Lex Cor-
nelia de Sicariis et Veneficis, had given jurisdiction
over all these three forms of crime to the same Permanent Commission. It seems too that this capricious
grouping of crimes affected the vernacular speech of
the Romans. People naturally fell into the habit of
designating all the offences enumerated in one law by
the first name on the list, which doubtless gave its
style to the Law Court deputed to try them all. All
the offences tried by the Quæstio De Adulteriis
would thus be called Adultery.

I have dwelt on the history and characteristics of
the Roman Quæstiones because the formation of a
criminal jurisprudence is nowhere else so instructively exemplified. The last Quæstiones were added by
the Emperor Augustus, and from that time the Romans may be said to have had a tolerably complete
criminal law. Concurrently with its growth, the analogous process had gone on, which I have called the
conversion of Wrongs into Crimes, for, though the
Roman legislature did not extinguish the civil rem
edy for the more heinous offences, it offered the suf
ferer a redress which he was sure to prefer. Still

even after Augustus had completed his leg_slation,
several offences continued to be regarded as Wrongs,
which modern societies look upon exclusively as
crimes; nor did they become criminally punishable
till some late but uncertain date, at which the law
began to take notice of a new description of offences
called in the Digest *crimina extraordinaria*. These
were doubtless a class of acts which the theory of
Roman jurisprudence treated merely as wrongs; but
the growing sense of the majesty of society revolted
from their entailing nothing worse on their perpetrator than the payment of money damages, and accordingly the injured person seems to have been permitted if he pleased, to pursue them as crimes *extra ordi-*
nem, that is, by a mode of redress departing in some
respect or other from the ordinary procedure. From
the period at which these *crimina extraordinaria*
were first recognised, the list of crimes in the Roman States must have been as long as in any community of the modern world.

It is unnecessary to describe with any minuteness
the mode of administering criminal justice under the
Roman Empire, but it is to be noted that both its
theory and practice have had powerful effect on
modern society.   The Emperors did not immediately
abolish the Quæstiones, and at first they committed
an extensive criminal jurisdiction to the Senate, in
which, however servile it might show itself in fact,
the Emperor was no more nominally than a Senator
like the rest.   But some sort of collateral criminal

jurisdiction had been claimed by the Prince from the first; and this, as recollections of the free commonwealth decayed, tended steadily to gain at the expense of the old tribunals. Gradually the punishment of crimes was transferred to magistrates directly nominated by the Emperor, and the privileges of the Senate passed to the Imperial Privy Council, which also became a Court of ultimate criminal appeal. Under these influences the doctrine, familiar to the moderns, insensibly shaped itself that the Sovereign is the fountain of all Justice and the depositary of all Grace. It was not so much the fruit of increasing adulation and servility as of the centralisation of the Empire which had by this time perfected itself. The theory of criminal justice had, in fact, worked round almost to the point from which it started. It had begun in the belief that it was the business of the collective community to avenge its own wrongs by its own hand; and it ended in the doctrine that the chastisement of crimes belonged in an especial manner to the Sovereign as representative and mandatary of his people. The new view differed from the old one chiefly in the air of awfulness and majesty which the guardianship of justice appeared to throw around the person of the Sovereign.

This later Roman view of the Sovereign's relation to justice certainly assisted in saving modern societies from the necessity of travelling through the series of changes which I have illustrated by the

history of the Quæstiones.   In the primitive law of
almost all the races which have peopled Western
Europe there are vestiges of the archaic notion that
the punishment of crimes belongs to the general
assembly of freemen; and there are some States—
Scotland is said to be one of them—in which the
parentage of the existing judicature can be traced
up to a Committee of the legislative body.   But the
development of the criminal law was universally
hastened by two causes, the memory of the Roman
Empire and the influence of the Church.   On the
one hand traditions of the majesty of the Cæsars,
perpetuated by the temporary ascendency of the
House of Charlemagne, were surrounding Sovereigns
with a prestige which a mere barbarous chieftain
could never otherwise have acquired, and were com-
municating to the pettiest feudal potentate the character of guardian of society and representative of
the State.   On the other hand, the Church, in its
anxiety to put a curb on sanguinary ferocity, sought
about for authority to punish the graver misdeeds,
and found it in those passages of Scripture which
speak with approval of the powers of punishment
committed to the civil magistrate.   The New Testament was appealed to as proving that secular
rulers exist for the terror of evil-doers; the Old
Testament, as laying down that " whoso sheddeth
man's blood, by man shall his blood be shed."
There can be no doubt, I imagine, that modern ideas
on the subject of crime are based upon two assump-

tions contended for by the Church in the Dark Ages—first, that each feudal ruler, in his degree, might be assimilated to the Roman Magistrates spoken of by Saint Paul; and next, that the offences which he was to chastise were those selected for prohibition in the Mosaic Commandments, or rather such of them as the Church did not reserve to her own cognisance. Heresy, supposed to be included in the First and Second Commandments, Adultery and Perjury were ecclesiastical offences, and the Church only admitted the co-operation of the secular arm for the purpose of inflicting severer punishment in cases of extraordinary aggravation. At the same time, she taught that murder and robbery, with their various modifications, were under the jurisdiction of civil rulers, not as an accident of their position, but by the express ordinance of God.

There is a passage in the writings of King Alfred (Kemble, ii. 209) which brings out into remarkable clearness the struggle of the various ideas that prevailed in his day as to the origin of criminal jurisdiction. It will be seen that Alfred attributes it partly to the authority of the Church and partly to that of the Witan, while he expressly claims for treason against the lord the same immunity from ordinary rules which the Roman Law of Majestas had assigned to treason against the Cæsar. " After this it happened," he writes, " that many nations received the faith of Christ, and there were many synods assembled throughout the earth, and among the English race also after they had received the faith of Christ, both of holy bishops and of their exalted Witan. They then ordained that, out of that mercy which Christ had taught, secular lords, with their leave, might without sin take for every misdeed the *bot* in money which they ordained; except in cases of treason against a lord, to which they dared not assign any mercy because Almighty God adjudged none to them that despised Him, nor did Christ adjudge any to them which sold Him to death; and He commanded that a lord should be loved like Himself."

APPENDIX

NOTES

NOTE A.

ANTIQUITY OF ROMAN LAW.

THE description of Roman law, in the preface to the first edition, as " bearing in its earlier portions the traces of the most remote antiquity," is literally correct unless, contrary to the usage of good authors, we press the superlative to its extreme construction, as if it had been meant to exclude the possibility that traces of still more remote antiquity may be found elsewhere. Maine obviously did not mean to deny that Germanic and Hindu law, for example, have at some points preserved more archaic features than those of the earliest Roman law known to us; much less to disparage the extremely modern character of classical Roman law, which gives it most of its value for modern jurisprudence: compare the passage cited from " Early Law and Custom " in Note F below. It may be still a natural temptation for a student unacquainted with other legal antiquities to suppose that the law of the Twelve Tables, or the law of the later Roman Republic as a whole, belongs to a more archaic type than it really does. Fifty years ago the temptation was almost inevitable; and we have to remember that Maine had been endeavouring, with indifferent success at the time, to revive the study of Roman law in a country where the educated public was in a state of absolute ignorance on the subject (as it probably still is), and the tradition of the civilians, confined, under the old division of jurisdictions and practice, to a small minority of the legal profession, was at least a century out of date. If Maine did use language tending to exaggerate the intrinsic merits and the practical importance of Roman jurisprudence, it was under those conditions a fault on the right side. But modern students must be warned not to assume that Roman law was in fact at any one time a perfect and symmetrical whole, or that its history can be deduced from any one formula. The Twelve Tables were no doubt regarded as an ultimate source of law for the field they covered, but they did not purport to include the whole of the recognised customary law. For the classical period of the Empire the most important and fruitful written embodiment of law was the Prætor's Edict, as almost every title of the Digest bears witness. Moreover, the Twelve Tables themselves were no mere consolidation, but a reforming code. It is certain that they incorporated Greek materials, and it is of very little importance whether the story of a special commission being sent to Greece is literally acceptable or not. In any case the means of information were at hand in the Greek cities of southern Italy, a region where the Greek language is not yet extinct. Borrowing of this kind from neighbours who have reached a more advanced stage is by no means abnormal in archaic legislation. Indeed, it is rather common for the lawgiver of the heroic age to be represented as a stranger, or as having learnt the wisdom of older and greater kingdoms; and even if the personal element of such a tradition is dubious, it is not likely to be a gratuitous invention. Ingenious paradoxical doubts have quite lately been cast on the antiquity of the Twelve Tables; but the hypothesis that they are really a compilation or fabrication of the second century B.C. has not met with a favourable reception: see Dr. A. H. J. Greenidge, "The Authenticity of the Twelve Tables," English Historical Review, January, 1905, and Professor Goudy in the Juridical Review, June, 1905. It is perhaps unnecessary to warn English students against implicit acceptance of the conjectural restorations of the Decemvirs' work essayed by various learned persons. The most elaborate of these, that of Voigt, is described by the no less learned M. Girard as containing " une restitution tout à fait inacceptable et un commentaire fort aventureux " (Manuel élémentaire du droit romain, 3e éd., 1901, p. 23). Dr. Roby (" Roman Private Law in the Times of Cicero and of the Antonines," 1902, vol. i., p. x) calls it in even plainer terms a house of cards.

NOTE B.

CUSTOMARY LAW IN HOMER.

Maine's reference to the Homeric poems as some of our best evidence for the archaic forms of legal ideas in Indo-European communities is a brilliant example of his insight. As he points out, the poet or poets had no conscious theory of the matter at all, and this is our best warranty for the witness of the poems being true. They describe a society in which custom is understood if not always observed, positive duties are definable if not easily enforceable, and judgments are rendered with solemnity and regarded as binding, although we hear nothing of any standing authority such as could be called either legislative or executive in the modern sense. And Maine is clearly right in holding (p. 2) that the description is not wholly idealised—we might even say not much—and is of a state of society known to the writer. To all appearance the usages described are real, and those of the singer's own time. The deliberate archaism of modern fiction has no place in Homer; only the wealth and prowess of the heroic age are exaggerated. The Chanson de Roland endows Charlemagne and his peers with the arms and manners of the twelfth century, as the Arthurian cycle attributes those of the fourteenth to the knights of the Round Table; and we cannot believe that Homer did otherwise.

Maine gives a hint (p. 6) that the analysis of positive law laid down by Bentham and Austin (following Hobbes, though Bentham seems not to have been aware of it) cannot be made to fit archaic society. For in communities like those of the Homeric age, or of Iceland as described in the Sagas, there is no sovereign (in Hobbes's sense) to be found, nor any legislative command, nor any definite sanction; and yet in Iceland there were regularly constituted courts with a regular and even technical procedure, as the Njáls Saga tells us at large. Maine afterwards worked out this position in the lectures on Sovereignty in "The Early History of Institutions," which are the foundation of sound modern criticism on the Hobbist doctrine. In those classical pages he dealt rather tenderly with Bentham and Austin, whom to some extent he regarded as his masters, in spite of the wholly unhistorical character of their work; and, apart from any particular feeling in this case, it was not his habit to exhibit the full consequences of his ideas.

Those who come after him are free to push the conclusion home, as Mr. Bryce has done (" Studies in History and Jurisprudence," Essay X). As to the absence of executive sanction in archaic procedure, cp. " Early Law and Custom," p. 170.

With regard to the " Themistes " of the Homeric chiefs, the word appears to be not an anomalous plural of θέμις, but distinct, and to mean principles of law or justice; " Themis," the singular noun, being " right " in the abstract sense (E. C. Clark, " Practical Jurisprudence," pp. 42-9). Once it means " tribute," which does not offer much difficulty when compared with the constant use of *consuetudo* in medieval Latin. Some of the language used here by Maine seems to imply that the decisions called by this name were or might be arbitrary; but Maine himself added the desirable qualification in his chapter on " The King and Early Civil Justice." " The Homeric King is chiefly busy with fighting. But he is also a judge, and it is to be observed that he has no assessors. His sentences come directly into his mind by divine dictation from on high." That is, if the king is just; we read in the Iliad, though it occurs only in the course of a simile, of unjust kings who give crooked judgments, disregarding the voice of the gods:

'Ωs δ' ὑπὸ λαίλαπι πᾶσα κελαίνη βέβριθε χθὼν
ἤματ' ὀπωρινῷ, ὅτε λαβρότατον χέει ὕδωρ
Ζεύς, ὅτε δή ῥ' ἄνδρεσσι κοτεσσάμενος χαλεπήνῃ,
οἳ βίῃ εἰν ἀγορῇ σκολιὰς κρίνωσι θέμιστας,
ἐκ δὲ δίκην ἐλάσωσι, θεῶν ὄπιν οὐκ ἀλέγοντες . . .

II. 384 sqq.

"These sentences, or θέμιστες—which is the same word with our Teutonic word ' dooms '—*are doubtless drawn from pre-existing custom or usage*, but the notion is that they are conceived by the king spontaneously or through divine prompting. It is plainly a later development of the same view when the prompting comes from a learned lawyer, or from an authoritative law-book " (" Early Law and Custom," p. 163).

Custom, indeed, is so strong in Homer that the gods themselves are bound by it. Zeus is the greatest of chiefs, but he owes justice to his people, and justice implies the observance of rule. Power is not wanting, but a sense of duty moderates it. Thus in the Iliad Zeus is tempted to rescue Sarpedon from his fate, but dares not break his custom in the face of Hera's rebuke ("Do it if thou wilt: but the rest of the gods in no wise approve " : II. 443): and in the Odyssey the Sun-God threatens to go down and shine among the dead men if he is not to be avenged for the sacrilege of Odysseus' men who have killed and eaten his oxen :—

> Ζεῦ πατέρ ἠδ' ἄλλοι μάκαρες θεοὶ αἰὲν ἐόντες,
> τῖσαι δὴ ἑτάρους Λαερτιάδεω 'Οδυσῆος,
> οἵ μευ βοῦς ἔκτειναν ὑπέρβιον, ᾗσιν ἐγώ γε
> χαίρεσκον μὲν ἰὼν εἰς οὐρανὸν ἀστερόεντα,
> ἠδ' ὁπότ' ἂψ ἐπὶ γαῖαν ἀπ' οὐρανόθεν προτραποίμην.
> εἰ δέ μοι οὐ τίσουσι βοῶν ἐπιεικέ' ἀμοιβήν,
> δύσομαι εἰς 'Αΐδαο καὶ ἐν νεκύεσσι φαείνω.
>
> μ. 377 sqq.

NOTE C.

EARLY FORMS OF LAW: "WRITTEN" AND "UNWRITTEN" LAW:
EARLY CODES.

It should be noted that the growth of institutions is much too complicated, even if we confine our attention to one society, to be represented as a simple series in order of time. We constantly speak of one rule or custom as belonging to a more advanced stage of ideas than another; but this does not mean that in every society where it is found it must have been preceded in fact by a less advanced institution belonging to the next lower grade of culture. Imitation of neighbours or conquerors, or peculiar local conditions, may materially shorten a given stage in the normal development, or even cut it out altogether. What we do mean is that the order is not found reversed. Chalk is not everywhere in England, nor red sandstone; but where red sandstone is, we know that chalk is not below it. Iron was known in Africa so early that Africa may be said not to have had a bronze age; but this does not make it more credible that any tribe should ever have abandoned iron for bronze. In like manner there may have been tribes that had lawgivers almost or quite as soon as they had judges. But no one has heard of a nation which, having acquired a body of legislation, reverted from it to pure customary law (cp. Kohler, "Zur Urgeschichte der Ehe," pp. 7-10).

A king's or chieftain's judicial dooms are very different from express laws promulgated for general observance; but it is noticeable that early traditions ascribe a divine origin to both. In the former case the judge enjoys, in some undefined way, the confidence of the gods; in the latter the human lawgiver is merely the scribe or reporter of a "Deity dictating an entire code or body of law," which, as Maine points out (above, p. 5), is a more artificial conception and belongs to a later stage. It appears, however, as early as anything that can be called legislation; and the tendency to refer the commandments of the law to a divine or semi-divine origin is quite regular. There is no reason, it may be added, why a lawgiver or recorder of divine law should not also be a speaker of dooms. A ruling ascribed to Moses, whom Sir Edward Coke claimed as the first law reporter, is at this day a practical decision, for it governs the civil law of succession in some Jewish communities (such as the Jews of Aden: Sir Courtenay Ilbert, "The Government of India," p. 397). Even if the Mosaic law has to admit the superior antiquity of King Hammurabi's code, we may safely say that the case of Zelophehad's daughters is the earliest recorded case which is still of authority.

When the king or chief ceases to bear all offices in his own person, and the political division of labour begins, those functions which had a sacred character naturally become attached to a priesthood or sacred tribe or family, and among them the custody and interpretation of the law. The distinction between religious and secular law is, one need hardly say, much later. Thus we find in both Germanic and Roman antiquity more than traces of priests, or nobles who claimed the priest's office as a birthright, being the first judges (Grimm, "D.R.A." 272, i. 378 in 4th ed.). In Iceland the rather vague but not ineffectual authority which was ascribed to the Speaker of the Law seems to have had a religious character. At any rate we read in the Njáls Saga that to him, and him alone, was left the momentous decision of the question, which had all but led to civil war, whether Christianity should be adopted (Dasent, "Burut Njal," ch. ci.). There seems to be no reason against accepting this incident as mainly historical. It is worth observing that Thorgeir would not make his award until both the Christian and the heathen party had given pledges to abide by it: a striking illustration of the voluntary and arbitral character of early jurisdiction. Edward I. of England, more than two centuries later, used similar precaution when he adjudicated on the claims to the crown of Scotland.

Whether a monopoly of legal knowledge is established in the hands of a privileged caste or order, or a tradition of learning is handed down in something like a school, or, without any profession of secrecy, certain persons enjoy for the time being the reputation of superior knowledge, appears to depend on the particular circumstances of each community. Besides the

Speaker of the Law, we find in the Iceland of the Sagas a few specially wise men, Njál himself, and after his death one or two others, whose advice is eagerly sought by their neighbours, and whose deliberate opinion is almost conclusive; yet there is no possible distinction of race or rank in that singularly homogeneous republic. A like position is ascribed to Nestor. This kind of reputation is obviously not less but more important in a society where jurisdiction and judicial power have not yet become compulsory; for the chances that any judgment or award will be observed will, in such a society, depend largely on the respect in which the acting judge or daysman is held.

Maine adds that law preserved as a kind of trade secret by a privileged class is the only real unwritten law. This may be literally true. But our current professional use of the term is really a matter of literary convention. We find it useful to confine the term " written law " to an enactment or declaration which is authoritative not only in matter but in form, so that its very words not only contain but constitute the law. An exposition whose very words are not binding is " unwritten law," however great its authority may be in substance. Consider the case of a judge in England, or any other jurisdiction under the system of the Common Law, making a careful statement of some point of law in a book written and published by him. This is only a private learned opinion, and has, properly speaking, no authority at all. But the same or another judge may adopt the statement in a reported judgment. It then acquires authority as a judicial exposition of the law, but still its actual terms are not binding, and it counts as " unwritten law." Finally, the proposition may be embodied in a statute. It then becomes " written law," and the Courts will have for the future to treat not only the substance but every word of it as authentic. The distinction is quite real, and no better way of expressing it has been found. French usage, moreover, presents a close analogy. Under the old monarchy the provinces of written law (*pays de droit écrit*) were those where the texts of Roman law were received as having binding authority, while in the *pays de droit coutumier* they were cited only for example and illustration, on the merits of the reason embodied in them, as they may be and sometimes are in England. Thus the same text might be " written " law in one province and "unwritten " (though there is no corresponding French term) in another. A learned modern writer says of the antithesis between *ius scriptum* and *ius*

non scriptum, after careful examination of the various mean-
ings with which they occur in the writings of the classical
Roman lawyers: " Its general practical use with them is as a
distinction between customary law, on the one hand, and law
drawn up and issued in any regular manner by any legislative
authority, on the other. . . . The above is also the practical
use of the distinction . . . by our English jurists, so far as
they use it at all. . . . With modern Continental writers *written* and *unwritten* in general designate respectively *enacted* and
customary law " (E. C. Clark, "Practical Jurisprudence," p.
272).

Maine's brief remarks on early codes (pp. 12-18) include
a few sentences on Hindu law; these were written at a
time when the existence of the books called by the names of
Manu and Narada was hardly known outside Anglo-Indian
official circles except to a few students of Sanskrit. In later
years, after having been a member of the Government of
India, he returned to the subject. The chapters in "Early
Law and Custom" on "The Sacred Laws of the Hindus,"
"Religion in Law," and "Classifications of Legal Rules,"
should be read accordingly as a supplement; and the second
and third lectures in "Village Communities" should also be
consulted as to the general nature of archaic customary law,
and the effect produced on it by contact with a modern system.

Timely codification of customs, as Maine observes (pp. 14,
15), may prevent degradation; I must confess that the ascription of such an effect to the Twelve Tables, though ingenious
and pleasing as a conjecture, appears to me to go beyond what
is warranted by our knowledge of the state and tendencies of
Roman society under the earlier Republic. It is certain that
conversely the fixing of law in a codified form at a later stage
may arrest a normal and scientific development. Such was the
result of the Ordinance which stereotyped the French law of
negotiable instruments in 1673 (Chalmers, "Bills of Exchange,"
Introduction, p. lvi). It would seem, indeed, that the Twelve
Tables themselves went near to stereotype an archaic and
formalist procedure, and that the Romans of later generations
escaped from great inconvenience only by the devices of legal
fictions and equity which Maine considers in the following
chapter.

CHAPTER II. Page 20.

NOTE D.

ENGLISH CASE-LAW AND FICTION.

ABOUT the middle of the nineteenth century, and somewhat later, the language currently used by text-writers was such as to warrant Maine's selection of the authority of decided cases in England as an example of legal fiction. But the twentieth-century reader, if he has taken to heart Maine's brilliant generalisation in the earlier part of the chapter, will hardly expect the ideas and formulas even of English lawyers to have remained stationary in the midst of a progressive society; and in fact, though probably no society has ever made progress at a uniform rate all along the line, and there may quite conceivably be stagnation or even falling back in some departments while there is advance in others, criticism of legal ideas has advanced a good deal in the English-speaking world. No intelligent lawyer would at this day pretend that the decisions of the Courts do not add to and alter the law. The Courts themselves, in the course of the reasons given for those decisions, constantly and freely use language admitting that they do. Certainly they do not claim legislative power; nor, with all respect for Maine, do they exercise it. For a legislator is not bound to conform to the known existing rules or principles of law; statutes may not only amend but reverse the rule, or they may introduce absolutely novel principles and remedies, like the Workmen's Compensation Act. Still less, if possible, is he bound to respect previous legislation. But English judges are bound to give their decisions in conformity with the settled general principles of English law, with any express legislation applicable to the matter in hand, and with the authority of their predecessors and their own former decisions. At the same time they are bound to find a decision for every case, however novel it may be; and that decision will be authority for other like cases in future; therefore it is part of their duty to lay down new rules if required. Perhaps this is really the first and greatest rule of our customary law: that, failing a specific rule already ascertained and fitting the case in hand, the King's judges must find and apply the most reasonable rule they can, so that it be not inconsistent with any established principle. They not only may but must develop the law in every direction except that of contradicting rules which authority has once fixed. Whoever denies this must deny that novel combinations of facts are brought before the Courts from time to time, which is a truth vouched by common experience and recognised in the forensic phrase describing such cases as " of the first impression " ; or else he must refuse to accept the principle that the Court is bound to find a decision for every case, however novel. It is true that at many times the Courts have been over-anxious to avoid the appearance of novelty; and the shifts to which they resorted to avoid it have encumbered the Common Law with several of the fictions which Maine denounces (p. 27) as almost hopeless obstacles to an orderly distribution of its contents.

Perhaps Maine's exposition hardly brings out the prevailing motive for introducing fictions, the desire of obtaining a speedier or more complete remedy than the strictly appropriate form of procedure affords. Among the regular though not invariable marks of fictions in modern English law is the use of the word " constructive " or the word " implied," as any careful student may note for himself. It would be rash to suppose that the age of legal fictions is wholly past. When " Ancient Law " was written, one example was quite recent in our Courts, the rule that a man who professes to contract as an agent is deemed to warrant that he has authority from his alleged principal. This is a fiction, but beneficent and elegant, and it is now fully accepted.

CHAPTER III. Page 42.

NOTE E.

THE LAW OF NATURE AND " IUS GENTIUM."

MAINE's third and fourth chapters need more supplemental criticism than any other part of " Ancient Law." The medieval doctrine of the Law of Nature, and its continuity with the classical Roman doctrine, had been forgotten or misunderstood in England for quite two centuries at the time when these chapters were written; and even many years later there was no obvious way for an English scholar to get back to the right historical lines. I owe my own guidance mainly to a somewhat belated acquaintance with Dr. Gierke's exhaustive treatment of the controversies which occupied the publicists of the Middle Ages and " the Renaissance " (" Johannes Althusius und die Entwicklung der naturrechtlichen Staatstheorien," Breslau,

1880; "Political Theories of the Middle Age," transl. with introduction by F. W. Maitland, Cambridge, 1900, from "Die Staats- und Korporationslehre," etc., Berlin, 1881; Pollock, "The History of the Law of Nature," Journ. Soc. Comp. Legisl., 1900, p. 418). Mr. Bryce's recent essay on the Law of Nature ("Studies in History and Jurisprudence," Oxford, 1901, ii. 112) should be read and considered by all students of legal history.

Maine was not a medievalist or a canonist, and shared the general ignorance of English lawyers and scholars of his time. Accordingly his statement practically neglects the Middle Ages, and suggests, though it does not assert in terms, that the law of nature as understood by the publicists of the seventeenth and eighteenth centuries was derived exclusively from the classical Roman lawyers; that the influence of Greek philosophy was only indirect and through Roman law; and that the conception of a primeval and innocent "state of nature" was an integral part of the doctrine. Not one of these inferences would be correct. The theory of Grotius is continuous with that of the canonists and schoolmen; the medieval doctrine is founded on Aristotle and Cicero, no less than on the Corpus Iuris; and the "state of nature" of eighteenth-century writers is an exaggerated perversion of what, in the traditional system, is a quite subordinate point.

Political justice is divided, according to Aristotle ("Eth. Nic." V. vii.; this is one of the books not written by Aristotle himself, but the substance is admitted to represent his teaching), into natural (τὸ μὲν φυσικόν, *naturale*) and conventional (τὸ δὲ νομικόν, *legale*). The Latin equivalents are from the current medieval translation directed by St. Thomas Aquinas. The rules of natural justice are those which all civilised men recognise. Those of conventional justice deal with matters indifferent in themselves or otherwise capable of being settled only by positive authority. Natural justice may tell me not to drive recklessly, but cannot tell me which is the right side of the road, a question which conventional justice answers one way in these kingdoms and the other in America and most, though not all, European Continental countries. Rules involving number and measure, again, cannot be fixed by natural justice alone. It is to be observed that Aristotle's conception of Nature implies rational design, and this was more fully worked out by the later Greek schools, and especially the Stoics. Maine, though he was an excellent classical scholar, omits all mention of Aristotle; but Aristotle is not prominent in the

later literature of the subject which he almost exclusively
made use of.

The Greek philosophical doctrine acquired an elegant Latin
form in Cicero's hands at the very time when thoughtful Roman lawyers were in need of a theoretical foundation for the
addition of the *ius gentium* to the old strict and archaic rules.
Now *ius gentium*, in its original meaning, has nothing to do
with distinct nations or tribes (which is not the meaning of
gentes), but signifies the rules accepted as binding by all people (Nettleship, "Contributions to Latin Lexicography," *s. v.*;
cp. E. C. Clark, "Practical Jurisprudence," p. 354). Towards
the end of the republican period, it would seem not before
Cicero's time, it became the special name of the rules administered by Roman magistrates in causes where Roman law
proper was inapplicable, by reason of the parties not being
both Roman citizens or allies, or otherwise. The personal and
religious laws of one community are incapable, in archaic
society, of being used by members of another; and such is still
the universal custom of India, broken only, so far as it is
broken, by the introduction of cosmopolitan ideas and habits
from Europe. Many Roman legal formulas involved a religious
element, and for that reason, we may be pretty sure, were available for Romans only: we know that in one case, that of the
words *Dari spondes? spondeo*, such a restriction was still in force
under the Empire. Similarly two strangers living under different laws of their own could not both be judged by either of
those laws any more than by Roman law. There is no necessary question of one law being thought better in itself than
another, or of "disdain for all foreign law"; still less of the
Romans having refused requests for the application of Roman
law which are most unlikely to have ever been made
(pp. 48, 49). What we find, at any rate, in the conflict of personal laws in the early Middle Ages is that every man wants
to be judged by his own law. This being out of the question,
the needs of business called for some practical solution in a
jurisdiction into which the growing power of Rome brought
merchants and traders from all parts of the Mediterranean.
It is hard to believe that there was not already some kind of
general custom among those merchants for matters of common occurrence, or that the Roman Praetor did not find it
easier to adopt any such custom, if satisfied of its existence,
than to frame a new rule by deliberate selection from the elements common to the domestic law of Rome and other Italian

States. The recognition of the Law Merchant in England by the Common Law seems a nearer modern parallel than the development of the rules of Equity. Maine himself pointed out, in a later work, that the *ius gentium* was in part originally a market law, and grew out of commercial exigencies (" Village Communities," pp. 193-4). It is significant in this connexion that in the later Middle Ages and down to the seventeenth century English books regularly treat the Law Merchant of Western Christendom as equivalent to the law of nature, or a branch of it (Pollock, Journ. Soc. Comp. Legisl., 1900, p. 431; " The Expansion of the Common Law," p. 117).

However this may be, the actual *ius gentium* agreed well enough with the rules of natural justice or natural law in the sense of the Greek philosophers, so far as these could be observed in practice. Accordingly the Roman lawyers, probably working on Greek materials now lost, identified *ius gentium* for most practical purposes with *ius naturale*: they regarded it as the sum of rules which were evident to natural reason, and received by all men because they were reasonable; " quod vero naturalis ratio inter omnes homines constituit, id apud omnes populos peraeque custoditur vocaturque ius gentium, quasi quo iure omnes gentes utuntur " (Gai. i. § 1). But this or any similar statement leaves it an open question whether *ius gentium* really coincides with *ius naturale*. There may possibly be rules that deserve to be recognised by all mankind, but in fact are not; and there may be universal or very widely prevailing usages which natural reason will not justify. Slavery was a recognised institution, part of the general customs of the Roman Empire if anything was; but the enlightened age of the Antonines could find no warrant for it in philosophy, and the incongruity pressed on at least one or two of the classical Roman jurists. Modern specialists in Roman law have not been able to agree what was exactly their doctrine as to the relation of the ideal to the actual usage of mankind, or whether there was any one accepted doctrine at all in the law schools of the empire. There is no apparent reason why there should have been any official or settled opinion on such a speculative point. Perhaps we should not be far from the truth if we said, in the language familiar to our own system, that *ius gentium* was presumed to follow *ius naturale* if the contrary did not appear.

As for the celebrated passage of Ulpian which defines the law of nature as common to man and other animals, " quod natura omnia animalia docuit," and distinguishes it on this ground from *ius gentium*, the rule confined to men, "solis hominibus inter se commune," we are not bound to believe that it was current among Roman lawyers in Ulpian's own time, or anything but a conceit borrowed from some forgotten Greek rhetorician. It stands alone in the classical texts, but its conspicuous adoption at the beginning of both the Digest and the Institutes of Justinian was the cause of endless trouble to the medieval commentators, for whom every word in the Corpus Iuris was of equal authority. Maine assumes the invention to have been Ulpian's own, and ascribes it to "the propensity to distinguish characteristic of a lawyer"; I can only say that it does not look to me like a working lawyer's point.[1]

Maine's suggestions, beginning at p. 55, as to "the exact point of contact between the old *ius gentium* and the law of nature," being given by a conjectured special sense of *aequitas* are ingenious, but hardly seem required. The general coincidence between *ius gentium* and the φυσικὸν δίακιον of Greek philosophy was obvious enough to jurists in search of a theory without being emphasised by any one special point of contact. *Aequitas* appears, in classical Latin usage, to come very near "reasonableness"; and in fact the word *reason* and its derivatives are the proper terms in the Common Law for conveying the ideas, or some of them, which are at the bottom of the law of nature, as St. German pointed out nearly four centuries ago in "Doctor and Student." Maine appears to have assumed that the Roman doctrine included the historical acceptance of a golden age: "the belief gradually prevailed among the Roman lawyers that the old *jus gentium* was in fact the lost code of nature," p. 54. I am bound to say that I do not know of any evidence that such was the belief of either lawyers or philosophers. Certainly no Greek philosopher would have admitted that the law of nature was lost, nor would Cicero; and as to the supposition that *ius gentium* was the law of the golden age in the opinion of the philosophic lawyers, "so far were they from such a delusion," says Mr. Bryce, "that they ascribe to *ius gentium* war, captivity, slavery, and all the consequences of

[1] The suggestion that it is the nature of lawyers to distinguish where there is no difference may possibly have been inspired by Hobbes's censure of Coke in his Dialogue of the Common Laws of England:—"Sir Edw. Coke does seldom well distinguish when there are two divers Names for one and the same thing; though one contain the other, he makes them always different, as if it could not be that one and the same Man should be both an Enemy, and a Traytor."

these facts, while in the golden age, the *Saturnia regna* of the poets, all men were free and war was unknown." *Ius gentium* is the common law or custom of mankind, actual not ideal custom. Just as little is there any traceable connection between the fables of a golden age and the fundamental conception of natural law, namely, that general rules of human conduct are at all times discoverable by human reason as being reasonable. The doctrine of the Roman jurists does not involve any historical assumption at all, neither, in itself, does that of the medieval doctors and commentators, although these, as good Catholics, accepted the Fall of Man and could give theological reasons for the law of nature not being sufficient in practice. Moreover, it is not probable that *ius gentium*, as a term of art, is much or at all older than *ius naturale* or *naturae*.

NOTE F.

EQUITY.

A peculiar historical development has given this word a technical meaning among English-speaking lawyers. "Reasonableness," as mentioned in the last note, appears to be the primary and general idea. This conception, when embodied for practical use as an appeal to the common sense of right-minded men, is closely akin to that of natural justice, and further resembles it in being traceable to Aristotle. It is of the utmost importance in many branches of our modern law; but we have specialised the name of Equity for one application of it, namely that administration of extraordinary justice by the king with the advice of his Chancellor and Council, and afterwards through the Chancellor alone, which produced the Court of Chancery. Maine, when he wrote "Ancient Law," seems to have doubted the historical truth of "the king's general right to superintend the administration of justice" (p. 68); but in "Early Law and Custom" (ch. vi., "The King and Early Civil Justice," p. 164), it is fully recognised. The king was held to retain a "pre-eminence of jurisdiction . . . as well for amendment as for supply of the Common Law," though he could not alter a regular jurisdiction once established; this "supplementary or residuary jurisdiction," as Maine aptly calls it, was exercised to form the Court of Chancery, and in due time it was held, as was inevitable, that this also had become an established Court, that the king's power to do equity as well as strict legal justice had been completely delegated, and

that accordingly he could not create any new equitable jurisdiction. It was no less inevitable that after this Equity should
become a technical system (cp. Pollock, "The Expansion of
the Common Law," pp. 67-73).

Maine pointed out (E. L. and C., p. 166) that the early Roman law, "a stiff system of technical and ceremonious law,"
"underwent a transformation through this very residuary or
supplementary royal authority," which under the Roman Republic was vested in the Praetor. "What has descended to so
large a part of the modern world is not the coarse Roman
law, but the Roman law distilled through the jurisdiction of
the Praetor, and by him gradually bent into supposed accordance with the law of nature."

As to the relation of our Court of Chancery to the law of
nature, I endeavoured to sum it up two years ago in a course of
lectures given in America: "The early Chancellors did not disclose the sources of their inspiration; probably they had as
good grounds of expediency for not talking about the law of
nature as the common lawyers." The law of nature was intimately associated with the canon law, and for English lay people in the Middle Ages canon law signified obnoxious meddling
of foreign ecclesiastics with English benefices and revenues,
besides the vexatious and inquisitorial jurisdiction of bishops'
and archdeacons' courts. "Certainly [the Chancellors] intended and endeavoured to follow the dictate of natural reason;
and if their version of natural justice was somewhat artificial in its details, and bore a decided civilian or canonical
stamp, this was only to be expected. Some centuries later,
when British judicial officers in India were instructed to decide, in the absence of any native law applicable to both parties, according to "justice, equity, and good conscience," the
results bore, even more manifestly, the stamp of the Common
Law" ("The Expansion of the Common Law," p. 114).

CHAPTER IV. Page 70.

NOTE G.

MEDIEVAL AND MODERN TREATMENT OF THE LAW OF NATURE:
BRACTON: FRENCH PUBLICISTS.

MUCH that has been written about the law of nature in modern
times is, as Maine says, extremely confused. This may be due
to several causes, but one cause which would alone be sufficient

is the neglect of the scholastic tradition, amounting to practical oblivion, which followed on the Reformation controversies. Hooker was the latest English writer who possessed the tradition, and accordingly stated a consistent and intelligible doctrine. What the canonists and schoolmen added to the classical Roman theory was the identification of the law of nature with the law of God revealed in human reason: in this way they reconciled the temporal authority of the Corpus Iuris and the moral authority of the philosophers (for Aristotle and Cicero, though heathens, had become almost sacred by orthodox commendations) with the spiritual authority of the Church. The natural revelation through reason and the supernatural revelation committed to the Church are equally divine, and cannot contradict one another; and the law of nature is no less paramount to any positive rule or custom of human origin than express revelation itself. The risk of this doctrine being turned against the Church or the Pope was, no doubt, serious, as later events proved; but it had to be taken. Hence the scholastic theory of the law of nature, though attempts were made to use it for the most opposite purposes, was on the whole rationalist and progressive. Indeed, it had several points of affinity with the utilitarian doctrine of our own times, although the founders of that school, who may be said to have neglected history on principle, were unaware of the fact. Natural justice had been identified by Epicurus with an agreement among men for their common advantage to abstain from harming one another (see Bryce, " Studies," ii. 127). In the fourteenth century we actually find *communis utilitas* a current term with William of Ockham and others, and it is used to denote a criterion for ascertaining what the law of nature prescribes; and this was only the development of a tendency already visible in St. Thomas Aquinas. Maine perceived the analogy, and suggested that it might not be too fanciful to call natural law the ancient counterpart of Benthamism (p. 76).

Beyond the fundamental principles of natural justice, we may deduce by natural reason various rules which may or might be convenient in the absence of competent jurisdiction, but, as they are in matter of convenience and not of absolute right, may be modified by the law of the land. Rules of this kind were said to be secondary; and the so-called " state of nature " is, from the point of view of the schoolmen, merely human society conceived as governed by the "secondary law of nature" in default of positive ordinance, or any human society so far as it is actually found in that condition. Thus during a great part of the Middle Ages most of what we know as the law of contract was left to the law of nature, which was supposed to be the ultimate authority for the custom of merchants. Nothing can more strongly illustrate the confusion which resulted from neglecting this distinction than the modern belief that natural law as a whole depends on the "state of nature," or assumes it to be better than civilisation. The scholastic habit of mind was alien from ours in many ways; but at any rate the schoolmen took some pains to know what they were talking about.

Hooker's statement of the first principles, as understood down to the sixteenth century, is quite accurate, and perhaps the most profitable for English readers. The law of nature is a law of reason. Its rules "are investigable by Reason, without the help of Revelation supernatural and divine . . . the knowledge of them is general, the world hath always been acquainted with them. . . . It is not agreed upon by one, or two, or few, but by all. Which we may not so understand, as if every particular man in the whole world did know and confess whatsoever the law of reason doth contain; but this law is such that being proposed no man can reject it as unreasonable and unjust. Again, there is nothing in it but any man (having natural perfection of wit and ripeness of judgment) may by labour and travail find out." But the law of nature does not include all binding laws: "we restrain it to those only duties, which all men by force of natural wit either do or might understand to be such duties as concern all men" ("Eccl. Pol." I. viii. 10). A strange contrast to Hooker's clear apprehension and intelligent use of the medieval tradition is presented by the loose talk about the law of nature and the law of reason (apparently supposed to be different things) in Sir Henry Finch's "Discourse of Law," published in 1613. Before the middle of the eighteenth century the conception of "the aboriginal reign of nature" had gained a footing, and the confusion was complete. No less a man than Montesquieu thought natural law could be defined merely as the rules that would have been appropriate for men living before the formation of civil society ("Esprit des Lois," I. ii.). The vitality of the old doctrine had in truth passed into the new science built on its foundations by Grotius and his successors; and such ornamental references to the law of nature as occur in Black-

stone and other English writers of his time are echoes of contemporary or recent Continental publicists whose real subject-
matter was the law of nations in its modern sense. In later
Continental and especially German usage natural law is taken,
by a considerable but legitimate extension, to denote all speculative construction in jurisprudence and politics as contrasted
with the purely historical or comparative study of institutions;
in the terms most familiar to English readers, it covers the
whole ground of general jurisprudence and the theory of legislation. Herbert Spencer's volume on Justice and the essays
of the Fabian Society would alike be classed as books of
Naturrecht. Writers of the historical school who consider the
law of nature obsolete include British utilitarian doctrine in
their condemnation as a matter of course, as being a mere
branch of it.

There are some incidental statements of Maine's in this connexion which need comment. What is said about the unques-
tioning respect paid in the Middle Ages to written texts is undoubtedly true, and is indeed rather understated. Reverence
for any plausible show of authority was not confined to theology or law, and it was not necessary that the text quoted
should purport to have any obligatory force, or that the sense
in which it was quoted should be the natural one. Aristotle
was nearly as good authority as the Bible, though not quite;
Cicero was only second to Aristotle; and the Corpus Iuris was
"written reason" even in jurisdictions where it was not binding. But in default of the Vulgate or the Philosopher, learned
writers were glad enough to quote Virgil or Ovid or Lucan,
though without any intention of putting them on a level with
Scripture. Maine's particular illustration from "the plagiarisms of Bracton" is unfortunate. I do not know on what
book or man having a pretended knowledge of Bracton he relied; certainly there were very few men living forty-five years
ago who had studied Bracton to such purpose as to be qualified to inform him, and certainly he had not then made any
critical examination of his own; but the solution of the historical enigma which Maine, with great reason, found in Bracton's alleged wholesale borrowing from Roman law is simply
that the fact is not so. Not one-thirtieth of Bracton's matter,
instead of a third as affirmed by Maine's unknown authority,
is taken from the Corpus Iuris (Maitland, "Bracton and Azo,"
Selden Soc. 1895, p. xiv, which see on the whole matter).
Bracton used Roman law, chiefly through Azo's famous gloss,

partly as a systematic framework and partly as a store of written reason to fill up gaps in English learning. He had no thought of putting it off on his countrymen as " pure English law," any more than a lawyer at Paris would have sought to put it off as pure Parisian custom; there is no concealment of its origin. When actual English custom was contrary to Roman law, Henry of Bratton (for such, it is now known, was his real name) did not hesitate to deny the Roman propositions.

Further, it is at least misleading to say that " the systematic study of the Roman law was formerly proscribed " in England. The only prohibition of which there is any evidence was confined to London; it is doubtful whether its purpose was to hold clerks in orders to their proper study of the canon as distinguished from the civil law, or to prevent London teachers from competing with the civilians of Oxford (Pollock and Maitland, " H.E.L.," i. 102). Roman law was not only taught at Oxford and Cambridge without interruption, but sometimes, though not often, cited, at least in a general way, in the King's Courts (Selden ad Fletam, pp. 528-530).[1] There is no reason whatever to suppose that any one thought it needful or expedient to protect the Common Law against a Roman invasion. Blackstone (" Comm.," i. 20-22) contrived, by accumulating mistakes, to draw an imaginary picture of English aversion and contempt for the civil law. In the case cited by him, Y. B. 22 Ed. III. 14 (not 24), what really happened was this. Counsel said, by way of preliminary objection, that the Court had no judicial knowledge of what the civilian—or rather, in the case in hand, canonist—process of *inhibitio novi operis* was: to which Justice Shardelowe replied in effect: " That is only what they call restitution in their law, so we think nothing of your point; you must answer to the merits "; and the argument proceeded accordingly. Nothing here shows very gross ignorance, although the language might not satisfy a learned civilian; the Court, so far from treating Roman words of art as nonsense, professed to understand them quite enough for the purpose in hand; and the only contempt in question was that of an abbot who was charged with having cited a prior to the Pope's Court at Avignon and persisted in disregard of the

[1] Selden speaks of two cases in a certain Inner Temple MS. of Year Books of Ed. II., where Roman texts are even cited with precise reference in the accustomed form of civilians. But this MS. is not now to be found, and, such references being otherwise unknown in other extant Year Books, it is safer, as my learned friend Professor Maitland suggests, to think that they were added by a specially learned scribe.

king's prohibition. But in the nineteenth century an over-zealous Romanising lawyer called Shardelowe an old savage on the strength of Blackstone's misunderstanding. What is really curious in the matter is that Blackstone appears to have been misled by Selden (ad Fletam, p. 533), who cites this to prove that Roman law had become unknown in the King's Courts in the reign of Edward III., though he does not use anything like Blackstone's rhetorical language about contempt and aversion. With all respect for Selden, I see no room for doubt that he did misunderstand the case; perhaps he was nodding a little, for he calls Shardelowe J. "Shardus." His general thesis that knowledge of Roman law in England, except among professed canonists, declined rapidly after the reign of Edward II., is doubtless correct. But there was no question of hostility. Not the fourteenth or thirteenth, but the sixteenth century was the time of recrimination between common lawyers and civilians, and perhaps of some real danger to the Common Law (Maitland, "English Law and the Renaissance" ; Pollock, "The Expansion of the Common Law," p. 88).

Maine's remarks on the enthusiasm of French lawyers for natural law (p. 80 sqq.) seem rather to ignore its general reception by Continental publicists; though the centralisation of the French monarchy no doubt made it easier for them to have something like uniform official doctrine. The enfranchising ordinance of Louis Hutin cited at p. 90, which asserts that all men ought to be free by natural law, repeats an earlier one issued by Philip the Fair in 1311 (" Journ. Soc. Comp. Legisl.," 1900, pp. 426-7). It is not very clear that the framers of this ordinance were thinking of the Roman maxim, " omnes homines natura aequales sunt " (or rather " quod ad ius naturale attinet omnes homines aequales sunt ": Ulpian in D. *de div. reg.* 50, 17, 32) ; for the general tone is decidedly more religious than secular, and the Church had always favoured manumission as a pious work. If they had wanted to vouch the authority of the Digest that slavery was not recognised by the law of nature, they might easily have made the reference more pointed. That Ulpian did not mean to preach an ethical or political creed of equality is, as Maine says, plain enough; his assertion is that slavery (like other inequalities of condition) is justified only by positive law. At the same time no medieval publicist who desired to use the passage for his own purposes would have troubled himself about the author's original intention.

At p. 82 there is a statement about Dumoulin's opinions which I have not been able to verify. Charles Dumoulin (properly Du Molin, latinised as Molinaeus, 1500-1566) was a profound jurist and a famous champion of Gallican liberties against the Papal claims. He was for some time a Calvinist, and afterwards a Lutheran, but his biographer Julien Brodeau, whose book[1] seems to be the ultimate authority, was anxious to make it clear that he died a Catholic; which from the Gallican point of view was only natural. His life was wandering and troubled, and is a striking example of the general disturbance into which the world of letters as well as of action was thrown by the Reformation controversies; twice he fled from Paris, and twice his house was sacked under colour of zeal for Roman orthodoxy. The standard edition of his works was printed at Paris in 1681 in five volumes, folio, and is copiously indexed. I have not found in them anything about the law of nature except one depreciatory remark in a note on the Decretum of Gratian (Annotationes ad ius canonicum, in vol. 4): "politia externa regitur iure naturali et politico, sed utrumque subest divino quod altius est naturali." This directly contradicts the received theory, which put the law of nature (principles of right revealed in human reason) before the Law of God (interpretation of specific precepts communicated by external revelation). I suspect that Du Molin, writing at that time as a Protestant, took the Law of God to be the text of Scripture, and meant that the text was to be preferred to the reasonings of the schools: compare the so-called Protestant declaration formerly in use on the admission of Fellows at Trinity College, Cambridge, "verbum Dei iudiciis hominum praepositurum." Whatever the exact significance may be, Du Molin's observation is the reverse of a panegyric on the law of nature. One can only suppose that the rhetorical passages of which Maine appears to have had a pretty distinct recollection occur in some other French jurist of the time, and that the introduction of Du Molin's name was due to a slip of memory or to some accidental dislocation or misreading of manuscript notes.

It has already been pointed out that Maine greatly exaggerated the place of the "state of nature" in the doctrines of natural law. This comes out again in a startling manner in

[1] La vie de Maistre Charles Du Molin, advocat au Parlement de Paris . . . et sa mort chrestienne et catholique. Par Mc Julien Brodeau, advocat au mesme Parlement. Paris 1654, 4°.

his remarks on Rousseau (p. 84).[1] Whatever Rousseau may
have said elsewhere, we shall not find anything about the original perfection of mankind in the " Contrat Social," to which
Maine apparently meant to refer. Rousseau believed, certainly,
in natural law, and to some extent in the virtues of the " natural man " as an individual; but his " state of nature " is not
much better than Hobbes's; it is unstable and becomes intolerable, and the social contract is dictated by the need of self-
preservation (liv. i. ch. vi.); justice, which did not exist in the
state of nature, is due to the establishment of political society
(ch. viii.). This is not the place to speak at large of Rousseau's influence on the founders of American independence and
the leaders of the French Revolution; but the careful research
of American scholars has lately shown that the Principles of
1789 owed more to the American Declaration of Independence
and the earlier Bills of Rights of several States than we used
to suppose, and less to Rousseau, and that the language of the
American constitutional instruments proceeded from the school
not of Rousseau but of Locke (Scherger, " The Evolution of
Modern Liberty," New York, 1904).

NOTE H.

THE ORIGINS OF THE MODERN LAW OF NATIONS.

Maine's statement (p. 92) seems to ignore the continuity of
Grotius and his immediate precursors with the scholastic doctrine. It is true that the spread of the New Learning, and still
more the Reformation, did largely increase the weight of the
classical and diminish that of the medieval elements; but it is
also true that Grotius did not rely exclusively on Roman or on
legal authorities. That Grotius and his contemporaries misunderstood the classical *ius gentium*, or supposed the modern
rules of conduct between sovereign states to be contained in
it, I am unable, with great respect for any suggestion of
Maine's, to believe. The term had become less common than
its practical synonym *ius naturale* in the Middle Ages, but came
into fashion again with the Renaissance. Grotius, like Al-
berico Gentili, takes *ius gentium* as the rule of natural reason
attested by general agreement, and makes it the starting-point

---

[1] " Nothing that Rousseau had to say about the state of nature was
seriously meant for scientific exposition, any more than the Sermon on
the Mount was meant for political economy " (John Morley, " Rousseau,"
i. 183).

of a new development. He may or may not have known that in its classical meaning it could, and sometimes did, include, among other rules of conduct sanctioned by general usage, whatever rules are reasonable and customary as between sovereign states. But as a scholar he must have known that *gentes* is not the plural of *civitas* or *populus*, which are the only apt words in classical Latin for a state or nation in its political capacity. At the same time Suarez had spoken of *iura gentium* with an approach to the modern " law of nations," and Hooker had used the English term in a fully international sense (" Eccl. Pol." I. x. § 12). There was no reason for Grotius to refuse the assistance of a verbal ambiguity, so far as it existed and could further his purposes (cp. L.Q.R. xviii. 425-8). The modern law of nations embodies certain distinctly legal conceptions. These are Roman and purely Roman. Inasmuch as, from the sixteenth century onwards, Roman law was generally received throughout Western Christendom, with the one material exception of England, as a kind of universal law, there is nothing surprising in this fact, and indeed nothing else could have happened. Maine's following observations (p. 98 sqq.) as to the application of Roman ideas in the modern law of nations, and especially the treatment of every independent State, with regard to its territory, as if it were an owner or claimant of ownership under Roman law, and the relatively modern character of purely territorial dominion, show the author at his best. The theoretical equality of independent States naturally follows from their recognition as analogous to free persons, who must have full and equal rights in the absence of any definite reason for inequality. This indeed is all that the maxim of men's equality before the law of nature declares or involves according to its classical meaning (p. 96).

It is interesting in connexion with Maine's thesis to observe how in our time the usual rules of international law cease to be applicable, or fail to give an adequate solution of difficulties, just in proportion as the fact of territorial sovereignty is not complete and definite. This is now of frequent occurrence in cases of " spheres of influence " in unsettled parts of the world, of protectorates, and of what are called semi-sovereign States dependent in various degrees on other and more powerful ones. In the last-named class we may notice a certain reversion to feudal conceptions. It would have been much easier to express the relations of Great Britain to the late

South African Republic in medieval than in classical Latin. As to the Anglo-Saxon kingship, it should be remembered that the English kings never owed or rendered any temporal allegiance to the Empire and any other power, or that the assumption of the imperial title " Basileus " involved a pretty strong claim to temporal supremacy within approximately certain territorial limits. In this respect the situation of England was peculiar. Modern national sovereignty may be regarded, in a general way, as a reaction against both the feudal and the imperial conceptions. Rulers of the Middle Ages, as and when they felt strong enough, expressly or tacitly renounced both homage to any overlord and submission to the Emperor. A German electoral prince or grand duke in the decadence of the Holy Roman Empire, say the Elector of Brandenburg, is from the strictly feudal point of view an overgrown tenant of the Emperor who has added one " immunity " to another till he has strained the tie of fealty to the breaking point. From the strictly imperial point of view, if it had been maintained to any practical purpose, he would or might be a rebel. Feudal tenure, however, probably led to the notion of the territory ruled by a sovereign prince being really—not by mere analogy to ownership in private law—his property. For, so long as overlordship was a reality, every principality, short of the Empire and the few monarchies which did not acknowledge the Emperor as superior, was in theory a " tenement "; and in the feudal system a tenement is indistinguishable from property; for absolute property is not recognised save in the supreme overlord, as is the strict theory of English and Scottish law to this day. This ultimate and now shadowy feudal superiority has nothing to do with the modern and purely political conception of Eminent Domain, though more than once they have been confused by able writers.

It must not be supposed, however, that medieval lawyers were incapable of distinguishing between territorial sovereignty and feudal overlordship. The distinction was clearly made in 1284 by the framers of Edward I.'s Statute of Wales. In its preamble the king is made to acknowledge the bounty of Providence whereby the land of Wales, formerly subject to him as a fief, has been wholly reduced into his lordship in possession and annexed to his crown as part of the body of the kingdom.

" Divina Providentia . . . inter alia dispensacionis sue munera quibus nos et regnum nostrum Anglie decorare dignata est terram Wallie cum incolis suis prius nobis iure feodali sublectam iam sui [*sic*] gratia in proprietatis nostre dominium . . . totaliter et cum integritate convertit et corone Regni predicti tanquam partem corporis eiusdem annexuit et univit " (" Statutes of the Realm," i. 55).

CHAPTER V. Page 109.

NOTE I.

MONTESQUIEU, BENTHAM, AND HISTORICAL METHOD.

MAINE'S judgment of Montesquieu is, in effect, that, notwithstanding inevitable defects of method and some individual faults, he came nearer than any other man to founding the historical and comparative study of institutions. It is true, as Sir Courtenay Ilbert has said in a fuller criticism (" The Romanes Lecture: ' Montesquieu,' " Oxford, 1904), that " his appreciation of the historical method was imperfect, and his application of it defective ": at the same time his work " prepared for and gave an enormous stimulus to those methods of study which are now recognised as indispensable to any scientific treatment either of Law or of Politics " (*op. cit.* pp. 35-6).

In 1903, on quitting the chair which I had the honour of holding in succession to Maine at Oxford, I thus endeavoured to sum up Montesquieu's relation to these studies:—

" If we hesitate to call him the founder, it is only because neither his materials nor his methods of execution were adequate to do justice to his ideas. He aimed (if I may repeat my own words, first written many years ago) at constructing a comparative theory of legislation and institutions adapted to the political needs of different forms of government, and a comparative theory of politics and law based on wide observation of the actual systems of different lands and ages. Hobbes was before him in realising that history is not a series of accidents, but Montesquieu was the first of the moderns to proclaim that a nation's institutions are part of its history, and must be considered as such if we are to understand them rightly. Much of his history is sound, and many of his judgments are admirable. Yet he failed to construct a durable system, and ' L'Esprit des Lois ' cannot even be called a systematic book. The materials were still too scattered and uncertain to be safely handled on Montesquieu's grand scale. Perhaps he would have done better to confine himself to Western Europe. The main defects of his method may be reduced, I think, to two. First, he overrated the influence of climate and other external conditions, and underrated, if he did not wholly neglect, the effects of race and tradition. Next, he had not even an inkling of what is now a fundamental rule of this kind of enquiry: namely, that there is a normal course of development for communities as well as for individuals, and that institutions which belong to different stages are not commensurable terms in any scientific comparison. This is as much as to say that even Montesquieu could not wholly escape from the unhistorical dogmatism of his time. It is perhaps a minor drawback that he constantly seeks for reasons of deliberate policy to account for seemingly eccentric features of outlandish customs, rightly or wrongly reported by missionaries or others, instead of endeavouring to connect them with their historic and racial surroundings. But the result is that many chapters of his great work amount, taken by themselves, to little more than collections of anecdotes and conjectures in which the most incongruous elements, such as the customs of China and the laws of Spain, are brought together at random. Also Montesquieu is not free from the very common error, especially prevalent in the eighteenth century, of attributing a constant and infallible efficacy to forms of government. In short, Montesquieu saw the promised land afar off, but was not equipped for entering it. I do not wish to be understood as affecting to find any fault with him. The greatness of Montesquieu's conception was his own, and the shortcomings in execution were at the time necessary, or at least natural" (" The History of Comparative Jurisprudence, a farewell Public Lecture ": Journ. Soc. Comp. Legisl., 1903, at pp. 83-4).

The " historical theory " ascribed to Bentham (p. 113) seems to be not quite so unfruitful as Maine's criticism supposes. If it is said that societies modify their laws according to modifications of their views of general expediency, this must mean views formed by actual observation and experience, as opposed to the application of dogmatic or traditional rules; and it must be implied that such views have a greater part in the changes of legal institutions than is avowed, or perhaps realised, by the actors and promoters. Doubtless Bentham underrated the power of tradition and custom. Probably he underrated it very much in the case of archaic societies. But his proposition, understood as above explained, is a substantial one and capable of discussion. It is not reducible to the truism that people make changes because they think change expedient, or in other words because they desire change; it signifies that the reasons professed or admitted for making particular changes are often not the real or the most operative reasons. Apparently the passages to which Maine alludes are scattered about various works of Bentham's and not expressed in clear or positive terms; it therefore does not seem practicable, in the absence of any specific reference, to identify them. But it was obviously natural for Bentham, with his thoroughgoing conviction that all ethical problems can be solved by the utilitarian calculus, to maintain that in fact the greater part of mankind are utilitarians without knowing it.

Maine's claim of scientific validity for the historical treatment of jurisprudence (p. 114) is now disputed by no one; indeed, if we now find any difficulty, it is in remembering that in 1861 it was still novel, and that its champion at that time had need of much insight and some boldness. His precepts as to the need of observing the caution approved by experience in other kinds of scientific enquiry, beginning with the best evidence and working gradually from what is known to what is obscure or unknown, are still in full force, and might easily be illustrated by the failure of ambitious reconstructions of later date whose authors have neglected them.

NOTE K.

THE PATRIARCHAL THEORY.

In the preface to the tenth edition, reprinted in all subsequent issues, Maine himself referred to the chapter on Theories of Primitive Society in " Early Law and Custom." The note on the Gens in the same volume (p. 286 sqq.) should also be consulted. In 1886 Maine replied in the Quarterly Review to the criticisms of the McLennan brothers (Q.R., vol. 162, p. 181); no secret was made of the authorship, though the practice of the Review, as it then stood, did not allow signature or public acknowledgment. It should be noted that the supposed ancient Slavonic poem cited at p. 196 of this article is a modern forgery: see Kovalevsky, " Modern Customs and Ancient Laws of Russia," p. 5. The last-named learned author made fuller contributions to the subject in his lectures delivered and published in French at Stockholm (" Tableau des origines et de l'évolution de la famille et de la propriété," 1890: some account of this book, which may not be easily accessible in England, was given in the Saturday Review of October 18 and 25, 1890). Still later Dr. Kohler of Berlin has dealt systematically with the whole topic of archaic marriage and kinship, following and applying Morgan's doctrine with less reserve than Lord Avebury and Dr. Tylor, who do not accept Morgan's inferences (" Zur Urgeschichte der Ehe: Totemismus, Gruppenehe, Mutterrecht," reprinted from " Ztschr. für vergleichende Rechtswissenschaft," Stuttgart, 1897: and see a more summary statement by the same learned author in the " Encyklopädie der Rechtswissenschaft," re-edited by him in 1904, vol. i. pp. 27 sqq.). Most English readers, however, will find in the latest edition (1902) of Lord Avebury's " Origin of Civilisation," and in Dr. E. B. Tylor's article on the Matriarchal Family System, Nineteenth Century, xl. 81 (1896), the easiest and certainly not the least profitable guides, among writings published since Maine's death, to what is now known or conjectured in this extremely difficult enquiry.

Much trouble and confusion might have been saved if Maine had in the first place expressly confined his thesis, as for all practical purposes it was confined, to the Indo-European family of nations. Herbert Spencer, whose courteous treatment of " Ancient Law " set a good example not always followed, gave a hint of this long ago. When Maine wrote " Ancient Law " there were no trustworthy materials for dealing with the social history of other races on a large scale. It is certain that from the earliest times at which we have any distinct knowledge of Indo-European society we find families—or communities which may be considered as expanded families—tracing descent through males, and living under the authority, more or less tempered by custom, of the eldest male ascendant. The worship of ancestors in the male line is of extreme antiquity in every branch of the stock; it is in full force at this day among the Hindus, and there are quite recent traces of it elsewhere. This is enough for the historian of Indo-European institutions; for the remaining evidences of a different earlier system are mere survivals at best, and of no importance for any subsequent development, however interesting they may be for prehistoric anthropology. My own judgment, so far as I have been able to form one, is that many of them are no better than ambiguous. Further, it is to be observed that local survivals of " matriarchal " institutions, where their existence is made out, may quite possibly not be Indo-European at all, but belong to the customs of the non-Aryan tribes who were subdued by Aryan invaders in India, or in Eastern Europe, or in the Mediterranean countries. We have been asked to regard the Erinyes prosecuting Orestes for matricide as the champions of a more ancient " mother-right " against the paternal system: as if the natural tendency of that system were to treat matricide as venial. Surely the question whether the son is bound to take up the father's blood-feud even against his own mother is hard enough to make a dramatic problem under any system which admits private vengeance at all. But in any case the Erinyes were autochthonous deities, looking on the gods of Olympus as intruders (τοιαῦτα δρῶσιν οἱ νεώτεροι θεοί). If their failure in the suit against Orestes is a symbol of anything, it may well symbolise the triumph of Hellenic over aboriginal customs. The existence of non-Aryan elements in the Mycenaean and even the later historical civilisation of Greece is accepted for independent reasons by some of our best archaeologists (P. Gardner in Eng. Hist. Rev. xvi. 744). Again (to take a Semitic example) we are told that Gideon avenged the sons of his mother upon the kings of Midian (Judges viii. 19). But there was no one else to do it, and the men of Israel who, as we read only a few verses below, said unto Gideon: " Rule thou over us, both thou and thy son, and thy son's son also," were certainly familiar with succession through males. The German, Scandinavian, and Celtic tribal customs as disclosed in the earliest known history of those branches appear to be thoroughly paternal, though not without traces of preference for relatives on the mother's side.[1] Summing up the results, Dr. Tylor says (Nineteenth Century, xl. 94): " There is no proof that at any period the maternal system held exclusive possession of the human race, but the strength with which it kept its ground may be measured by its having encompassed the globe in space, and lasted on from remote antiquity in time." For different views as to the significance of some archaic Indo-European customs, see J. D. Mayne in L.Q.R. i. 485, 494, and Kovalevsky, " Droit coutumier Ossétien," Paris, 1893, p. 181. It is no doubt possible, as suggested by Mr. Kovalevsky, that survivals from an earlier system may be maintained under a later one for reasons different from the original ones. But if patriarchal reasons are enough to account for the custom as we find it, we can hardly assume that in a given case it was formerly matriarchal, merely because for all we know it might have been. This would be to assume the very thing to be proved, namely that the society in question was in fact maternal at some earlier time.

On the whole the safest opinion appears at present to be that the Indo-European race may have gone through a stage of " matriarchy " at some remote time, but at any rate before

---

[1] It is now admitted that marriage by capture was part of the earliest Germanic law, but it is very doubtful whether it survived the introduction of Christianity in England. The Anglo-Saxon bride-price appears to have been paid not for the wife's person but for the rights of wardship (Hazeltine, " Zur Geschichte der Eheschliessung nach angelsächsischem Recht," Berlin, 1905).

the great migration which dispersed the several branches. This was Ihering's conclusion in his brilliant posthumous work, " Vorgeschichte der Indo-Europäer " (p. 40 of Eng. tr., 62 of original). It would seem, again, that the transformation, if such a transformation there was, must not only have taken place very early, but must have been singularly rapid and complete. Thus we are brought face to face with Maine's original problem: How and why did the Indo-Europeans become progressive? In this connexion I cannot forbear from citing some profitable words of my learned friend Professor F. W. Maitland, though their immediate subject-matter is the history not of the family but of property.

"Even had our anthropologists at their command material that would justify them in prescribing a normal programme for the human race and in decreeing that every independent portion of mankind must, if it is to move at all, move through one fated series of stages which may be designated as Stage A, Stage B, Stage C, and so forth, we still should have to face the fact that the rapidly progressive groups have been just those which have not been independent, which have not worked out their own salvation, but have appropriated alien ideas and have thus been enabled, for anything that we can tell, to leap from Stage A to Stage X without passing through any intermediate stages. Our Anglo-Saxon ancestors did not arrive at the alphabet, or at the Nicene Creed, by traversing a long series of 'stages'; they leapt to the one and to the other " (" Domesday Book and Beyond," p. 345).

The accident of borrowing one alphabet rather than another, or in one stage rather than another, may determine the affinities of a literature and a civilisation for many generations. All the tendency of modern research is to show that deliberate imitation was earlier, easier, and commoner than scholars formerly supposed; and that people will imitate pretty odd things is amply shown by modern experience.

Maine was not the first to discover that the ancient Indo-European tribe or city, as the case may be, is an expanded family with the tie of actual kindred supplemented, so far as needful to keep the community together, by adoption or even by bolder fictions; indeed, the conception is in its essential points as old as Aristotle. But he was, I think, the first to call attention in an adequate manner to the general existence and importance of this feature in archaic society. His view has been strikingly confirmed by the researches in the history of Slavonic institutions which are mentioned in " Early Law and Custom" under the head of East European House Communities. The family element in the Indo-European community has now and then been unduly suffered to drop out of sight. Thus the exclusiveness of the archaic village or township is simply and adequately explained as the exclusiveness of a community which had been or pretended to be a clan, and no deeper mystery need be sought in the much discussed Salic rule *De Migrantibus.*

Maine's original thesis was further developed by himself in the lecture on Kinship as the Basis of Society in " The Early History of Institutions," pp. 64 sqq.

It is impossible here, and I hardly think it would be relevant if possible, to enter at large on discussion of the " matriarchal " or, as Dr. Tylor prefers to call it, maternal family system. But it may be pointed out that, whatever else it is or has been, primitive it is not. It goes along with an elaborate and complex nomenclature of kindred and affinity, of which the interpretation is much disputed,[1] and often though not always with other usages of the most artificial kind, of which the explanation is no less conjectural, and as obscure to the modern historian as the facts to be explained are repugnant to modern civilised manners. Dr. Tylor has observed that its real characteristic point is the continuance of the wife in her own family, who do not lose her property or the value of her work, and gain the husband's alliance. If these or such-like politic motives were the true determining causes of " matriarchy "—and Dr. Tylor makes out a case which is none the less strong for being simple and using the general known materials of human nature instead of hypothetical superstitions— we are a long way off from primitive man, and the problem of what came before all this remains open. Here Maine's appeal to the Homeric description of the savage (not merely barbar-

---

[1] J. F. McLennan's opinion, which he intended to develop farther and prove in detail, was that this classification had nothing to do with consanguinity, but was a system of modes of salutation; and this is also maintained by Dr. Westermarck. Morgan, on the other hand, would allow no merit to McLennan's work and thought the term " exogamy," now generally adopted, useless. Professor Kohler, and less decidedly Mr. Kovalevsky, are, I believe, the only recent authors prepared to accept as a whole the consequences drawn by Morgan himself from the " classificatory " system. Subject to what McLennan might have added if he had lived, his particular line of objection just mentioned does not seem sufficient. Mr. Andrew Lang's conclusions are about equally remote from both schools: see the additional paragraph at the end of this note.

ous) Cyclopes is probably nearer to the truth than the state of promiscuity—surely the least likely state of nature ever heard of—which some anthropologists have postulated. At any rate it has, in substance, Dr. Tylor's support. "The claim of the patriarchal system to have belonged to primitive human life has not merely long acceptance in its favour, but I venture to think that those who uphold it have the weight of evidence on their side, provided that they do not insist on its fully developed form having at first appeared, but are content to argue that already in the earliest ages the man took his wife to himself, and that the family was under his power and protection, the law of male descent and all that belongs to it gradually growing up afterwards on this basis. . . . Among the great ancient and modern nations within the range of history, the paternal system becomes so dominant as to be taken for granted, and the existence of any other rule seems extraordinary" (Nineteenth Century, xl. 84, 85). So far as the evidence has gone, the maternal system appears to be unstable when people who live under it come into contact with paternal families: in such cases the husband's predominance pretty soon begins to assert or re-assert itself. It is also remarkable that a received custom so lax as not to seem to civilised administrators fit to rank as any kind of marriage law has been found compatible with fairly strict monogamy in practice (on both these points see H. H. Shephard, "Marriage Law in Malabar," L.Q.R. viii. 314). It seems fairly certain that both the frequency and the importance of polyandry have been exaggerated, and that, where it occurs, it can be explained, by those who regard "group-marriage" as proved, as a limiting case of group-marriage determined by special conditions. Thus we are rather led to regard the maternal system as a product of social necessities, not yet very well understood, which, although they have prevailed at some time in many or most inhabited parts of the world, may be fairly called abnormal with respect to the most original and persistent instincts of mankind as a species. When the maternal is supplanted by the paternal society, those instincts come to their own again in surroundings that no longer demand the highly artificial discipline of matriarchy. Much more evidence is needed both as to the origins of the maternal family, and as to the causes and manner of its transformation into the paternal type, before anything like a comprehensive statement can be made. We should remember that, as Professor Maitland says, continuing

the passage already quoted, " we are learning that the attempt
to construct a normal programme for all portions of mankind
is idle and unscientific." Probably no one would now maintain
that either marriage by capture or matriarchy is primitive.
Any such position is formally disclaimed, for example, by a
recent learned and ingenious author, Dr. Richard Hildebrand,
" Recht und Sitte auf den verschiedenen Kulturstufen," 1ter
Teil, Jena, 1896. It is perhaps needless at this day to refute
the formerly current opinion that the customs of savages are
the result of degradation from a more ancient state of innocence or civilisation. Partial backsliding into barbarism over
a considerable range of both time and space is of course possible, as shown in the decline of the Roman and the Mogul
empires. But trying to account for the systems of kinship
(if it is kinship) investigated by Morgan as fallings off from
monogamy or patriarchal polygamy is, if I may repeat an
illustration I have already used in an earlier note, like expect-
ing to find chalk under granite.

With regard to the extreme form of paternal power which,
as Maine says (p. 130), we may conveniently call by its later
Roman name of Patria Potestas, it is not clear that it is a
mere incident of family headship. Some competent persons,
such as Mr. Kovalevsky, hold it to be derived from the notion
that the wife is the husband's property, and therefore her offspring must be in his power too. If this be so, the right, being
proprietary and not merely social, would belong exclusively to
Private Law, and the " maxim of Roman jurisprudence that
the Patria Potestas did not extend to the Jus Publicum " would
be strictly logical as well as politic. But some, again, think
that the paternal family itself was developed through marriage by capture or purchase, causing the wife so acquired to
be regarded as the husband's chattel (Kohler, " Encykl. der
Rechtswissenschaft," i. 30, 33; " Das Vaterrecht entwickelt
sich . . . zunächst als Herrschaftsrecht: der Ehemann ist
Herr der Frau und damit Herr ihrer Frucht "). Not that lordship in a rudimentary society can safely be identified with our
modern legal ownership. *Dominus* is an ambiguous word except in strict Roman law. At all events we cannot disregard
the testimony of Gaius that the Patria Potestas of the Roman
family law was, in the time of Hadrian, singular among the
Mediterranean nations; and, so far as we know anything of the
provincial customs of the empire, they seem to have been not
less but more archaic than the law of Rome. The responsibili-

ties of the Roman paterfamilias, on the other hand, are not distinguishable in character or extent from those of the patriarch
in other Indo-European family systems.

Another reason against regarding the Roman Patria Potestas as of the highest antiquity is that at an earlier time the
paterfamilias was regarded not as owner, but as an administrator of the family property which in some sense already belonged to the heirs as well as himself. Indeed, this idea survived as late as the classical ages of Roman law in the untrans-
latable term of art *sui heredes*, of which " necessary heirs " is
perhaps the most tolerable rendering, and the comments of the
jurists upon it (Paulus in D. 28, 2, *de liberis et postumis*, 11,
cited by Holmes, " The Common Law," p. 342). We are fully
confirmed in this by the history of the Hindu Joint Family.
In Bengal the change from the position of an administrator
with large powers to that of an owner is known to have taken
place in relatively modern times.

Finally, I venture to record, for what it may be worth, my
impression that recent inquirers, with the notable exception of
Mr. J. G. Frazer, have somewhat neglected the part of superstitions and magical or pseudo-scientific beliefs in the formation of social customs. There is no presumption whatever that
the true explanation of any savage practice is that which to
us appears most reasonable or natural. The fundamental difference between religion and magic has been explained by Lord
Avebury and Sir Alfred Lyall. Religious offerings and ceremonies, apart from the higher ethical and philosophical devel-
opments of advanced theology, seek to propitiate supernatural
powers, magical ritual to control both natural and supernatural agencies. The priest is, in the current phrase, a minister, that is to say a servant of whatever gods he worships;
he begs their peace and alliance with tribute in his hand. The
magician or wizard acts as a master; he aims at using the
secrets of nature, or commanding for his own use or that of
his clients, and at his own will, the " armies of angels that soar,
legions of demons that lurk." Solomon's seal is magical, his
dedication of the temple is religious. But this has little, if
anything, to do with the present subject.

Since the foregoing note was in type Mr. Andrew Lang's
book, " The Secret of the Totem " (London, 1905), has been
published. Mr. Lang, agreeing in the main with Darwin on

this point, wholly rejects the hypothesis of a promiscuous horde having been the earliest state of human life, and holds that " men, whatever their brutal ancestors may have done, when they became men indeed, lived originally in small anonymous local groups, and had, for a reason to be given "—the jealous despotism of the eldest male, as is explained in a later chapter—" the habit of selecting female mates from groups *not* their own." McLennan's explanation of exogamy is dismissed as wholly inadequate, and the facts supposed by Morgan and his school to establish a general epoch of " group-marriage " are treated as exceptional and belonging to a relatively advanced stage. I do not presume to appreciate Mr. Lang's theory, or make any critical comparison of it with those of other anthropologists who differ widely from Mr. Lang and from one another. But it is legitimate to observe that Mr. Lang, as well as Dr. Tylor, appears to justify Maine's opinion as to the primitive character of the Cyclopean family, and that it is less plausible now than it was twenty years ago to regard Maine as an old-fashioned literary scholar standing out against the lights of modern research. No doubt Maine, when he wrote " Ancient Law," conceived the transition from the savagery of the Cyclops to the archaic civilisation of a Roman paterfamilias under the Kings or the early Republic as having been a far more direct and simple process than we can at this day think probable. This is so common an incident of historical speculation, in the absence of full and trustworthy material, that there is nothing in it to derogate from Maine's credit.

NOTE L.

STATUS AND CONTRACT.

Maine's now celebrated dictum as to the movement from Status to Contract in progressive societies is perhaps to be understood as limited to the law of Property, taking that term in its widest sense as inclusive of whatever has a value measurable in exchange. With that limitation the statement is certainly just, and has not ceased to be significant. The movement is not yet complete, for example, in England, where the emancipation of married women's property has been proceeding in a piecemeal fashion for more than a generation, and is at present in a transitional state capable not only of raising hard questions but of producing, within a few years, decisions not easy to reconcile. As regards the actual definition of different personal conditions, and the more personal relations incidental to them, it does not seem that a movement from Status to Contract can be asserted with any generality. For example, the tendency of modern legislation has been to make the dissolution of marriage less difficult, and in some jurisdictions this has gone very far. But it has nowhere been enacted, and I do not think any legislator has yet seriously proposed, that the parties shall be free to settle for themselves, by the terms of the marriage contract, whether the marriage shall be dissoluble or not, and if so, on what grounds. Assimilation of marriage, as a personal relation, to partnership is not within the scope of practical jurisprudence. Again, a minor who has attained years of discretion cannot advance or postpone the date of his full age by contract with his parent or guardian, and we do not hear of any one proposing to confer such a power. The test which Maine suggests as alone justifying the preservation of disabilities—that the persons concerned do not possess the faculty of forming a judgment on their own interests—will hardly be received as adequate for either of the cases just put. In fact, the interests which these rules of law regard are not those of the parties alone. Paramount considerations of the stability of society, or the general convenience of third persons, override the freedom usually left to parties in their own affairs. The law of persons may be and has been cut short; but, so long as we recognise any differences at all among persons, we cannot allow their existence and nature to be treated merely as matter of bargain. Status may yield ground to Contract, but cannot itself be reduced to Contract. On the other hand Contract has made attacks on Property which have been repulsed. There was a time in the thirteenth century in which it seemed as if there was no rule of tenure that could not be modified by the agreement of parties. Our settled rules that only certain defined forms of interest in property can be created by private acts, our rule against perpetuities, are the answer of the Common Law to attempts to bring everything under private bargain and control. The importance of Contract in the feudal scheme of society is pointed out by Maine himself in this book, ch. ix *ad fin.* (cp. Pollock and Maitland, "H.E.L." ii. 230).

One department of the law of Persons is increasing, not diminishing, in importance, namely the law of corporations or " moral persons." We are beginning to find that the law cannot afford to ignore collective personality—that of a trade union, for example—where fact and usage have conferred a substantially corporate character on a more or less permanent social group. Modern company law is largely, no doubt, a law of contract; but of contract whose action is regulated and modified at every turn by the fact that one of the chief parts is borne by a corporate and not an individual person.

Maine guarded his position, however, to a considerable extent in the final words of this chapter, for he seems not to include Marriage—at all events marriage among Western nations, which is preceded by and results from agreement of the parties—under the head of Status. And, if the term is thus restricted, the gravest apparent exception to Maine's dictum is removed. This, of course, involves a sensible narrowing of the term Status, a much discussed term which, according to the best modern expositions, includes the sum total of a man's personal rights and duties (Salmond, "Jurisprudence," 1902, pp. 253-7), or, to be verbally accurate, of his capacity for rights and duties (Holland, "Jurisprudence," 9th ed. p. 88). It is curious that the word "estate," which is nothing but the French form of "status," should have come to stand over against it in an almost opposite category. A man's *estate* is his measurable property; what we call his *status* is his position as a lawful man, a voter, and so forth. The liability of every citizen to pay rates and taxes is a matter of status; what a given citizen has to pay depends on his estate, or portions of it assigned as the measures of particular imposts. We have, too, an "estate" in land, which so far preserves the original associations of "status" that, as we have just noted, contract may not alter its incidents or nature. Again, as Professor Maitland has pointed out (Introduction to Gierke's "Political Theories of the Middle Age," Camb. 1900, p. xxv), the Roman Status has also become the State of modern public law, and in that form has refused to be reduced to a species of contract by the ingenious efforts of individualist philosophers, notwithstanding the widespread acceptance of the Social Contract for a century or more.

It is not clear how far Maine regarded the movement of which he spoke as a phase of the larger political individualism which prevailed in the eighteenth century and great part of the nineteenth, or what he would have thought of the reaction against this doctrine which we are now witnessing. At all events the questions at issue between publicists of various schools as to the proper limit of State interference with trade, or of State and municipal enterprise, do not seem to have much to do with simplifying the tenure and transfer of property, nor with removing obsolete personal disabilities.

Professor Dicey says indeed (" Law and Public Opinion in England," p. 283) that " the rights of workmen in regard to compensation for accidents have become a matter not of contract, but of status." But many other kinds of contracts have long had incidents attached to them by law, and those incidents are not always subject to be varied at the will of the parties. A mortgagor cannot enter into an agreement with the mortgagee which has the effect of making the mortgage irredeemable, or even tends that way by " clogging the equity of redemption." It would be a strong thing to say that this peculiar doctrine of English courts of equity has created a status of mortgagors.

CHAPTER VI. Page 166.

NOTE M.

TESTAMENTARY SUCCESSION.

THE burden of this chapter is that the Will or Testament of modern law, with its specific characters of being secret, revocable, and posthumous in operation, is unknown to archaic law, and is of comparatively recent introduction wherever we find it. Maine's position is amply confirmed by later historical research, and one or two seeming exceptions which he felt bound to notice have been removed.

Jurists of the seventeenth century, we read in Maine's text, resorted to the law of nature to explain and justify testamentary power. This is almost enough of itself to show that no such power was commonly found in customary law. For the doctrine of natural law was, as we have already seen, a progressive and rationalist doctrine. Its use was to override the commonplace objections founded on lack of authority or even on the existence of contrary custom; and at the time of the Renaissance and even earlier it served speculative publicists in much the same way as the principle of utility (with which it has considerable affinities) has served modern reformers. In fact, the whole conception of individual succession to property, even without a will, is relatively modern. The archaic Indo-European family was, Maine tells us, a corporation, of

which the patriarch for the time being was the representative
or public officer—or at most, we may add, managing director.
Evidently we are not meant to take this statement as if a definite legal doctrine of persons, much less artificial persons, was
to be ascribed to the patriarchal stage of society. For in that
stage, as Maine also says, a man was not yet regarded as an
individual, but only as a member of his family and class; and
this is still true to a great extent in Hindu law. Now the modern doctrine of corporations assumes that the "natural person" or individual, considered as a subject of rights and duties, or "lawful man," as our English books say, is the normal
unit of legal institutions, and that the collective personality of
a group of men acting in a common interest or duty and be-
having like an individual is something which needs to be explained. But for archaic society the collective body and not
the individual is the natural person.

We find the same conditions existing in full force among
the German tribes in a much later period of time than that
which Maine is directly considering in this chapter. A recent
learned writer in France, dealing with precisely the same subject as it occurs in the medieval history of French law, has
forcibly contrasted the Roman conception, as it was established in the classical law of the empire, with the German.

"Le droit romain consacre le triomphe de l'individualisme;
la volonté personnelle du chef de famille, voilà le facteur juridique essentiel, l'agent de toutes les transactions, la force cré-
atrice de tous les droits. Cette volonté est si respectée et si
puissante, qu'elle continue d'agir après la disparition de celui
qui l'a exprimée. Le père règle le sort de sa fortune et de sa
famille pour le temps où il ne sera plus, et cela par un acte
souverainement libre, qu'il est toujours à même de modifier.
. . . . L'individu *sui juris* est, dans le monde romain, l'unité
juridique et social.

"Chez les Germains, c'est bien plutôt la famille. Il serait
sans doute excessif, surtout pour le temps des Leges [the custumals collectively known as 'Leges Barbarorum'], de dé-
clarer en termes absolus que la famille est tout et que l'individu n'est rien; la vérité sous cette forme serait exagérée et
dénaturée. Mais il est certain cependant que l'exaltation de
l'individu est beaucoup moins complète qu'à Rome, et que
d'autre part la famille forme une association, une sorte d'être
collectif armé de droits inconnus des jurisconsultes de l'Empire. L'énergie individuelle est limitée dans le temps, et les

Germains ne peuvent pas concevoir qu'elle s'exerce au delà de la tombe; sitôt l'homme mort, toutes ses volontés s'évanouissent. Au même moment ses prérogatives juridiques sont recouvertes et absorbées par celles de ses parents, car de son vivant même sa famille jouissait de droits autonomes qu'il ne dépendait pas de lui de supprimer: sa mort les développe, mais elle ne les crée pas" (Auffroy, "Evolution du testament en France," Paris, 1899, pp. 173-4. Cf. Brunner, "Grundzüge der deutschen Rechtsgeschichte," § 56; "Das germanische Erbrecht war ein Familienrecht." For examples of analogous customs among various uncivilised tribes, see Lord Avebury, "Origin of Civilisation," 6th ed. pp. 489-91.

The suggestion in Maine's text of regarding the Roman ancestor in his representative character as a kind of corporation sole may be helpful to English students, but we can hardly trust it to throw light on the actual formation of Roman legal ideas. For our English category of corporations sole is not only, as Maine calls it, a fiction, but modern, anomalous, and of no practical use. When a parson or other solely corporate office-holder dies, there is no one to act for the corporation until a successor is appointed, and, when appointed, that successor can do nothing which he could not do without being called a corporation sole. In the case of the parson even the continuity of the freehold is not saved, and it is said to be in abeyance in the interval. As for the king, or " the Crown," being a corporation sole, the language of our books appears to be nothing but a clumsy and, after all, ineffective device to avoid openly personifying the State. The problems of federal politics in Canada and Australia threaten to make the fiction complex. Is " the Crown " a trustee for Dominion and Province, for Commonwealth and State, with possibly conflicting interests? or is there one indivisible Crown being or having several persons for different purposes? (F. W. Maitland, L.Q.R. xvi. 335, xvii. 131; W. Harrison Moore, L.Q.R. xx. 351; Markby, "Elements of Law," §145). The whole thing seems to have arisen from the technical difficulty of making grants to a parson and his successors after the practice of making them to God and the patron saint had been discontinued, as tending to bring the saints into the unseemly position of litigants before secular courts. All this we may now think makes for historical curiosity rather than philosophical edification.

But in any case the chief part of Maine's argument, his insistence on " the theory of a man's posthumous existence in the person of his heir," and the intimate connection of that theory with the ancestor's representative character as head of the family, goes to the root of the matter. Mr. Justice Holmes, now of the Supreme Court of the United States, writing twenty years after Maine, summed this up with concise elegance ("The Common Law," p. 343):

"If the family was the owner of the property administered by a *paterfamilias*, its rights remained unaffected by the death of its temporary head. The family continued, although the head died. And when, probably by a gradual change, the *paterfamilias* came to be regarded as owner, instead of a simple manager of the family rights, the nature and continuity of those rights did not change with the title to them. The *familia* continued to the heirs as it was left by the ancestor. . . .

"The aggregate of the ancestor's rights and duties, or, to use the technical phrase, the total *persona* sustained by him, was early separated from his natural personality. For this *persona* was but the aggregate of what had formerly been family rights and duties, and was originally sustained by any individual only as the family head. Hence it was said to be continued by the inheritance; and when the heir assumed it, he had his action in respect of injuries previously committed."

Maine proceeds to trace the development of the Roman testament from a distribution of property, taking effect at once, made in contemplation of impending death or great peril, and requiring, in its earliest form, something like legislative sanction (cp. Girard, "Manuel," pp. 792-5), through the intermediate stage of a conveyance reserving a life interest, which may be seen in the provincial customs of the Roman Empire, and much later in medieval and even modern systems. Muirhead ("Historical Introduction to the Private Law of Rome," pp. 66, 168) pointed out a remedy for the difficulty suggested at p. 200, that a will by mancipation must have left the testator penniless. Usufruct might very well be reserved on a mancipation, Gai. ii. 33, "and a reservation of a life interest in one's own *familia* would possibly be construed even more liberally than an ordinary usufruct." Still, usufruct is not among the earliest institutions, and it would be rash to say that the difficulty may not have been real at one time. But men have been driven all over the world, by an imperfect state of property law or by special reasons for avoiding publicity, to put very large trust in the honour of chosen friends and assistants; and there is nothing about the Roman *familiae emtor* in his most archaic stage to surprise an English student who has made acquaintance with our medieval feoffee to uses. Indian practice will furnish a parallel in the *benámi* (literally, " anonymous ") conveyances to a nominal purchaser, to hold on a secret trust for the real one, which appear to have survived the original reasons for them. Sohm, however, holds (" Institutes," § 99, p. 569, in Ledlie's translation, 2nd ed.) that the testament *per aes et libram* was coupled with a mandate to the *familiae emtor*, which was binding under the well-known provision of the Twelve Tables, " uti lingua nuncupassit ita ius esto." This would of course simplify the matter. The same learned author's suggestion that the institution of an heir was a modified form of adoption—that is, an adoption deferred to the testator's death—does not seem to be generally accepted (Girard, " Manuel," p. 793).

What is said in this chapter about Hindu law would no doubt have been fuller if a convenient and trustworthy textbook like Mr. Mayne's had existed at the time when it was written. I am not aware, however, that any modification is needed except on one point, namely that the strict determination of the order of succession among an ancestor's next of kin according to the spiritual efficacy of their sacrifices is found only in the school of Bengal, and is thought to be a deliberate Brahmanical innovation. As Maine himself said in 1883, " we now can discern something of the real relation which the sacerdotal Hindu law bears to the true ancient law of the race " (" Early Law and Custom," p. 194; see also the chapter on Ancestor Worship and Inheritance). The general importance of keeping up the family ritual both in Hindu and in other archaic law remains undoubted. Some addition has to be made as regards the Hindu will. Quite unknown to early Hindu law, will-making came into use in modern times, though not in imitation of European practice according to the best authorities, and was not recognised in any of the Presidency Courts before 1832, when it was allowed in Bengal. When " Ancient Law " was published the law was not yet quite settled in Madras and Bombay; but the courts of those Presidencies followed the same course within a few years. Apparently the first form of the Bengal will was a gift *mortis causa* to religious uses. The reader will perceive the resemblance to the development of the testament of chattels, under ecclesiastical influence, in medieval English law. The English history, however, is for the most part too complex and peculiar to throw much light on the normal type of evolution. As for the Anglo-Saxon will, even if it can be assimilated to modern wills, which is doubtful, it was a special and anomalous kind of document, and disappeared after the Norman Conquest. Probably language is still to be found in popular books asserting or implying that before the Conquest there was general freedom of alienation; but this is due to pure misunderstanding, the privileged class of transactions which are recorded in the Anglo-Saxon charters having been taken as typical and indigenous. Early English " post obit gifts " (Pollock and Maitland, " H.E.L." ii. 317, sqq., and see Note Q below) do present some analogy to the Roman will by mancipation; and this appears in a strengthened form in the conveyance to feoffees to uses to be declared by the feoffee's will which was common in the later Middle Ages. In the thirteenth century divers learned clerks made an ingenious and, it seems, almost a successful attempt to create posthumous disposing power by grants *inter vivos*, containing in what we now call the " habendum " such words as " cuicunque dare vel etiam legare voluerit." A clause so framed is quite common in deeds of the third and even fourth quarters of that century, and inconsistent utterances in Bracton show that learned opinion fluctuated (18*b*, 412*h*, *pro*, 49*a*, fuller and seemingly more deliberate, *contra*, cp. Pollock and Maitland, ii. 27). We may believe[1] that for some time and to some extent the power such clauses purported to confer was exercised without objection. But this was a transitory experiment, and has nothing to do with any real testamentary distribution or succession. Local customs to devise land or, at any rate, purchased land existed, but their origin and early history are still obscure.

In Scotland we find the most remarkable illustration of the præ-testamentary stage, as we may call it, of property law. Properly there is no such term as Will in Scots law, and there was no true will of lands before 1868. " Heritage could only be transmitted by a deed containing words of *de praesenti* disposition, and the use of the word ' dispone ' was essential " (Green's " Encycl. of the Law of Scotland," s.v. *Will.*). The accustomed form was (and apparently still is, notwithstand-

---

[1] Extant wills of the period which purport to devise parcels of land (Madox, Form. Anglic. DCCLXVIII., DCCLXIX., DCCLXXI.) are not conclusive as to the practice in the absence of a known previous grant with which they can be connected, as other explanations are possible.

ing that it is no longer necessary) a "trust disposition and settlement," a present conveyance reserving a life interest to the grantor. Scotland, in fact, is the last home of the old Germanic *Vergabung von Todes wegen* (Goffin, "The Testamentary Executor," 1901, pp. 19, 99). It may survive many generations yet, for aught we know, as in the customs of Egypt and other parts of the Roman Empire essentially similar forms continued in use long after true wills had become familiar in the law of Rome. Original examples of the second century A.D. found at Naucratis might be seen in London some years ago. Notwithstanding the marks of Roman influence which the modern English will bears, its practical scope and effect remain as different as possible from those of the Roman testament. As a rule the wills of Englishmen having any considerable property to dispose of aim not at investing any one person with the whole of the testator's control over his estate, subject to payment of debts and legacies, but rather at postponing absolute control and preserving the estate under the sanction of a trust which will not be finally determined while any child of the testator is a minor or his widow living. The capital is to be intact as long as possible, while the income is enjoyed or applied according to the testator's directions. If any one is at all like a Roman heir, it is the executor, who does not necessarily take any beneficial interest, and whose origin is quite different (Goffin, *op. cit.* p. 33; O. W. Holmes, L.Q.R. i. 165-6; Gierke, "Grundzüge des deutschen Privatrechts," § 126, in "Encykl. d. Rechtswiss." i. 555). The Roman horror of intestacy mentioned in the early part of the following chapter was equalled or surpassed among medieval Englishmen (Pollock and Maitland, ii. 356); but the reason was not one that would have occurred to any Roman from the time of Labeo to that of Justinian, being the danger to the intestate's soul if he died without having assigned a fitting part of his estate to pious uses (Du Cange *s. v. intestatio*).

CHAPTER VII. Page 209.

NOTE N.

PRIMOGENITURE.

MUCH has been written in recent years about the origins of medieval jurisdiction and land tenure, and the peculiar complication of tenure with personal lordship and jurisdiction which we call feudalism; we mention, almost at random, the names of Brunner, Waitz, Fustel de Coulanges, Flach, Luchaire; but there is nothing to throw doubt on the general soundness of the luminous sketch given in this chapter. Maine returns to the subject in the latter part of ch. viii. At the end of that chapter an opinion is adopted, it seems from Kemble, that "some shade of servile debasement" attached to a Germanic king's or chieftain's personal companions. I have never been able to discover Kemble's authority for this supposition, or to meet with any other acceptance of it. See, *contra*, Konrad Maurer in "Kritische Überschau," ii. 391.

Further observations on Primogeniture by Maine himself will be found in "The Early History of Institutions," pp. 124, 198-205. We may add to the brief mention of "parage" at p. 205 that the "paragium" of the Norman custumals has an important part in the Anglo-Norman nomenclature of Domesday Book. Groups of co-heirs holding "in paragio," and represented, for the purposes of the service due to their lord, by one of them who is sometimes called the senior, are common in several counties (Maitland, "Domesday Book and Beyond," p. 145; Pollock and Maitland, "H.E.L." ii. 263-4, 276; Pollock in Eng. Hist. Rev. 1896, xi. 228, note 65). This arrangement is a strong illustration of the practical convenience of primogeniture for the lord when feudal service was really military service. Maine's view that primogeniture originally had an official character seems to be thoroughly accepted; it would probably be found, if we had all the facts, that the occasional examples of primogeniture in servile or inferior tenures are to be explained by the tenement having been attached to some manorial or communal office. It would seem that, whether for reasons of convenience or because men liked to imitate the fashion of their lords, the general introduction of primogeniture in England was to some extent a popular movement. In 1255 the burgesses of Leicester alleged that they were being ruined by partible tenures, and procured a charter from their lord, Simon de Montfort, which Henry III. shortly afterwards confirmed, to change the course of descent to primogeniture ("Records of the Borough of Leicester," ed. Bateson, Nos. xxiii. xxiv., the latter indorsed "carta quod hereditas sit ad communem legem"). On the whole subject Mr. Evelyn Cecil's book "Primogeniture: A Short History of its Development in Various Countries, and its Practical Effects," Lond. 1895, may be studied with advantage.

CHAPTER VIII. Page 237.

NOTE O.

CAPTURE, OCCUPATION, POSSESSION.

THE statements made in the early part of this chapter about
the Roman doctrine of capture in war, its relation to the ordinary rules of *occupatio,* and the relation of both to the modern law of nations, are not easy to follow. Maine's general
results do not depend on the accuracy of these statements, but
it is necessary to indicate the points on which a reader unacquainted with Roman and international law might find the text
misleading. First, there is really no authority for attributing
to the Roman jurists the unqualified opinion that all spoil of
war belonged to the individual captor, nor for deducing the
rule of war from the law of *occupatio* in time of peace. Next,
it is by no means clear that the Roman law of *occupatio* was
more than one of many elements which went to form the modern rules as to belligerent rights. It is necessary to examine
the authorities in some detail.

Maine seems to have relied on a passage of Gaius in the title
of the Digest " de adquirendo rerum dominio " (41, 1, ll. 5, §7,
7, §1; l. 6 is clumsily interpolated by the compilers from
another writer, and is not to our purpose). Gaius has spoken
of the " occupation " of *res nullius,* such as wild animals, and
goes on to other classes of cases in which occupation or something like it confers ownership (and not merely possession)
iure gentium. This last term would seem, in relation to hostile capture, to point to the actual usage of war rather than
to the ideal law of nature, which at all events would not justify
treating captives of free condition as slaves. " Item quae ex
hostibus capiuntur iure gentium statim capientium finat . . .
adeo quidem ut et liberi homines in servitutem deducantur."
Then Paulus says, at the head of the next title, " de adquirenda
vel amittenda possessione ": " Item bello capta et insula in
mari enata et gemmae lapilli margaritae in litoribus inventae
eius fiunt, qui primus eorum possessionem nanctus est." Obviously no proof or authority was needed to show that a public enemy in arms could have no civil rights. The point is
not that spoil of war ceases to belong to the enemy, but that
capture, when it occurs, makes the captor an owner and not
merely a possessor as between himself and his fellow-citizens.

This docs not tell us what is lawful spoil of war according to any specially Roman usage, nor does it exclude the restrictions of military discipline. Under the Empire, in fact, the commanding officer might distribute booty if he pleased, but plunder for the individual soldier's benefit or any kind of subsequent private appropriation was distinctly forbidden. "Is, qui praedam ab hostibus captam subripuit, lege peculatus tenetur et in quadruplum damnatur": Modestinus in D. 48, 13, *ad legem Iuliam peculatus* 15 (ed. Mommsen, *vulg.* 13). Indeed, it may well be that the dicta of Gaius and Paulus contemplate only the case of enemy property found on Roman ground at the outbreak of a war: "quae res hostiles *apud nos* sunt non publicae sed occupantium fiunt": Celsus, D. 41, 1, 51. Grotius comments on this dictum of Celsus, understanding it in this sense, and holds the right of private capture to be confined to acts not in the course of service, "extra ministerium publicum": De Iure Belli ac Pacis, III. vi. xii. § 1; and so Girard, "Manuel," p. 314. There is no doubt that land seized in war was acquired and distributed by the State: Pomponius in D. 49, 15, *de captivis*, 20, § 1. In considering these passages it is just as well to remember that problems arising out of a state of war between Rome and a civilised or wealthy enemy must have seemed a mere archaic curiosity to the jurists who flourished under the Antonines.

Then as to Grotius's use of the Roman law, he certainly quotes the words of Gaius already set·out; but almost in the same breath he quotes the Old Testament, Plato, Xenophon, and Aristotle (*op. cit.* III. vi. ii. § 4). He denies (iv. § 1) that enemy's land can be acquired by mere invasion short of permanent occupation in force. He seems to think private plundering admissible in strict right, but elsewhere, under the head of *temperaments*—a kind of counsels of perfection to mitigate the rigour of war, most of which have since been adopted as rules—he suggests that captured property should be restored on the conclusion of peace, so far as practicable (III. xiii., "temperamentum circa res captas"). Again, an early trait of Grotius, " De Iure Praedae," published only in our own time (ed. Hamaker, Hag. Com. 1868), altogether repudiates the occupation theory of the right to spoil of war. He likens it to the right of judicial execution, and explains away the dictum of Gaius by holding that the captor takes only as the servant and in the name of the State; and he fortifies his doctrine, after the manner of the time, which he continued to follow in his own later work, with Hebrew, Homeric, and other Greek examples. It is difficult to find here much adoption of the Roman law of Occupancy. Perhaps other publicists of the seventeenth or eighteenth century may have been less discriminating than Grotius. If this is to be verified, it must be by some one more familiar with their writings than myself. No further light is thrown on the point in Maine's Cambridge lectures on international law, which he did not live to revise finally for publication. These questions, however, have long been antiquarian; modern practice has abrogated the old harsh customs of war, and the seizure of movables or other personal property in its bare form has, except in a very few cases, become illegal (Hall, " Intern. Law," 5th ed. p. 427: the whole chapter should be consulted).

Maine observes at p. 241 that the Roman law of Occupancy was altogether unequal to the task of settling disputes of title between different nations claiming new territories in right of their respective subjects who had discovered and more or less taken possession of them. Undoubtedly this is true, and it could not be otherwise. The difficulties have arisen in almost every case, down to the recent boundary question between Venezuela and British Guiana, from attempts to treat isolated, slight, and partial acts of dominion as equivalent to effective possession. Roman law knows nothing of any " occupation " which does not amount to full and actual control. Hence the learning of occupation had to be supplemented by that of possession. Roman law, like the Common Law, recognises the fact that a man cannot physically hold or control at the same time every square foot of a parcel of land, and therefore it allows legal possession to be acquired by entry on a part in the name of the whole and with intent to possess everything included in the boundaries. " Quod autem diximus et corpore et animo adquirere nos debere possessionem, non utique ita accipiendum est, ut qui fundum possidere velit omnes glebas circumambulet: sed sufficit quamlibet partem eius fundi introire, dum mente et cogitatione hac sit, uti totum fundum usque ad terminum velit possidere " (Paulus in D. 41, 2 *de adq. vel amitt. poss.* 3, §1). In order to apply this rule, however, we have to assume that the boundaries are known or ascertainable, and also that there is no effective opposition; and when the facts to which the application is to be made are those alleged to amount to a national occupation of unsettled territory, it is often far from easy to say whether these conditions are satisfied. In case of dispute whether possession has been established, we must resort to the rule of common sense, which is expressly adopted by the authorities of the Common Law, and does not contradict anything in the Roman Law, namely that regard must be had to the kind of use and control of which the subject-matter is capable (authorities collected in Pollock and Wright on Possession, pp. 31-5). On the question what is the " terminus " in the occupation of unsettled territory, certain conventional rules, which must be sought in the regular text-books of international law, have been more or less generally adopted by the custom of nations, and in some cases express agreements have been made (Hall, *op. cit.* p. 114). The doctrine that occupancy produces ownership is of course not of the highest antiquity. Besides the reasons given by Maine, the conception of individual ownership as a legal right, the *dominium* of Roman law, is itself relatively modern. How and why Roman law developed that conception as early as it did is a historical problem which, so far as I have learnt, we cannot solve with our materials. We only know that Roman property law, for whatever reason, was already quite individualist at the time of the Twelve Tables. I am not sure that I fully understand Maine's passing remark about the influence of Natural Law in this point (p. 250). At all events the transformation of the Hindu Joint Family to its modern type can hardly be set down to any such influence, and, so far as it has gone, the example appears fairly parallel.

Blackstone's account of the origin of property is loose enough to deserve nearly all of Maine's criticism. He wholly fails to distinguish between physical control or " detention," possession in law, and ownership, and he talks as if our refined legal conceptions had come to primeval man ready made, and in exactly the form and language of eighteenth-century publicists. But perhaps it was needless cruelty to suggest that Blackstone either did not understand the technical meaning of Occupation or intended to impose on his readers by playing with a verbal ambiguity. The word *occupare* is, after all, not purely technical in Latin; it certainly has no technical meaning in the passage of Cicero which Blackstone quotes (" Comm." ii. 4; Cic. " de Fin." iii. 20, § 67). Cicero was neither an original philosopher nor a great jurist; but no one would charge him with supposing that the right of a spectator in a theatre to the place he has taken (" eum locum quem quisque occuparit ") had anything to do with the permanent acquisition of *dominium*. It would be more plausible to credit him with an inkling of the historical truth pointed out by Maine in these pages, that the notion of absolute legal ownership, and still more the presumption that everything ought to have an owner, or that, as our own books say, "the law must needs reduce the properties of all goods to some man," are rather modern than primitive. Blackstone's neglect to observe that the detached individual man whom he postulates is a kind of person altogether unknown to archaic institutions is the common and fatal fault, as Maine has in effect said, of all individualist theories of society: of Hobbes's, which Locke's was intended to refute, no less than of Blackstone's, which is a slight modification of Locke's.

Incidentally, but with provoking brevity, Maine speaks of Savigny's aphorism that property is founded on adverse possession ripened by prescription. This aphorism is certainly true for English law. Property in goods is, in the terms and process of the Common Law, not distinguishable from a right, present or deferred, to possess them; and it is only under statutory provisions of very recent introduction and partial application that we know any means of proving title to English land other than showing continuous undisturbed possession, under a consistent claim of title, for a time long enough to exclude any reasonable fear of adverse claims. The conventional fixing of that time first by the usage of conveyancers and latterly by positive law makes no difference to the principle, nor do the elaborate rules which have been developed in various matters of detail. Title-deeds, as I have said elsewhere, are nothing but the written history of the possession and of the right in which it has been exercised. This is essentially a Germanic institution, as any one who pursues the subject will find; and when we consider the ideas of early Germanic law, we shall perhaps be less apt to find any problem in the fact of a possessor's rights being recognised by Roman law than to wonder how Roman law came so early by the full and clear conception of an owner's rights as distinct from possession. As to the historical origin of the Roman doctrine of Possession there are now several theories in the field, and none of them can be said to be generally accepted, certainly not Savigny's, which was dominant when Maine wrote.

NOTE P.

THE INDIAN VILLAGE COMMUNITY.

AFTER Maine had acquired official knowledge of Indian affairs, he gave a hint in his lecture on "Village Communities" that the local customs of India are neither so simple nor so uniform in type as an ordinary European reader of "Ancient Law" might infer. "I shall have hereafter to explain," he said,[1] "that, though there are strong general resemblances between the Indian village communities wherever they are found in anything like completeness, they prove on close inspection to be not simple but composite bodies, including a number of classes with very various rights and claims." The publication in more than one form (most conveniently in "The Indian Village Community," Lond. 1896) of B. H. Baden-Powell's authoritative researches on the Land Systems of British India has since made it common or at least easily accessible[2] knowledge that Indian villages are divisible into two principal and widely different types, of which the "assemblage of co-proprietors," formerly assumed to be the only normal one, is not the more ancient. Sir Alfred Lyall (L.Q.R. ix. 27) has approved Baden-Powell's "conclusion that the oldest form of village was *not*, as is usually supposed, a group of cultivators having joint or communistic interests, but a disconnected set of families who severally owned their separate holdings." There is a headman and there are village officers; we may say there is administrative unity for many purposes; but there is not communal ownership or tenure. There is no evidence that in villages of this kind, usually called *raiyatwārī*, and prevalent in Central and Southern India, the holdings were ever otherwise than separate and independent; "the so-called joint village followed, and did not precede, the village of separate holdings." In the joint or "landlord" villages of Oudh, the United (formerly North-West) Provinces, and the Panjāb, we find a dominant family or clan, oligarchs and in fact landlords as regards the inferior majority of inhabitants, and more or less democratic (for the shares are not always

[1] I cannot find any fulfilment of this intention in Maine's published work. See the Preface to the first edition of "Village Communities" for the probable explanation.

[2] Baden-Powell's work appears to have been wholly unknown to a learned gentleman resident at Madras, who published some notes on "Ancient Law" a few years ago.

equal) among themselves. This type of village, which is in some ways curiously like a smaller reproduction of a Greek city-state, may be due to several causes. Conquest may produce it, or a deliberate new settlement, or joint inheritance among descendants of a single founder. In the case of conquest it may be superimposed on a former *raiyatwārī* village. Baden-Powell points out that all writers on the subject down to a time later than the publication not only of " Ancient Law " but of "Village Communities " had to generalise on incomplete materials.

"It can hardly be doubted that the information available when Sir H. S. Maine wrote was very far from being what it has since become. None of the reports on the Panjāb frontier tribal-villages were written—or at least were available in print; and the greater part of the best Settlement Reports of the North-West Provinces, Oudh and the Panjāb, are dated in years subsequent to the publication of 'Village Communities.' Further, the Settlement Reports of the Central Provinces, the District Manuals of Southern India, and the Survey Reports and Gazetteers of the Bombay districts were many of them not written, and the others were hardly known beyond the confines of their presidencies. In this fact I find the explanation of the total omission in Sir H. S. Maine's pages of any specific mention of the *raiyatwārī* form of village, and the little notice he takes of the tribal or clan constitution of Indian races in general, and of the frontier tribal villages in the Panjāb " ("The Indian Village Community," p. 4).

It will be quite a mistake, however, as we may learn at large from Baden-Powell, to assume that the family tenure or property which is the unit of the *raiyatwārī* village system is equivalent to individual ownership or any kind of ownership as understood in modern Western law. What is certain is that there is no such thing as *the* village community of Hindu times, any more than there is any such thing as *the* village community of the Middle Ages in Europe. But there remains much profit to be derived from comparing the effects of more or less similar causes in fixing the customs of land tenure in the East and the West, whether those effects are, as they sometimes are, closely similar, or varied by the presence of other and different conditions. We no longer expect to find complete and parallel survivals of a common prehistoric stock of institutions, but it is not less interesting to find how easily parallel types may be developed at very distant times and places; and we are free to hold as a pious opinion that the Indian village council still known as the Five (*panchâyat*)—though that has long ceased to be the usual number in practice, and the institution belongs only to the "landlord" type of village—may go back to the same origin as our own reeve and four men, who flourish in Canada to this day. Robuster faith might be needed to find more than accident in the number of five hearths and five lawful men on Horace's estate ("habitatum quinque focis et Quinque bonos solitum Variam dimittere patres," Ep. i. 14). A system of dividing land so as to give every man a share of every quality, which resembles our medieval common-field system even in minute detail, is described by Baden-Powell (*op. cit.* pp. 191, 414).

With regard to the supposed corporate or quasi-corporate ownership of European and especially English village communities, Professor Maitland's section thereon in "Domesday Book and Beyond," pp. 340-56, gives a sound and much needed criticism of the loose language which was current among historical writers a generation ago.

NOTE Q.

RES MANCIPI; ALIENATION IN EARLY LAW.

MAINE'S opinion that the *res mancipi* of ancient Roman law were "the instruments of agricultural labour, the commodities of first consequence to a primitive people" is entirely confirmed by the best recent authors. Professor Girard, agreeing with Ihering, Sohm, and Cuq, considers the soundest explanation ("la doctrine la moins aventureuse") to be that the category consists of the necessary elements of the original Roman farmer's goods, to which alone, therefore, the early "Roman forms of alienation" were applicable. It is further suggested that at first only *res mancipi* were the subjects of full ownership, and that, at a time before individual property in land was alienable, the distinction *mancipi—nec mancipi* coincided with that of *familia* and *pecunia*, which had become obsolete at the date of the Twelve Tables (Girard, "Manuel," p. 247). Muirhead's explanation ("Private Law of Rome," p. 63) is similar, adding that the things constituting the *familia* were those which determined a Roman citizen's political qualification after the Servian reforms. Alienation of such things might affect the owner's political standing, and was therefore of public importance; but I am not clear that this reason is not superfluous. Muirhead observes, deliberately not following Gaius, that the fundamental notion of *mancipium* is *manum*—not *manu*—*capere*, the acquirement of *manus* in the sense of legal dominion (*op. cit.* p. 61), which seems highly probable.

As to the fetters on alienation usually found in early systems of property law, Maine set it down as "remarkable that the Anglo-Saxon customs seem to have been an exception" to the prevailing Germanic usage which forbade alienation of land without the consent of the family or at least the sons of the grantor. Maine's insight is now justified. The freedom which he thought anomalous, though it was accepted as a fact by the best authorities then accessible on Anglo-Saxon law, was really very partial indeed, being confined to land, or rather lordship over land, held by privileged persons and bodies under the privileged instruments known to contemporaries as "books" and to us as charters. Only after the Norman Conquest did the charter become a "common assurance." As I tried not long ago to sum up in the simplest form practicable what is known and not known about customary land tenure before the Conquest, I may as well repeat my words:—

"We know next to nothing of the rules under which free men, whether of greater or lesser substance, held 'folk-land,' that is, estates governed by the old customary law. Probably there was not much buying and selling of such land. There is no reason to suppose that alienation was easier than in other archaic societies, and some local customs found surviving long after the Conquest point to the conclusion that often the consent of the village as well as of the family was a necessary condition of a sale. Indeed, it is not certain that folk-land, generally speaking, could be sold at all. There is equally no reason to think that ordinary free landholders could dispose of their land by will, or were in the habit of making wills for any purpose. Anglo-Saxon wills (or rather documents more like a modern will than a modern deed) exist, but they are the wills of great folk, such as were accustomed to witness the king's charters, had their own wills witnessed or confirmed by bishops and kings, and held charters of their own; and it is by no means clear that the lands dealt with in these wills were held as ordinary folk-land. In some cases it looks as if a special license or consent had been required; we also hear of persistent attempts by the heirs to dispute even gifts to great churches" ("The Expansion of the Common Law," pp. 156-7).

The analogy which Maine points out (p. 279) between the Roman *cessio in iure* and the Fines and Recoveries of medieval English law is of course genuine; but much earlier Germanic examples of a like device may be found, though not in England. *Auflassung* is the modern German term. Methods of this kind, when once ascertained to be efficient, are often used merely by way of abundant caution in spite of the additional trouble and expense involved. But in the classical real property law of the fifteenth century Fine and Recovery were already taking their places as regular specialised parts of a technical machinery.

CHAPTER IX. Page 295.

NOTE R.

CONTRACT IN EARLY LAW.

REMEMBERING that Maine did not profess to write a treatise on Roman law, we shall not follow this brilliant and suggestive chapter with a critical eye for details. But we must note that Savigny's explanation of the Stipulation as an "imperfect conveyance"—a truncated form of the Nexum (about which, by the way, little seems to be really known)—is not accepted by any recent author. The origin is now sought in an earlier religious obligation, probably by oath; opinions differ, as might be expected, as to the conjectural details (Muirhead, 22-7; Girard, 481, sqq.; Pacchioni, "Actio ex sponsu," Bologna, 1888; Zocco-Rosa in Annuario dello Istituto di storia di diritto Romano, vol. 8, Catania, 1902). To such an origin the fact that the words "spondes? spondeo" could be used only by Roman citizens appears to point, though Savigny strangely failed to see this; and in medieval English law we actually find the religious sanction of the spiritual courts interposed, in the name of correcting the sinful breach of plighted faith (*fidei loesio*), to enforce promises which were still mere words for temporal courts, bound as they were to the archaic categories of forms of action. English example also shows how improbable it is that contract should be derived from an imperfect conveyance. In medieval English law a debt is constituted not by the debtor's promise to repay, but by a supposed grant of the sum to the creditor, and the creditor's action alleges no promise, but is in exactly the same form as an action to recover land, and is expressly called an action of property. Here we have conveyance enough. But the action of debt was quite incompetent to become the starting-point of any true law of contract, and when a way was found to sue on informal promises outside its limits, that way was altogether different. All this is in no degree prejudicial to the substance of Maine's argument, which is to show that the law of contract, or, to be exact, any comprehensive doctrine of contract, appears everywhere only at an advanced stage of legal development. This is undoubtedly sound. Even the classical Roman law in its final form never attained a really general theory of contracts. Ultimately the want was supplied, but it would hardly be too much to say of the canonists on the Continent, certainly not too much to say of the common lawyers in England, that they took the kingdom of heaven by violence (cp. my "Oxford Lectures," 1890, pp. 59-62; details and references for the English history in Pollock on Contract, 7th ed. 136, 170; the use of the specially English term Consideration to represent the Roman *causa* is too dangerous a liberty to be allowed to any lesser man than Maine).

Maine censures unnamed English critics (p. 322) for identifying the quasi-contracts of the Civil Law (the term is, of course, not classical) with the implied contracts of the Common Law. But the truth is that this latter expression is, or very lately was, ambiguous. Real agreements manifested by acts and conduct, and not by words, were constantly spoken of as " implied " contracts in English books, as Maine says, at the time when he wrote and long afterwards. Thus the Indian Contract Act of 1872 declares that a promise made otherwise than in words is said to be implied. Here a real agreement is inferred as a fact. But also many " relations resembling those created by contract " (to use again the language of the Indian Act) arise from facts which in Roman law would produce an obligation *quasi ex contractu*. Such facts, under the Common Law, may produce an obligation ascribed in the old system of pleading to a fictitious promise, which promise was said to be " implied " by the law. There are therefore so-called implied contracts in our law which may quite properly be compared with the quasi-contracts of the Roman law; they cover, indeed, much of the same ground. Of late years the term Quasi-contract has been fully naturalised in the American law schools, and by this time it is fairly well known in England. " Constructive contract " would have been correct and in harmony with the general usage of the Common Law, but no one seems ever to have used it.

One result, and a somewhat important one of observing how late and slow of growth any general doctrine of contract has been in any system of civilised law is to strengthen the conviction that a huge anachronism is involved in those political theories which seek to make contract the foundation of all positive law and even of government itself. It should be noted that the doctrine of the Social Contract is much earlier than appears in Maine's statement, and that the theory of the divine right of kings, to which Maine alludes very briefly, was in its origin directed not against popular liberty but against papal and ecclesiastical claims to supremacy in temporal as well as spiritual affairs, as Mr. J. Neville Figgis has shown at large in his learned and acute monograph (" The Theory of the Divine Right of Kings," Cambridge, 1896).

We have said that the classical Roman system of contracts was not theoretically complete; but this did not prevent the discovery that rights could be freely and largely modified by contract (for a discovery this was to the men of the Middle Ages, when the revived study of Roman law made the fact prominent) from exercising a fascination which is not at all exaggerated in Maine's remarks at the end of this chapter. For a time there was a tendency to assume that estates and interests in land could be modified without limit at the will of parties, and this was not effectually checked in England until the latter part of the thirteenth century.

CHAPTER X. Page 355.

NOTE S.

ARCHAIC PROCEDURE.

THE account given by Maine of the symbolism involved in the Legis Actio Sacramenti may be taken as generally correct. The Sacramentum itself, however, seems, according to the generally received modern opinion, to have had the definite and practical purpose of bringing the matter in dispute within the highest jurisdiction. Each party swears to the justice of his cause under a conventional forfeit, and thus the king, who is also chief priest, is brought in to decide which of them is perjured: " il faut au roi, chef de la religion et de la justice crimi-

nelle, chercher qui a raison." The separation of civil and
spiritual jurisdiction under the Republic led to the abolition
of the oath (Girard, "Manuel," pp. 13, 977). If this opinion is
right, the Praetor does not represent a discreet passer-by, nor
yet (as might also be conjectured) the village elders, but intervenes as the minister of the king's justice, conceived in the
first instance (as it was in England in the early Middle Ages)
as an extraordinary justice applicable only for special reasons.
English readers hardly need to be reminded of the fictions by
which the King's Bench and Exchequer extended their jurisdiction to ordinary pleas between subjects.

Maine's reference to the trial scene described in the Iliad,
Σ. 497-508, as adorning the shield of Achilles, is very brief;
but the whole scene is of such interest for early legal history
that we may be allowed to dwell on it a little. The point specially made by Maine is that the two talents of gold are a fee
for the member of the court who shall be thought to speak the
law best. On this he is confirmed by Dr. W. Leaf's very careful interpretation of the passage in his notes *ad loc.*, and his
earlier paper in Journ. Hell. Stud. viii. 122. There is no difficulty about the magnitude of the sum, for the Homeric talent
represents only the value of one ox (Ridgeway in Journ. Hell.
Stud. viii. 133). We shall now give Dr. Leaf's version.

"The people were gathered in the place of assembly, and
there had sprung up a strife; two men were striving about
the price of a man slain. The one averred that he had paid in
full [namely by tender of the blood-fine then and there before
the assembly; but Dr. Leaf's alternative in his later notes to
the Iliad, Appendix I., 'claimed to pay,' is as good or better
for the grammar of εὔχετο πάντ' ἀποδοῦναι, and makes better
sense], and made declaration thereof to the people, but the
other refused to accept aught [this is the proper idiomatic
meaning of ἀναίνετο μηδὲν ἑλέσθαι: 'denied that he had received
anything' is, even apart from the context, barely admissible];
and both were desirous to take an issue at the hand of a daysman [this person, ἴστωρ, summons the council and presides,
but the judgment has to be theirs; he is more like the sheriff
in the old county court than a modern judge or referee]; and
the people were shouting for both, taking part for either side
[not unlike such glimpses as Bracton's Note Book and other
sources afford us of the behaviour of medieval county courts].
And the heralds were restraining the people, and the elders
sate on polished stones in the holy circle [such stones may be

seen on Dartmoor to this day], and in their hands they held the clear-voiced herald's staves. With these they rose up and gave sentence in turn; and in their midst lay two talents of gold to give to him among them that spake the justest doom."

In addition to Dr. Leaf's reasons for rejecting the view formerly current that the dispute is on the mere question of fact whether a blood-fine admitted to be due has been paid or not, we may observe that such a payment would surely be made in a notorious manner and with ample witness, to say nothing of the physical difficulty of handing over some score of cattle (for such would be the most likely form of payment) as privately as modern debtors hand over cash or post a cheque.

The result is that we are confronted with an ancient Greek blood-feud in an interesting stage of transition, that in which the slain man's kindred are no longer free to accept or refuse compensation at their will, but are expected to abandon the feud, in a proper case, on receiving a sum fixed either by custom or by the judgment of the assembly. Homicide aggravated by treachery or the like would probably not fall within such a rule; and the amount of the fine, if we may judge by the practice of Iceland as described in the Sagas, might give matter enough for discussion among the wise men even if no preliminary question arose. Indications of a similar stage, though not clear enough to amount to proof if they stood alone, may be found in the Anglo-Saxon laws.

There is no question in the Homeric text of a formally compulsory jurisdiction; the parties have agreed to put themselves on the judgment of the assembly whether in all the circumstances, whatever they were, tender of the customary fine ought to be accepted. But when such voluntary references have become common practice we are near the point at which they cease to be voluntary, and the party who stands out for what formerly would have been his right incurs, at all events, public reprobation which will be an efficient sanction for most purposes.

Maine's opinion that in the infancy of criminal jurisdiction the sum paid to the king, or the State, was not penal, but a fee for hearing and determining the cause at the request of the parties, " the fair price of its time and trouble," is borne out by later researches in the antiquities of Germanic law. Such was probably at one time the *wite* of the Anglo-Saxon laws, though it is treated as penal in the earliest documents we have. If one feature in early procedure may be fixed on more than another as marking the recognition of criminal and civil responsibility as distinct in character, though one and the same act may be and quite commonly is both a wrong and an offence, perhaps it is the appearance of a special fine for breaking the peace. The development of the king's peace in England from a privilege attached to certain persons, places, and occasions, to the common right of every lawful man belongs to another and later stage.

INDEX.